The GARDEN EXPERT
Dr. D.G. Hessayon

First published in Great Britain
by pbi Publications 1986

All Editions & Reprints: 830,000 copies

This Edition published 1993
by Expert Books
a division of Transworld Publishers Ltd

A catalogue record for this book is available from the British Library

TRANSWORLD PUBLISHERS LTD
61–63 Uxbridge Road, London W5 5SA

TRANSWORLD PUBLISHERS (AUSTRALIA) PTY LTD
15–25 Helles Avenue, Moorebank, NSW 2170

TRANSWORLD PUBLISHERS (NZ) LTD
3 William Pickering Drive, Albany, Auckland

EXPERT BOOKS
LONDON · NEW YORK · TORONTO · SYDNEY · AUCKLAND

Contents

Acknowledgements

The author wishes to acknowledge the painstaking work of Gill Jackson and Pauline Dobbs.
Grateful acknowledgement is also made for the help or photographs received from
Angelina Gibbs, Joan Hessayon, Constance Barry, Jacqueline Norris, Gerard McEvilly,
Hozelock-ASL, Harry Smith Horticultural Photographic Collection, Pat Brindley and Michael Warren.

John Woodbridge provided both artistry and design work. Norman Barber, Yvonne Still,
Henry Barnett, Deborah Achilleos and Brian Watson prepared the paintings for this book.

Printed and bound in Great Britain by Jarrold & Sons Ltd, Norwich

CHAPTER 1
LOOKING AT YOUR GARDEN

Your garden may cover many acres, with a stately home at its centre. Or it may be no larger than one of the small rooms in that grand house. In either case it is your garden — to change, care for and use as a refuge from a world filled with stress.

You will never learn everything there is to know about gardening, but you can become an expert gardener. This book attempts to set out the fundamental principles — becoming an expert calls for combining the knowledge gained from books with a great deal of careful observation and practical experience.

For most people the aim is to create a good example of the typical British garden — the lawn, Roses and flower beds which make up such a distinctive feature of our urban scenery. Beloved by foreigners, but not part of our ancient heritage.

Much has been written about gardening on the grand scale. Britain, often thought of as the country which gave gardening to the world, went to the Continent to learn what to do. So our early gardens stretching around 17th century mansions were copies of the highly formal European style. In the 18th century we stopped copying. We invented the Landscape Garden — rolling parkland, artificial lakes, trees on top of man-made hills. William Kent, Capability Brown and the other architects of this naturalism made England the most respected gardening nation on earth.

It was all on the grand scale. Around ordinary homes these changes in fashion meant nothing — the Cottage Garden remained an untidy but useful jumble of vegetables, herbs and sweet-smelling flowers. Then came the Industrial Revolution. Whilst the cottage and its garden slept on, there appeared a new phenomenon — the villa of the middle classes and the terrace house of the millworker. The villa owners turned to Mr & Mrs Loudon for guidance, and it was these two tireless journalists who popularised the Victorian Villa Garden — lawns, geometric flower beds, shrubberies, annual bedding and so on. Later designers such as Gertrude Jekyll softened the line a little with herbaceous borders. From these Victorians the home garden of today has arisen, and it continues to develop. Nowadays we happily mix Roses, shrubs, perennials and bulbs in the same bed in a way which would have horrified the rule-book writers of 50 years ago. Perhaps the only rule is to remember the words of Gertrude Jekyll — "A garden is for its owner's pleasure".

THE ELEMENTS OF A GARDEN

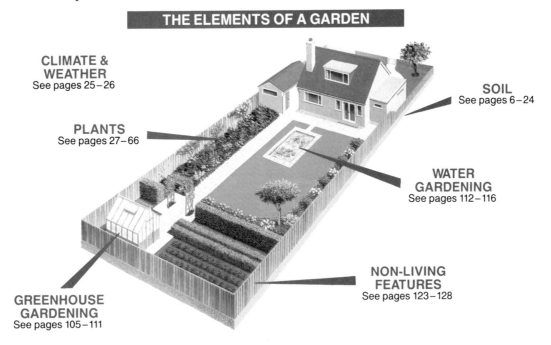

CLIMATE & WEATHER
See pages 25–26

SOIL
See pages 6–24

PLANTS
See pages 27–66

WATER GARDENING
See pages 112–116

GREENHOUSE GARDENING
See pages 105–111

NON-LIVING FEATURES
See pages 123–128

THE TYPICAL GARDEN

LAWN

You will find a lawn in 80 per cent of Britain's gardens. It is a prominent feature — grass covers an average of 1,000 sq. ft, which is about half the total area.

Once a power mower was a luxury, now more than 50 per cent of gardeners have one. Each year about 1 in every 10 lawn owners buys a new model and very, very few buy a hand-pushed one — 80 per cent choose an electric mower.

OUTDOOR LIVING AREA

The concept of using the garden as an outdoor living area has at last become popular. A patio is now present in 1 in every 4 gardens (1973: 1 in 10). Fifteen years ago only a minority of gardeners had some form of outdoor furniture — now 73 per cent have chairs, tables and/or an umbrella. Fifteen years ago fewer than 40,000 barbecues were sold — now more than 500,000 are sold each year.

ROSES

Roses are present in 85 per cent of Britain's gardens — the average number of plants is 11. Of these 90 per cent are Hybrid Teas or Floribundas — Shrub Roses, Ramblers, Climbers and Miniatures remain much less popular. Two new Roses are planted each year in the average garden.

FRUIT

One in 3 gardens has fruit trees or bushes. Raspberry, Strawberry, Apple and Pear dominate the picture, with about 40 per cent of our total consumption of soft fruit being home-grown.

GREENHOUSE

There are 3 million greenhouses in Britain — the most popular type and size used to be a wooden 10 ft × 8 ft structure, now it is an aluminium 8 ft × 6 ft house. About half are heated.

Tomatoes are the popular crop — they are grown in three-quarters of all greenhouses. Other popular uses include raising seedlings (60 per cent) and growing Chrysanthemums (34 per cent).

VEGETABLES

A vegetable plot is present in about half our gardens. Economic necessity does not seem to be the reason for growing vegetables — seeds are more often bought for large gardens than small ones. The advent of home deep freezing is probably an important factor. Seeds are the most popular planting material — 40 million packets are bought every year with Lettuce, Runner Beans, Cabbage, Peas, Carrots and Beetroot as the top six. Tomato plants are bought for 20 per cent of Britain's gardens — other purchases include Seed Potatoes (13 per cent of gardens) and Onion Sets (12 per cent).

THE GARDEN & THE GARDENER

Of the 20 million households in the U.K., more than 17 million have a garden and nearly all are cared for to some extent — only 5 per cent are completely neglected. The proportion of households with a tended garden varies from one region to another — the Midlands and Wales top the ratings:

Region	Households with a tended garden
Midlands, Wales	86%
South	85%
North	75%
Scotland	70%

The size of the average plot is 2,250 sq. ft — equivalent to 32 ft × 70 ft. There are, however, enormous variations. Only 20 per cent are 'average' gardens of 1,500 – 2,500 sq. ft. About 1 in 6 are smaller than 300 sq. ft and 1 in 10 are larger than 10,000 sq. ft.

Not every adult having access to a garden works on the plot. In a typical spring month about 1 in every 2 men and 1 in every 3 women do some work outdoors. The time the gardener spends outdoors in an average week is 6–7 hours, and either husband or wife takes the responsibility for the garden — shared responsibility is claimed in only 25 per cent of households. The time spent in the garden does not change as they get richer, but it does increase as people get older. The time spent out in the garden is less in the North than in the South.

The average household with a plot to look after spends about £45 per year. Expenditure has sharply increased in recent years — in 1974 the average expenditure was only £10.

WHERE THE MONEY GOES

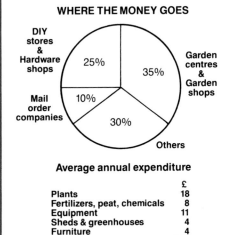

DIY stores & Hardware shops 25%

Garden centres & Garden shops 35%

Mail order companies 10%

Others 30%

Average annual expenditure

	£
Plants	18
Fertilizers, peat, chemicals	8
Equipment	11
Sheds & greenhouses	4
Furniture	4
	45

BORDER

A border is a planted area which is designed to be viewed from one, two or three sides but not from all angles.

Herbaceous border: An essential feature of the larger garden in the early years of the 20th century. It is long and narrow with a backcloth of a wall or clipped hedge and hardy perennials planted in tiers, the tallest at the back and clumps of low-growing plants at the front. Dividing up plants and obtaining cuttings from friends remain important ways of stocking the border.

Shrub border: A labour-saving alternative to the herbaceous border with colour from the spring Rhododendrons to the autumn Hydrangeas. Unfortunately, it can be dull for part of the season if not carefully planned.

Mixed border: A fairly recent innovation which has become the most popular way of growing hardy perennials. The shape is often irregular and there is a framework of flowering shrubs and decorative evergreens. Roses and hardy perennials form large and colourful patches, and in the remaining pockets low-growing items such as bulbs and annuals are grown.

BED

A bed is a planted area which is designed to be viewed from all sides. The **flower bed** is the traditional home for annuals, biennials, bulbs and half-hardy perennials. The occupants are usually planted ('bedded out') in autumn for a spring display and in late spring for a summer show.

Island bed: Designed for hardy perennials, with the tallest at the centre and the shortest around the edge.

Formal bed: Outline and planting arrangement strictly geometrical.

Raised bed: Retaining walls support the soil surface above the surrounding level.

Peat bed: A variation of the raised bed — the retaining walls are made up of peat blocks and the in-fill is a peat-rich compost.

Scree bed: Designed for alpines — the deep and sloping bed contains stone chippings mixed with a small amount of loam.

Sunken bed: Surface below surrounding level.

Beds are usually associated with bedding plants. About 12 million trays are bought each year, and countless millions are raised from seed.

ROCKERY

A rockery is an area of the garden which contains rocks and is used for growing plants. If natural rock formation is copied, the correct term is **rock garden.** Rockery perennials, bulbs, dwarf conifers and small annuals are grown — true **alpines** are from mountainous areas. This term is often used for rock plants in general — about 8 per cent of gardeners buy some each year.

TREES

An ornamental tree is a single-trunk woody plant grown for its blossom, its attractive foliage or shape. When planted on its own as a focal point it is known as a **specimen tree.**

Standard: Main trunk bare — the usual form for large trees.   **Fastigiate:** Column-like growth, branches upright.

Weeping: Branches borne vertically, either naturally or by training.

CHAPTER 2

SOIL

Pick up a handful of soil in your garden. Ordinary, unexciting earth. Yet it is one of Nature's miracles, and one of her most complex products. Your success as a gardener will largely depend upon its condition, so take the first bold step in gardening ... get to know your soil.

All soils are composed of four basic components — mineral particles, organic matter, air and water. The physical quality of the resulting blend we know as soil is described as its texture or structure, but these two terms do not mean the same thing.

Soil texture refers to the proportions of the different-sized mineral particles which are present. When coarse particles predominate, the soil is described as light. If the particles are minute, the soil is called heavy. The ideal lies half-way between the extremes — the coarse and minute particles are evenly balanced to produce the medium-textured soil known as loam.

Soil structure refers to the way the mineral particles are joined together — they may be grouped as clods, plates or crumbs. A crumb structure is ideal — it is 'friable soil' with a 'good tilth'.

Your soil may be nothing like a crumbly loam. It may be a back-breaking clay or sandy stuff which always needs feeding and watering. Don't despair — read page 10 and see how its structure can be improved. Organic matter will cement sand grains into crumbs — digging, liming and organic matter have the same effect on clay particles.

The improvement may be spectacular, but you cannot change the basic texture unless you add vast quantities of the deficient mineral particle. So your soil will remain basically clayey, sandy etc, which means you should wherever possible choose plants which the catalogues recommend for your particular soil type.

TOPSOIL is the fertile and living part of the soil. It is fertile because it contains nearly all of the humus, and it is living because it supports countless bacteria, which change various materials into plant foods. This layer varies from 2 in. in chalky soils to several feet in old, well-tended gardens. **When digging, this layer should be turned over, not buried under the subsoil.**

SUBSOIL lies under the topsoil, and is relatively dead and starved. It can be recognised by its lighter colour, due to lack of humus. **When digging, it should not be brought to the surface.**

A **SOIL PAN** is a horizontal layer, on or under the soil surface, which prevents the free movement of air and water to the region below. A surface pan is formed by the action of heavy rain on certain soil types — remove by hoeing or forking. Cultivating to the same depth year after year can cause sub-surface pans — another cause is the leaching down of iron, aluminium and manganese salts to a level where they form a chemical pan. Break through sub-surface pans by double digging (page 12).

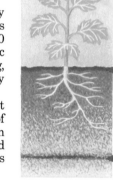

Soil structure is crumbly — crumbs range from lentil- to pea-sized. Both large and small pores are present

Sufficient plant nutrients, both major and minor, to ensure vigorous and healthy growth, flowering and fruiting

Sufficient organic matter to ensure high bacterial activity and humus production

The ideal garden soil

Soil texture is medium loam with few or no stones

Sufficient lime to counteract soil sourness

Sufficiently free-draining to prevent waterlogging of the topsoil during periods of heavy rain

The Basic Constituents

WATER

Water is essential for the support of both plant and soil life — it is also the carrier of nutrients. Water is absorbed into humus and adsorbed on to the surface of particles. Water adheres tightly to clay, restricting both drainage and uptake by the roots.

AIR

Air is essential for the support of plant and desirable soil life — it is also required for the breakdown of organic matter to release nutrients. Movement of air is necessary to avoid the build up of toxic gases — this movement takes place through the soil pores.

MINERAL PARTICLES

The non-living skeleton of the soil is derived from the decomposition of rocks by weathering. The parent rock usually (but not always) lies under the soil and both the fertility and size of the particles are governed by the type of parent rock.

ORGANIC MATTER

Fertile soils contain a minimum of 5% organic matter. This is present as a mixture of living, dead and decomposed organisms, both animal and vegetable. True humus is a dark, jelly-like substance which binds mineral particles into crumbs. For more details see page 22.

Particle name	Particle size	Comments
GRAVEL & STONES	More than 2 mm	'Stones' usually refers to larger pieces of rock whereas 'gravel' generally describes smaller weathered fragments, but there is no precise distinction.
COARSE SAND	0·6–2 mm	**Distinctly gritty.** Feels like granulated sugar when rubbed between the fingers.
MEDIUM SAND	0·2–0·6 mm	**Gritty.** Feels like table salt when rubbed between the fingers.
FINE SAND	0·02–0·2 mm	**Slightly gritty.** Not easy to detect when rubbed between the fingers, but grittiness can be heard if fingers are held close to the ear.
SILT	0·002–0·02 mm	**Silky-soapy when moist.** The half-way house in particle size — neither gritty nor sticky.
CLAY	Less than 0·002 mm	**Sticky when moist.** A moist ball can be easily shaped and is polished when rubbed.

Soil Texture

The classification of soil texture is based on the content of sand, silt and clay — stones and gravel are ignored. These proportions can be measured exactly by laboratory analysis but it is much easier to use the hand method described on page 9. Soil scientists recognise 17 or more types of mineral soil texture, but for the gardener there are just 8 basic types.

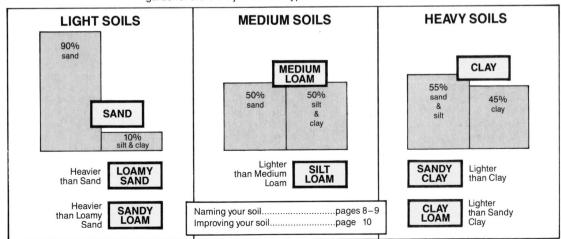

LIGHT SOILS

90% sand

SAND

10% silt & clay

Heavier than Sand — **LOAMY SAND**

Heavier than Loamy Sand — **SANDY LOAM**

MEDIUM SOILS

MEDIUM LOAM

50% sand | 50% silt & clay

Lighter than Medium Loam — **SILT LOAM**

Naming your soil............................pages 8–9
Improving your soil........................page 10

HEAVY SOILS

CLAY

55% sand & silt | 45% clay

SANDY CLAY — Lighter than Clay

CLAY LOAM — Lighter than Sandy Clay

Putting a Name to Your Soil

You have probably met them — people who can tell you the specific names of the plants in the border but cannot give you the specific name of the soil below. Knowing your soil type is more than a means of satisfying your idle curiosity — the proper soil improvement programme (page 10) depends on correct identification.

The two essential tests are the walkover test and the hand test — both cost nothing and take only a few minutes to complete. The pit test takes a little effort and the soil kit test costs money, but both are worthwhile for the keen gardener.

The walkover test

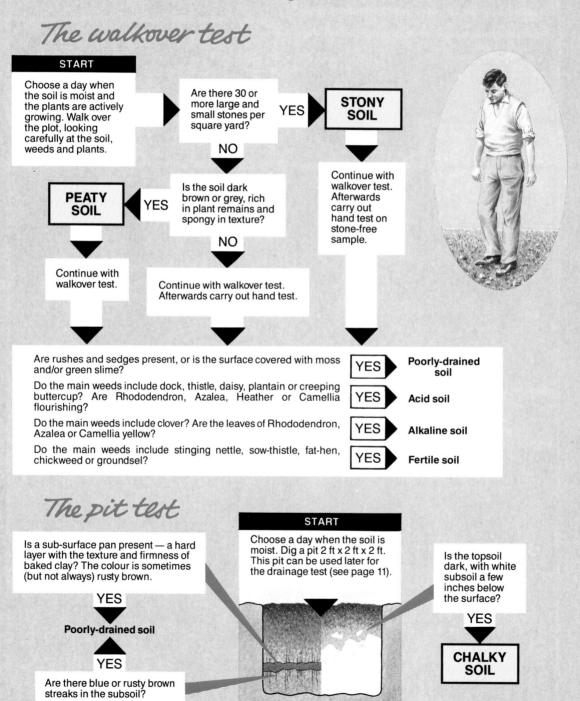

START

Choose a day when the soil is moist and the plants are actively growing. Walk over the plot, looking carefully at the soil, weeds and plants.

Are there 30 or more large and small stones per square yard?

YES → **STONY SOIL**

NO

Is the soil dark brown or grey, rich in plant remains and spongy in texture?

YES → **PEATY SOIL**

NO

Continue with walkover test. Afterwards carry out hand test on stone-free sample.

Continue with walkover test.

Continue with walkover test. Afterwards carry out hand test.

Are rushes and sedges present, or is the surface covered with moss and/or green slime? | **YES** | **Poorly-drained soil**

Do the main weeds include dock, thistle, daisy, plantain or creeping buttercup? Are Rhododendron, Azalea, Heather or Camellia flourishing? | **YES** | **Acid soil**

Do the main weeds include clover? Are the leaves of Rhododendron, Azalea or Camellia yellow? | **YES** | **Alkaline soil**

Do the main weeds include stinging nettle, sow-thistle, fat-hen, chickweed or groundsel? | **YES** | **Fertile soil**

The pit test

Is a sub-surface pan present — a hard layer with the texture and firmness of baked clay? The colour is sometimes (but not always) rusty brown.

YES

Poorly-drained soil

YES

Are there blue or rusty brown streaks in the subsoil?

START

Choose a day when the soil is moist. Dig a pit 2 ft x 2 ft x 2 ft. This pit can be used later for the drainage test (see page 11).

Is the topsoil dark, with white subsoil a few inches below the surface?

YES

CHALKY SOIL

The hand test

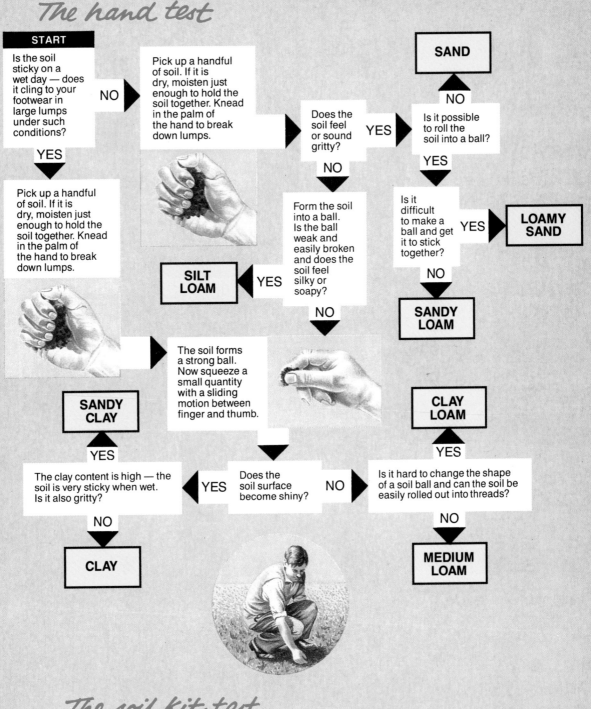

START

Is the soil sticky on a wet day — does it cling to your footwear in large lumps under such conditions?

NO → Pick up a handful of soil. If it is dry, moisten just enough to hold the soil together. Knead in the palm of the hand to break down lumps.

YES ↓

Pick up a handful of soil. If it is dry, moisten just enough to hold the soil together. Knead in the palm of the hand to break down lumps.

Does the soil feel or sound gritty?

YES → Is it possible to roll the soil into a ball?

NO → **SAND**

YES ↓ Is it difficult to make a ball and get it to stick together?

YES → **LOAMY SAND**

NO ↓ **SANDY LOAM**

NO ↓ Form the soil into a ball. Is the ball weak and easily broken and does the soil feel silky or soapy?

YES → **SILT LOAM**

NO ↓

The soil forms a strong ball. Now squeeze a small quantity with a sliding motion between finger and thumb.

Does the soil surface become shiny?

YES → The clay content is high — the soil is very sticky when wet. Is it also gritty?

YES → **SANDY CLAY**

NO ↓ **CLAY**

NO → Is it hard to change the shape of a soil ball and can the soil be easily rolled out into threads?

YES → **CLAY LOAM**

NO ↓ **MEDIUM LOAM**

The soil kit test

There are several kits available for testing the nitrogen, phosphates, potash and pH content of the soil. Some involve test-tubes and indicator solutions — others are based on a probe which is inserted into the ground. These kits provide a reasonably accurate way of discovering whether your soil needs liming or not (page 15), but are less useful for determining fertilizer needs (page 16). The problem lies in the difficulty of translating the results into practical plant nutrient requirements.

IMPROVING YOUR SOIL

Even small improvements in soil structure can produce noticeably better plants. Despite the claims which are sometimes made, there is no 'magical' method which can transform poor soil into fertile loam. Each type requires its own special treatment, as shown below.

SOIL TYPE	ADVANTAGES	DISADVANTAGES	THE WAY TO IMPROVE IT	MOST IMPORTANT TREATMENTS
STONY	Usually free draining. Generally dry enough to work early in the season.	Dries out very quickly in summer. Difficult to cultivate.	Remove the larger stones lying on the surface. Do not attempt to free the soil from stones. Stony soils tend to be very free draining, so that the 'goodness' in them is quickly washed through. Plenty of manure or compost and fertilizers are the answer. These must be applied close to the surface; digging should always be kept shallow. If the soil is also sandy or clayey, appropriate treatments should be followed.	Addition of HUMUS-MAKING MATERIALS (page 22) and FERTILIZERS (page 16)
PEATY	Easily worked. Best soil type for several shrubs (especially Azaleas, Rhododendrons and Camellias). Fertile when limed and drained.	Too acidic for most plants. Poor drainage.	Such soils can be made to produce excellent results, because basically they are very fertile. To bring this about, good drainage and generous liming are essential. The addition of loamy topsoil is very helpful.	DRAINAGE (page 11) and LIME (page 15)
CHALKY	Best soil type for several flowers and shrubs (especially rockery plants).	Sticky and soft in wet weather. Often too alkaline for many plants.	These soils are not easy to manage, but they can be greatly improved. Digging should be kept shallow, and plenty of humus-making materials and fertilizers must be added because such soils are free draining and therefore 'hungry'. Green manuring (page 23) is a great help. Although the subsoil is chalk, topsoil is occasionally acid. If the area is not large, add topsoil to the surface.	Addition of HUMUS-MAKING MATERIALS (page 22) and FERTILIZERS (page 16)
Light Soils / **SAND** / **LOAMY SAND** / **SANDY LOAM**	Warm — most suitable for early crops. Easily worked, even when wet. Free draining, due to open texture.	Hungry — usually short of plant foods. Dries out very quickly; needs frequent watering during summer. Shallow-rooting plants may die. Cools down rapidly at night.	"The soil with the least backache and the most heartache". The main trouble with sandy soils is that they lose food and water very quickly. The only way to improve matters is to add as much humus-making material as possible. Sticky manure (such as cow or pig manure) is best. Fertilizers are also essential, and should be applied in spring and summer. Humus-makers and fertilizers should not be dug in deeply.	Addition of HUMUS-MAKING MATERIALS (page 22) and FERTILIZERS (page 16)
Medium Soils / **MEDIUM LOAM** / **SILT LOAM**	Good crumb structure. Possesses all the advantages, to a lesser degree, of both sandy and clayey soils. Good water- and food-holding properties.	Some Silt Loams are difficult — surface caps in rainy weather.	Lucky gardener if you have a Medium Loam. The only thing you have to do is keep it as it is, with regular light dressings of lime, humus-making materials and fertilizers. Dig the ground over in the autumn.	Addition of HUMUS-MAKING MATERIALS (page 22) and FERTILIZERS (page 16)
Heavy Soils / **CLAY** / **SANDY CLAY** / **CLAY LOAM**	Generally well supplied with plant foods. Nutrients are not leached away by rainfall.	Cold — not suitable for early crops. Heavy to work under wet conditions. Tends to waterlog in winter. Cakes hard and cracks in dry weather.	Artificial drainage may be necessary. Attend to this point first. Your next task is to dig thoroughly in the autumn to expose the soil lumps to winter frosts. A generous dressing of lime will help to build up a crumb structure. Humus-making materials are necessary to preserve the crumb structure obtained in this way. Strawy stable manure is best. Clayey soils are usually quite rich in plant foods, but the proper use of fertilizers will make for still better results.	DRAINAGE (page 11) and DIGGING (page 12) followed by LIME (page 15) and HUMUS-MAKING MATERIALS (page 22)

IMPROVING YOUR SOIL BY
DRAINAGE

Excessive drainage in sandy soil is a nuisance — you have to water frequently in dry weather and it is necessary to build up a water-holding structure by adding as much organic matter as you can obtain. Faulty drainage is more than a nuisance — it is a plant killer. Stagnant water around the roots starves them of air. Helpful bacterial activity is slowed down and harmful organisms flourish. Toxic gases build up and the overall result is poor growth at first and the eventual death of the plants if conditions do not improve.

Poor drainage is associated with heavy topsoil. Water moves very slowly through clay, and so the answer is to improve the structure by cultural means. Impeded drainage is a more serious problem, as the downward movement of water is not just slowed down — it is blocked. There are three prime causes — non-porous rock below the soil, a sub-surface pan below the topsoil (page 6) or a high water table (the level at which porous rock is saturated with water). Soils with impeded drainage are waterlogged for long periods during the winter months — some remedial action is essential.

Drainage test

A vital job in soil improvement is to find out whether drainage is satisfactory. The simple test outlined below will give you the answer.
Dig a hole 2 ft square and 2 ft deep at the lowest part of the garden. Look inside the hole after heavy rain and see how much water is present at the bottom.

An hour after rain — no water in the hole	**Excessive drainage** If topsoil is sandy — addition of humus is essential (page 22)
A few days after rain — no water in the hole	**Satisfactory drainage** No help is needed
A few days after rain — some water still present at the bottom of the hole	**Poor drainage** One or more cultural aids (see below) are needed
A few days after rain — water has seeped in from surrounding soil; hole partly filled	**Impeded drainage** An artificial aid (see below) as well as cultural aids may be needed

Cultural Aids

● Poor drainage caused by a high clay content in the topsoil can be improved by double digging in autumn (page 12). On no account should the rough clods be broken down at the time of digging — leave them to be crumbled by the action of wind and frost during the winter months.

● Double digging will break up a thin soil pan and so allow water to drain through. Sometimes the sub-surface pan is too thick to be penetrated by an ordinary garden fork — use instead a pickaxe or a steel bar and sledgehammer. In some cases the pan cannot be broken — you will then have to use an artificial drainage system (see below) or else raise the level with brought-in soil.

● The crumbs created by digging provide temporary relief — you must build up a permanent crumb structure by applying heavy dressings of organic matter at regular intervals (page 22). Add calcium in the form of lime or chalk if the soil is acid — use gypsum if it is neutral or alkaline.

● If the cause of impeded drainage is either non-porous rock close to the surface or an abnormally high water table, an artificial aid is usually recommended. Laying drains is an expensive, difficult and time-consuming job — it is often better to tackle the problem by raising the soil level. Buy good quality topsoil and add it to the whole surface if the garden is small or use it to fill raised beds.

Artificial Aids

● A tile drainage system consists of a herringbone pattern of plastic or earthenware tile drains. A rubble drainage system is created in the same way, but the drain pipes are omitted.

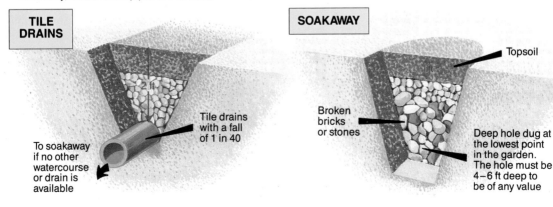

TILE DRAINS

2 ft

Tile drains with a fall of 1 in 40

To soakaway if no other watercourse or drain is available

SOAKAWAY

Topsoil

Broken bricks or stones

Deep hole dug at the lowest point in the garden. The hole must be 4–6 ft deep to be of any value

IMPROVING YOUR SOIL BY
DIGGING

Digging brings several benefits to the garden. Its basic role is to break up compacted soil by the direct action of the spade and the indirect action of frost and drying winds on the upturned clods. In this way drainage is improved, air is introduced and the natural process of organic matter breakdown is speeded up, thereby releasing more plant nutrients into the soil.

There are additional benefits — humus-makers such as peat or compost can be incorporated below the surface, roots of perennial weeds can be removed and annual weeds can be buried. Despite these benefits, digging has declined a little in popularity and the complex, over-deep methods have almost disappeared. The general advice is to cultivate to 2 spits (2 spade-depths or 20 in.) by double digging if the plot has not been cultivated before. This is also used every few years by the keen vegetable grower, but for most gardeners single digging (cultivating to 1 spit) is all that is required. Trenching (cultivating to 3 spits) is virtually never worthwhile.

Some gardeners believe that digging is not necessary at all. By the no-digging method, a thick layer of well-rotted compost is applied to the surface each year and seeds are sown in it. Everyone agrees on the need for humus-makers, but most experts believe that the spade is more effective than the worm in burying compost and breaking up the soil.

Using the spade

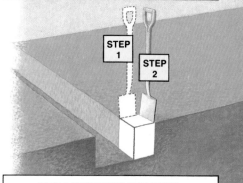

CUT OUT THE SPADEFUL
Drive in the spade vertically to its full depth (approx. 10 in.). Press (do not kick) down on the blade. The first cut (Step 1) should be at right angles to the trench. The next cut (Step 2) should be parallel to the trench, 6–8 in. behind the face.

STEP 1

STEP 2

LIFT & TURN THE SPADEFUL
Pull (don't jerk) back on the handle and lever the soil on to the blade. Lift, and with a flick of the wrist turn the earth into the trench in front — turn the spadeful right over to bury the weeds.

SINGLE DIGGING *Other names:* Plain digging Forking Ordinary digging	Single digging is the standard method for ordinary garden use. If the soil is not heavy no other method is necessary. Single dig every year, except where the land is planted with permanent subjects. With uncultivated heavy land or with soil which forms a compacted layer below the surface after a few years, double digging may be preferable — see below.	A B C
DOUBLE DIGGING *Other names:* Bastard trenching Spading Half trenching	Double digging is used on land which has not been cultivated previously — it must be used instead of single digging if the drainage is poor. Though not vital for most cultivated gardens, keen gardeners still follow this method every 3 years on the vegetable plot and about every 4 years on flower beds.	A B C
RIDGING	Ridging was once widely used for stiff clay soils in autumn, as it exposes the maximum possible area to the pulverising action of frost and wind. It is, however, best avoided. A large quantity of the frost-created crumbs can fall below the clods when the surface is raked down in the spring.	B A C

The elements of digging

DIG AT THE RIGHT SEASON: Autumn and early winter are the best times for medium and heavy soils — very heavy soil should be cultivated before the end of November. Sandy soil can be dug in winter or early spring. Do not dig your plot too early in the season — turning the soil over in September can produce a flush of weeds.

DIG AT THE RIGHT TIME: Never dig when the land is frozen or waterlogged. The soil should not be wet enough to stick to your boots, nor should it be dry and hard. If possible pick a time of settled weather.

DO NOT UNDERESTIMATE THE JOB: About 30 minutes digging is quite enough for the first day if you are not used to strenuous exercise. Work steadily, but not too fast.

NEVER BRING SUBSOIL TO THE SURFACE: Raw clay, chalk or sand will ruin the fertility.

CHOOSE THE RIGHT TOOL: Use a spade for general work or a fork if the soil is very heavy or stony. A pickaxe may be required for breaking up heavy clay subsoil. Carry a scraper and use as necessary to keep the blade clean when digging.

BE METHODICAL: Dig out a trench 1–2 ft wide at one end of the plot and cart the soil to the other end. Work in strips, turning each one into the trench in front until the plot is dug. Then use the carted soil from the first trench to fill the last one. If the plot is wide, divide it into sections and deal with each one separately.

DO NOT DISTURB THE DUG EARTH: Leave the clods in lumps to ensure maximum benefit from the crumb-forming frosts of winter. At least 3 weeks must elapse between digging and the preparation of the land for planting or seed sowing.

Dig out a trench about 10 in. wide and 1 spit (spade-depth) deep. Transport this soil to the other end of the plot. Spread compost or manure over the bottom of the trench, using 1 bucketful per 10 ft of trench. It is useful to incorporate Bone Meal at this stage (1 oz per 3 ft of trench).

Turn strip A into the trench, using the digging technique shown on page 12. Annual weeds will be buried at the bottom of the spadeful of soil, but the roots of perennial weeds such as Docks, Dandelions and Nettles should be removed.

A new trench will be created when you have dug from one side of the plot to the other. Add Bone Meal, compost or manure as before, and turn strip B into the trench. Continue with C etc. Use soil from the first trench to fill the final trench.

Dig out a trench about 2 ft wide and 1 spit (spade-depth) deep. Transport this soil to the other end of the plot. Spread compost or manure over the bottom of the trench, using 1 bucketful per 5 ft of trench. It is useful to incorporate Bone Meal at this stage (2 oz per 3 ft of trench). Fork over the bottom of the trench to the full length of the prongs.

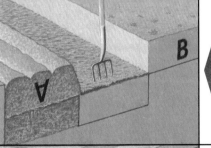

Turn strip A into the trench, using the digging technique shown on page 12. Annual weeds will be buried at the bottom of the spadeful of soil, but the roots of perennial weeds such as Docks, Dandelions and Nettles should be removed.

Dig from one side to the other until all of the forked-over area has been covered. You will then have created a new 2 ft wide trench. Add Bone Meal, compost or manure to the new 2 ft wide trench and turn strip B into it. Continue with C etc. Use soil from the first trench to fill the final trench.

Mark out the plot into a number of strips, each one about 2 ft wide. Beginning with the first strip, dig out a trench about 10 in. wide and 1 spit (spade-depth) deep. Transport this soil to the other end of the strip.

Now turn the centre spadeful A forward into the trench. Turn B and C on to the side of the upturned centre spadeful so as to form a ridge. Continue with this ridging until the whole strip has been dug — use soil from the first trench to fill the final trench. Move across to the next 2 ft wide strip and continue the operation until the whole plot has been dug.

IMPROVING YOUR SOIL BY
APPLYING DRESSINGS

A dressing is a material (usually solid but occasionally liquid) which is applied to the soil. Its purpose is to improve the soil's structure and/or the growth of the plants it supports. Dressings work by adding one or more factors which are missing from a poor soil or have been removed by roots or rain from a fertile one.

Some dressings, such as animal manure, are as old as gardening itself. Others appeared for the first time this year, proudly proclaimed as improvements on standard materials. Yet nobody has discovered a single product which will do all the tasks we expect from dressings, and so we must continue to rely on products from each of the three basic groups.

WHAT THEY ARE	WHAT THEY ARE USED FOR	AVERAGE APPLICATION RATE
LIME page 15 Liming materials are added to the soil to provide calcium. Several types are available — quicklime, magnesium limestone, chalk, ground limestone and so on. By far the most popular liming material is hydrated lime (slaked lime). Gypsum improves crumb structure without removing soil sourness.	Improving crumb structure Removing soil sourness	1 lb per sq. yd
FERTILIZERS pages 16–21 Fertilizers are materials containing one or more major plant nutrients in concentrated form. They are added to the soil to **feed the plants**. These dressings are applied at a rate of a few ounces or even less per square yard. Because of this, they cannot be expected to make any significant contribution to the humus content of the soil, even when they are organic-based and are claimed to improve the soil. This means that **humus-makers have to be used if you want to get the full benefit from fertilizers.**	Feeding the plants	1/8 lb per sq. yd
HUMUS-MAKERS pages 22–24 Humus-makers are bulky organic materials. They are added to the soil to add fibre and/or to build up the bacterial population. In this way they **improve the texture of the soil**. These dressings are applied at a rate of several pounds per square yard. Nutrients are present, but only in the case of top quality and properly composted animal manure applied at high rates is the supply adequate. The plant nutrients present in humus-makers are generally slow-acting, wrongly balanced and insufficient for the plants' needs. This means that **fertilizers have to be used if you want to get the full benefit from humus-makers.**	Improving the texture of the soil	10 lb per sq. yd

How dressings are used

Base Dressing

A base dressing is applied to the soil before planting or seed sowing. Lime is used in this way, but the main role of a base dressing is to provide humus and/or a steady supply of plant foods during the months to come. It is therefore HUMUS-MAKERS and SLOW-ACTING FERTILIZERS which are generally used. Base dressings are dug into the topsoil. The favourite humus-makers are compost and peat — the most popular fertilizers are the granular solids Bone Meal and Growmore.

Top Dressing

Once plants are established and actively growing, extra nutrients are often applied to the surface of the soil around the plants. This is a top dressing, and its role is to provide readily-available nourishment to the roots. Therefore QUICK-ACTING FERTILIZERS are used. A few rules — keep solid dressings off the leaves and a little way from the stems. A little light hoeing or raking is permissible after treatment in the case of shrubs or large herbaceous plants, but never work to a depth which could damage the roots. Water in if the weather is dry.

IMPROVING YOUR SOIL BY
ADDING LIME

Rain steadily washes lime out of the soil at an average rate of ½ oz per sq. yd. Slowly the land becomes more sour, and neither humus-makers nor the majority of fertilizers are of any help in correcting this condition. The answer is to apply lime — the oldest and still the best soil conditioner.

● **Lime neutralises sourness.** Very few garden plants grow well under acid (sour) conditions.

● **Lime brings life into your soil.** When soils are sour, beneficial bacteria and earthworms tend to die out. Lime helps them to flourish.

● **Lime breaks up heavy clay soil.** Lime binds the tiny clay particles together into 'crumbs' and so makes heavy soils easier to work, warmer, and better draining. You can prove for yourself this property of lime.

 Add a teaspoonful of clayey soil to a glass of water and stir until it is all in suspension. When you stop stirring, the liquid will remain muddy because the minute particles of clay are not heavy enough to fall to the bottom of the glass. Now stir in a ¼-teaspoonful of hydrated lime. The clay particles group together into clearly visible soil crumbs, which quickly sink to the bottom of the tumbler.

● **Lime is a plant food.** Calcium, the main component of lime, is an essential nutrient for all plants.

● **Lime makes other plant foods available.** Lime acts on humus, setting free the elements needed for healthy plant growth.

● **Lime discourages pests.** Some soil diseases (club root, for example) are checked by liming. Soil pests such as slugs, leatherjackets and wireworms hate it.

How much to lime

Your garden can have too much of a good thing. If an excessive amount of lime is used, humus breaks down too quickly and plant leaves turn yellow because of the lock-up of iron in the soil. It is easy to avoid overliming by testing your soil and applying these rates.

Hydrated lime is the usual liming material. Other types include quicklime (unpleasant) and chalk or limestone (slower-acting). To improve soil texture without changing the pH, use gypsum at ½ lb per sq. yard.

Hydrated Lime application rate			
	Sandy soil	Loam	Clayey or Peaty soil
VERY ACID	1 lb per sq. yd	1½ lb per sq. yd	2 lb per sq. yd
ACID	½ lb per sq. yd	1 lb per sq. yd	1½ lb per sq. yd
NEARLY NEUTRAL	¼ lb per sq. yd	½ lb per sq. yd	1 lb per sq. yd
ALKALINE	do not lime	do not lime	do not lime
NOT TESTED	½ lb per sq. yd	½ lb per sq. yd	¾ lb per sq. yd

Whether to lime

Do not try to guess the answer to this question. Buy a simple test kit — this will tell you the pH of your soil. The term pH is a measure of acidity and alkalinity. The middle point is pH 7.0 and this indicates neutrality (neither acid nor alkaline). Soils vary between 3.5 and 8.5 but practically every garden soil lies in the 4.5-8.0 range.

pH	TO LIME OR NOT TO LIME
4·5–5·5 **VERY ACID** Seriously short of lime	Strongly acid soil is ideal for Azaleas, Camellias, blue Hydrangeas, most Heathers, Rhododendrons and Blueberries. For other plants liming is essential — if a lawn is to be laid on this soil make sure that you do not overlime as fine-leaved grasses require acid conditions.
5·5–6·5 **ACID** Short of lime	Acid soil is ideal for most fruit trees and bushes (Apples, Pears, Raspberries, Strawberries) and some vegetables (Potatoes, Tomatoes, Marrows, Cucumbers). It is also ideal for lawn grasses and Roses, but for nearly all other garden plants a dressing of lime is desirable.
6·5–7·3 **NEARLY NEUTRAL** Correct amount of lime	Neutral soil is suitable for nearly all flowers, shrubs, trees and vegetables. Peat will be necessary if you want to grow an acid-lover, but for other plants no treatment is necessary. A light dressing of lime every few years will be necessary to maintain this neutral state — rain steadily washes lime out of the soil.
7·3–8·0 **ALKALINE** Too much lime	Alkaline soil is satisfactory for Carnations, Wallflowers, Delphiniums, Cabbages, Brussels Sprouts, many shrubs and many alpines. Too much lime or chalk is generally a bad thing in the garden as plant foods are locked up. Never lime soil of this type.

When to lime

The best time to add lime to the soil is after digging, in autumn. If autumn manuring has been carried out, postpone liming until February. Spread the powder evenly over the surface, leaving rain to carry it down into the soil.

Vegetable plot: Lime every 3 years. If you follow a crop rotation, lime the plot which is intended for the Cabbage family. Do not lime land which is to be used for Potatoes.

Flower garden: Lime every 2 years on sandy soils, and every 3 years on heavy soils and loam.

Remember that lime likes to be alone, so do not mix it with other soil dressings. To avoid the loss of plant foods, lime should not be applied until at least 2–3 months after manuring, and 1 month after fertilizers.

Manures, composts, fertilizers and seeds can safely be added to the soil 1 month after liming.

IMPROVING YOUR SOIL BY
ADDING FERTILIZERS

We have to eat to live. Without a regular supply of starch, protein and other complex nutrients we should very soon die. Plants have a different arrangement. They use carbon, hydrogen and oxygen from the air and soil water in order to manufacture their own starch and sugars. All they need from the soil is a number of simple chemicals which they then use to create all the amino acids, proteins, vitamins, enzymes, etc.

All soils have a stock of these vital simple chemicals known as plant nutrients — they come from the mineral part of the soil (sand, clay, etc) and from the humus it contains (fallen leaves, dead roots, etc). When the ground is cultivated and garden plants grown in it, the balance is upset. Essential elements in the soil diminish more rapidly than they can be replaced by natural means.

The most serious loss concerns three elements — nitrogen, phosphorus and potassium. These are known as the major plant nutrients, and are required in large amounts if the plants are to grow satisfactorily. This means that these major plant nutrients must be applied regularly. A proportion will be provided if organic dressings such as compost or manure are applied, but we must rely on fertilizers as the main source of supply. *A fertilizer is a material which provides appreciable quantities of one or more of the major plant nutrients without adding significantly to the humus content of the soil.*

A bewildering variety of fertilizers is available — organic and inorganic, straight and compound, liquid and solid. These terms are explained on page 18 and the choice is yours. Do remember, however, there are no 'good' and 'bad' fertilizers — all have a job to do and the correct choice depends on the plant, soil type, area involved, time of year and so on. The golden rule is to feed plants regularly but no more often than the package recommends. If you are undecided whether to feed or not, be guided by the vigour of the plants. Fertilizer test kits are available, but the interpretation of the results is difficult for the ordinary gardener.

Methods of application

BY HAND
The standard method for solid fertilizers in most situations

FERTILIZER SPREADER
The standard method for solid fertilizers on large lawns, and on large beds and borders before planting

WATERING CAN
The standard method for liquid fertilizers in most situations

SPRAYER
The standard method for foliar fertilizers

HOSE-END DILUTOR
The standard method for liquid fertilizers on large areas

The meaning of the words and figures on the package

The **nitrogen** content: this fertilizer contains 3.0% N (nitrogen)

The **phosphorus** content: this fertilizer contains 6.0% P_2O_5 ('phosphates' or 'phosphoric acid')

Net weight of contents in the package

The **potassium** content: this fertilizer contains 9.0% K_2O ('potash')

By law the manufacturer of a product described as a 'fertilizer' must declare the nitrogen, phosphates and potash content on the package.
The content of most other nutrients must also be declared if they have been added to the product.

3:6:9
5 kg

NITROGEN (N)
PHOSPHORUS PENTOXIDE (P_2O_5)   3%
Phosphorus pentoxide (P_2O_5)   6%
soluble in water
Phosphorus pentoxide (P_2O_5)   5%
soluble in neutral ammonium
citrate and in water   5.5%
Phosphorus pentoxide (P_2O_5)
soluble only in mineral acids   0.5%
POTASSIUM OXIDE (K_2O)
soluble in water   9%

NPK FERTILIZER

Statutory declaration of fertilizer type:

NPK fertilizer	Inorganic compound fertilizer
Compound fertilizer	Compound fertilizer containing organics and/or weedkillers

Detailed analysis:

N	Total nitrogen
P_2O_5	Total phosphates
P_2O_5 soluble in water	Phosphates which are immediately available
P_2O_5 soluble in neutral ammonium citrate and in water	Phosphates which are immediately or quite quickly available
P_2O_5 soluble only in mineral acids	Phosphates which are slowly available
K_2O	Total potash

Plant Nutrients

PLANT NUTRIENT	PLANTS MOST IN NEED	SOILS MOST IN NEED	SIGNS OF SHORTAGE	HOW TO AVOID SHORTAGE
MAJOR PLANT NUTRIENTS			Large amounts required for satisfactory plant growth	
NITROGEN (N) the LEAF MAKER	Grass • Vegetables grown for their leaves • Root-bound plants	Sandy soils • Rainy areas	Stunted growth • Small, pale green leaves • Weak stems	Apply a base dressing before sowing or planting • Top dress in spring and summer with a nitrogen-rich fertilizer. Repeat if recommended, as quick-acting nitrogen is rapidly washed down by rain
PHOSPHATES (P_2O_5) the ROOT MAKER	Young plants • Root vegetables • Fruit and seed crops	Sandy soils	Stunted roots and stems • Small leaves with a purplish tinge • Low fruit yield	Apply a base dressing of Bone Meal or a compound fertilizer with a high P_2O_5 content • Use a compound fertilizer when top dressing plants
POTASH (K_2O) the FLOWER and FRUIT MAKER	Fruit • Flowers • Potatoes	Sandy soils	Edges of leaves turn yellow and then brown • Low fruit yield — fruit and flowers poorly coloured • Low disease resistance	Apply a base dressing of a compound fertilizer with a high K_2O content • Use a compound fertilizer when top dressing plants
INTERMEDIATE PLANT NUTRIENTS			Moderate amounts required for satisfactory plant growth	
CALCIUM (Ca)	Fruit • Flowers • Vegetables	Acid soils • Potash-rich soils	Similar to nitrogen shortage — stunted growth and pale green leaves	Apply lime — see page 15 • If the soil is sufficiently alkaline, use gypsum instead of lime
MAGNESIUM (Mg)	Roses • Tomatoes	Sandy soils • Peaty soils • Potash-rich soils	Yellow or brown patches between the veins of older leaves • Young leaves may fall	Apply a base dressing of a compound fertilizer containing magnesium • Use MultiTonic if symptoms are seen during the growing season
SULPHUR (S)	All plants	Rural areas	Similar to nitrogen shortage — stunted growth and pale green leaves	No remedial action is necessary if a sulphur-containing product such as Growmore, Multirose, Multiveg etc is used during the year
TRACE ELEMENTS			Minute amounts required for satisfactory plant growth — application of large amounts can lead to damage	
IRON (Fe)	Rhododendrons • Azaleas • Camellias	Chalky soils	Yellowing of younger leaves	In good growing conditions no action is required. Use humus-makers in the usual way and these, together with the impurities present in fertilizers, will provide sufficient trace elements required for satisfactory growth
MANGANESE (Mn)	Rhododendrons • Azaleas • Camellias	Chalky soils	Yellowing between the veins of older leaves	Trouble can occur on chalky, peaty, very light and distinctly acid soils. Here one or more trace elements may be either absent or locked up by other elements. Iron and manganese shortage in chalky soils is due to lock-up by calcium. Growth of some plants such as Rhododendrons, Azaleas and Camellias is difficult or impossible in such situations. Use peat at planting time — apply MultiTonic if deficiency symptoms appear
MOLYBDENUM (Mo)	Brassicas	Acid soils	Narrow leaves	
BORON (B)	Root vegetables	Sandy soils	Brown heart	
ZINC (Zn)	Fruit • Vegetables	Sandy soils	Dieback	
COPPER (Cu)	Fruit • Vegetables	Sandy soils	Dieback • Brown spots on leaves	

Fertilizer Types

Over the years a vast mythology has grown up around the magic of fertilizers. The head gardeners of the pre-war estates had their secret potions. Today there are feeds which are claimed to be ideal for everything in the garden.

The truth is much less exciting. All nutrient-providing ingredients have to be reduced to the same simple compounds before the roots are able to absorb them. This means that the nutrients in a liquid fertilizer containing inorganic salts may be immediately available to the plant roots — on the other hand the plant foods locked up in a coarsely-ground organic may have to wait months before release.

There is no 'good' or 'bad' here — the desired speed of release and the ideal balance of nutrients will depend on the soil type, the season and the plant. No single fertilizer can be the best in all situations.

Every gardening expert agrees that nitrogen, phosphates and potash must be added to the soil. The fertilizers which provide these nutrients are described as either 'organics' or 'inorganics'. Most authorities agree that both kinds do important but rather different jobs.

ORGANIC FERTILIZERS

These materials are of animal or vegetable origin. Most of them provide nitrogen, and this organic nitrogen must be transformed into a simple inorganic form before it can be absorbed by the roots. This breakdown is performed by soil bacteria. It is important to remember that these organisms are not active in cold, acid or waterlogged soils, so speed of action depends on soil conditions.

Organics are generally slow-acting, providing plants with a steady supply of food over a long period. They are less likely than inorganics to scorch leaves, but are usually more expensive. Do not regard them as soil improvers — they are used at a few ounces per square yard and so provide very little humus.

or

INORGANIC FERTILIZERS

Some of these fertilizers are minerals extracted from the earth — Chilean Potash Nitrate is every bit as natural as Bone Meal. Others are manufactured and have earned the titles of 'synthetic' or 'artificial' fertilizers. Plants are unable to tell the difference between plant foods from natural or synthetic sources — breakdown to the same nutrients occurs before uptake.

Inorganics are generally quick-acting, providing plants with a boost when used as a top dressing. They are usually less expensive than organics and have become much more popular than the old-time favourites. Just one organic fertilizer, Bone Meal, has kept its place amongst the best-selling plant foods.

SOLID FERTILIZERS

Garden shops display a wide array of solid fertilizers — powders or granules which are sprinkled on the soil by hand or applied through a fertilizer distributor. Powders are dustier to use than granules but are generally quicker acting. Sticks of concentrated fertilizer for insertion in the soil are available.

or

LIQUID FERTILIZERS

Liquid feeding means applying fertilizer diluted with water around the plants. It began with soaking bags of manure in a barrel of water — bottles of concentrated liquid fertilizer then became popular and in recent years soluble powders have taken pride of place. All are applied through a watering can or hose-end dilutor.

STRAIGHTS

A straight fertilizer is based on a single active ingredient. It nearly always contains just one major plant nutrient, although a few (e.g Bone Meal) contain a small amount of a second one.

or

COMPOUNDS

A compound fertilizer is based on a mixture of active ingredients. It nearly always contains all three major plant nutrients, although a few contain only nitrogen and phosphates.

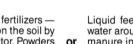

Which ones to buy?

No two experts will ever agree about which products are the best to buy — the choice must be yours.

As a guide, buy a granular compound fertilizer for base feeding and as a spring top dressing. Make sure that the major nutrients are 'balanced' (present in approximately equal proportions). Growmore (7:7:7) is an excellent choice.

For top dressing in late spring or summer use a balanced liquid fertilizer. Liquids are the right choice here because you want quick action.

There are areas of the garden which require a specific rather than a general fertilizer. Buy a lawn fertilizer which is high in nitrogen — for the Roses and Tomatoes choose fertilizers which are rich in potash.

FOLIAR FERTILIZERS

Several foliar feeds are sold, either as leaf-feeding fertilizers or mixed with pesticides as multipurpose products. When sprayed onto leaves the nutrients enter the sap-stream in a few hours, even where root action is restricted by poor soil conditions. A useful technique, especially for Roses and sick plants. For maximum effect ensure that sufficient leaf is present and spray in the evening when rain is not forecast.

STEADY-RELEASE FERTILIZERS

Many popular compound fertilizers contain both quick- and slow-acting sources of nutrients, so feeding goes on for some time. A true steady-release fertilizer, however, is a complex chemical which provides a prolonged supply of nutrients as it breaks down in the soil or as the outer coating dissolves. The best-known example is Urea-formaldehyde.

An A–Z of Fertilizers

Fertilizer	Nitrogen %N	Phosphates %P$_2$O$_5$	Potash %K$_2$O	Organic/ Inorganic	Speed of Action	Application Rate	Notes
BASIC SLAG	1	10–20	—	I	S	4–8 oz/sq. yd	Apply in autumn/winter. Good for acid, wet soils.
BIO LAWN TONIC	40	10	—	I	Q	¼ oz/sq. yd	Apply to lawns in spring/summer. Produces very quick green-up.
BIO PLANT FOOD	5	5	6	O/I	Q	5–15 ml/gal	Apply regularly during growing season as a general liquid feed.
BIO TOMATO FOOD	6	5	9	O/I	Q	5 ml/gal	Apply at every watering or at 10–14 day intervals.
BONE FLOUR	1	20–28	—	O	FQ	2–4 oz/sq. yd	Quicker to act but dustier to use than Bone Meal.
BONE MEAL	4	20	—	O	S	2–4 oz/sq. yd	Apply in autumn/early spring. Use 'heat treated' grade for safety.
CHILEAN POTASH NITRATE	15	—	10	I	Q	1–2 oz/sq. yd	Apply in spring/early summer as a general top dressing.
DRIED BLOOD	12	trace	trace	O	FQ	1–2 oz/sq. yd	Apply in late spring/summer. Quick-acting under glass.
FILLIP	8	8	6	I	Q	27 ml/gal	Foliar fertilizer. Apply during growing season.
FISH MEAL	6–10	6–12	1	O	S-FQ	2–4 oz/sq. yd	Apply in winter/spring as a base dressing.
GROWMORE	7	7	7	I	Q	1–4 oz/sq. yd	Apply in spring as a general dressing. Very popular.
HOOF & HORN MEAL	14	2	—	O	S-FQ	2–4 oz/sq. yd	Apply in spring. Speed of action depends on fineness.
MIRACLE-GRO	15	30	15	I	Q	18 ml/gal	Apply around roots of plants or foliar feed.
MURIATE OF POTASH	—	—	60	I	Q	½–2 oz/sq. yd	Best avoided — damaging to some plants.
NITRATE OF POTASH	13	—	45	I	Q	1–2 oz/sq. yd	Apply in spring — much used in liquid fertilizers.
NITRATE OF SODA	16	—	—	I	Q	½–1 oz/sq. yd	Very quick acting, but scorches leaves on contact and makes clays stickier.
NITRO-CHALK	16	—	—	I	Q	1–2 oz/sq. yd	Contains lime — useful on acid soils. Store in a dry place.
PHOSTROGEN	10	10	27	I	Q	1 tsp/2 gal	Apply regularly during growing season as a general liquid feed.
POULTRY MANURE (DRIED)	4	3	2	O	S-FQ	2–8 oz/sq. yd	Apply as a base (high rate) or top dressing (low rate).
ROCK PHOSPHATE	—	30	—	I	S	4 oz/sq. yd	Apply in autumn/winter. Good for acid soils.
SOOT	3–6	—	—	O	Q	4 oz/sq. yd	Allow to weather before use. Apply as a base or top dressing.
SULPHATE OF AMMONIA	21	—	—	I	Q	½–1 oz/sq. yd	Basic source of nitrogen. Makes soil more acid — good for lawns.
SULPHATE OF POTASH	—	—	48	I	Q	½–1 oz/sq. yd	Basic source of potash. Apply as a base or top dressing.
SUPERPHOSPHATE OF LIME	—	18	—	I	Q	2–4 oz/sq. yd	Basic source of phosphates. Apply as a base dressing.
TOPLAWN	10	5	3	I	Q	2 oz/10 sq. ft	Powder feed and weed product. Apply in spring/summer.
TOPROSE	5	6	12	I	FQ	2 oz/sq. yd	Apply in spring/summer and at planting time.
TRIPLE SUPERPHOSPHATE	—	47	—	I	Q	1–2 oz/sq. yd	Apply as a base dressing — less popular than standard superphosphate.
UREA	46	—	—	I	Q	½ oz/sq. yd	Apply in spring — much used in liquid fertilizers.
UREA-FORMALDEHYDE	38	—	—	I	FQ or S	1–2 oz/sq. yd	Any time of year — nitrogen steadily released for months.
WOOD ASH	—	—	5–10	O	Q	4–8 oz/sq. yd	Use young wood. Keep dry. Do not use on chalky soils.

O=derived from plants or animals

S= slow
FQ= fairly quick
Q= quick

Using and Storing Fertilizers

- Do not sprinkle fertilizer along seed drills.

- Do not feed plants with solid fertilizers right up to the stems. The feeding roots are some distance away from this region.

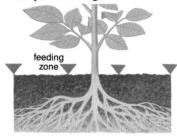

feeding zone

- A granular or powder fertilizer is of no value when lying on a dry soil surface. Its nutrients must get to the roots, so hoe or rake in after application and water if rain seems unlikely.

- Keep solid fertilizers off leaves and flowers. Wash off with water if these parts are accidentally treated.

- If the application rate is 1 oz or less per sq. yard, mix the fertilizer with sand to improve the evenness of the cover obtained. Do not dilute fertilizer/weedkiller products in this way.

- If a large area is to be treated, use a hose-end dilutor rather than a watering can for liquids, and a fertilizer spreader rather than handfuls for solids.

- Liquid fertilizers are often recommended in teaspoons or tablespoons per gallon. Don't use kitchen spoons — their capacity is variable. Buy a set of standard plastic measures from any hardware store.

- The soil should be moist before liquid feeding. If ground is dry, water first.

- Make sure that you use the amount recommended on the package. Double the amount does not give twice the benefit — it can in fact lead to unbalanced growth or scorch.

- Do not store fertilizer bags or cartons in a damp place. Always close the top after use and keep the packages off the floor.

Applying fertilizer by hand

The package and textbook tell you how much to use, but not how to do it. It is not surprising, therefore, that so many gardeners run out of fertilizer before the whole area has been treated.

Before you begin, cover any cuts on your hands with sticking plaster. Wear gloves if you are allergic to dusts. Choose a still day, especially if you are using a powdery product and a large plot is to be fed.

SMALL AREAS, SUCH AS BEDS OR AROUND PLANTS

STEP 1 — Weigh out the recommended quantity per sq. yard, sq. metre, per plant etc into a suitable container, such as a matchbox or small bowl.

STEP 2 — Mark out the area to be covered — sq. yard, sq. metre etc. Use string and canes if necessary.

STEP 3 — Sprinkle the measured fertilizer evenly over the marked-out area. Do this slowly and carefully so that all the ground is uniformly treated.

STEP 4 — Look at the density of powder or granules over this treated region. Now sprinkle the fertilizer by hand over the whole area to be treated. Try as far as possible to copy the cover obtained in Step 3.

STEP 5 — Keep any left-over fertilizer in a closed container. Store in a dry place. Wash hands and face.

LARGE AREAS, SUCH AS LAWNS

Carry out Steps 1 to 4, but use only half the recommended quantity to go up and down the area. Then repeat the process, going from side to side with the rest of the fertilizer. Step 5 is the final stage.

How much is a handful?

A 'handful' is an extremely unreliable measure — it depends on the product, size of hand and tightness of the grip.

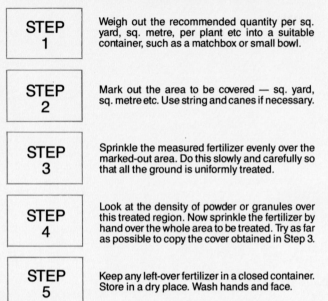

	LARGE HAND	SMALL HAND
CLOSED HANDFUL fingers touching palm	Bone Meal ▷ 3½ oz Growmore ▷ 2½ oz	Bone Meal ▷ 1½ oz Growmore ▷ 1¼ oz
OPEN HANDFUL fingers and palm cupped	Bone Meal ▷ 5 oz Growmore ▷ 4½ oz	Bone Meal ▷ 2½ oz Growmore ▷ 2 oz

Feeding Your Plants

Fertilizers put back what the rain and plants take away. It's as simple as that, but the details of correct fertilizer usage are not so simple. Garden plants vary greatly in their requirements, and correct timing is often all-important.

The usual plan is to buy a branded compound fertilizer. It is possible to prepare a home-made mix, but some skill is needed. Not all straight fertilizers can be blended — for instance, avoid mixing lime and sulphate of ammonia or superphosphate of lime and nitrate of soda. Some mixtures quickly set rock-hard if conditioning agents are not added — one of the best conditioners is Bone Flour.

LAWNS

Every lawn needs a nitrogen-rich compound fertilizer when growth becomes active in spring. Use one such as Toplawn which contains a weedkiller. If the lawn appears pale in midsummer, water on a liquid Lawn Tonic or sulphate of ammonia. Autumn treatment is for the keen gardener. Never use quick-acting nitrogen — this is the time for a product with phosphates, potash and a small amount of slow-acting nitrogen. Using quick-acting nitrogen can lead to disease.

ROSES

Use a mixture of 1 part soil, 1 part moist peat and 3 handfuls of Bone Meal per barrowload for filling the holes at planting time. With established plants, use a potash-rich compound fertilizer which contains magnesium and gypsum. Spread 1 oz of Toprose around each bush before the leaves are fully open and repeat the treatment in June or July. Do not feed Roses after the end of July or frost-sensitive growth may occur.

GREENHOUSE TOMATOES

Regular feeding is vital for greenhouse vegetables such as Tomatoes, Cucumbers, Aubergines etc. The best plan is to buy a potash-rich liquid fertilizer. Trials have shown that the little-and-often technique is better than a few heavy feeds. Use a low-strength solution for each watering until the plants are in full fruit. Increase the strength once heavy cropping has started. Outdoor Tomatoes should be fed every 10–14 days.

TREES & SHRUBS

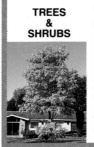

The standard recommendation is to apply a routine dressing of Growmore around the plants in spring, but the problem with trees is to get the fertilizer down to the roots. A better plan is to use a specific Tree & Shrub Fertilizer and pour it over the leaves and around the base of shrubs in the spring. For trees spike the ground under the leaf canopy with a fork to the full length of the tines before feeding.

VEGETABLES

A base dressing should be applied shortly before sowing or planting — Growmore is the old favourite and remains as popular as ever. Fast-maturing crops will need no further feeding — vegetables which take some time to mature will need one or more top dressings during the season. Use a soluble fertilizer, such as Instant Bio, which is dissolved in water and then applied through a watering can. Sulphate of ammonia can be used to give a quick boost to greens.

HOUSE PLANTS

There are many house plant feeding techniques these days. There are sticks, steady-release granules, tablets, feeding mats and so on. Whichever method you use, remember to reduce the amount of nutrients when the plants are resting — the winter months for foliage plants. Adding a few drops of liquid fertilizer to the watering can remains by far the most popular method as it is easy, inexpensive and provides control of the nutrient supply.

FRUIT TREES & BUSHES

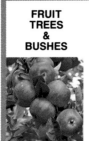

The general principles set out on the right for ornamental trees and shrubs apply to top and bush fruit, but there are a few additional factors. The greatest demand for nutrients is when the small fruits are beginning to swell, and at this stage it is necessary to use a potash-rich feed. Never use a feed which is richer in nitrogen than potash once fruit has formed. Most fruit trees and bushes respond to foliar feeding, especially after pest damage.

FLOWERS

Work a powder or granular fertilizer into the surface during soil preparation prior to planting. Most flowers will need feeding in spring — sprinkle Growmore around border perennials. Feed large and leafy plants such as Chrysanthemums and Dahlias with a liquid fertilizer on a regular basis. Annuals and alpines, however, need much less feeding — just once when they are coming into flower.

IMPROVING YOUR SOIL BY
ADDING HUMUS

Plant and animal remains are gradually decomposed in the soil. The agents of decay are the millions of bacteria and other microscopic organisms which live in every ounce of earth. They break down dead roots and underground insects as well as fallen leaves carried below the surface by worms. Partially-decomposed organic matter with the horde of living and dead bacteria is known to the gardener as **HUMUS.**

Soil without humus is nothing more than finely-ground rock. Humus is vital because it contains and maintains the vast population of microscopic organisms in the soil. These bacteria are the key to fertility, and have a beneficial effect both before and after death.

When alive they produce heat and transform complex organic materials into forms which will later be available to the roots. When dead they release these plant foods together with colloidal gums. To the soil scientist it is these gums and not plant remains which are humus — the magical material which cements the soil crumbs.

Under natural conditions there is a rough balance which maintains the humus level of the soil. Under cultivation, however, the humus content declines and so in the garden it is necessary to regularly replenish the supply. Last year's dead plants and dead worms are not enough — you have to add humus-makers. Many types are available, and they all fall into one or other of three basic types.

What is manure?

There are many humus-makers to choose from — compost, peat, farmyard manure and so on. The term 'manure' used to be employed to cover all these materials, and also to cover organic fertilizers such as dried blood and dried poultry 'manure'.

This group is far too large and far too different in action to be covered by a single term. It is best to restrict manure to cover bulky organic materials which add significantly to the humus content of the soil and also release major plant nutrients plus trace elements. By this definition compost is a manure but peat and dried blood are not.

Types of Humus-makers

RAW HUMUS-MAKERS

These organic materials contain sufficient readily-available nutrients to stimulate active bacterial growth. Heat is produced and soil structure is improved — hot beds made with fresh manure were producing early vegetables before electricity was discovered.

Common examples are grass clippings, fresh dung, dug-in weeds and seaweed. Using raw humus-makers is a good way of warming the earth and building up the humus content . . . provided you know the limitations. The sudden increase in the bacterial population robs nitrogen from the soil. Always add some nitrogen when using a raw humus-maker.

As a general rule, humus-makers of this type are used some time before planting or in an area some distance away from plant roots. The generation of heat and the nitrogen-robbing effect can be damaging to nearby roots.

MATURED HUMUS-MAKERS

These organic materials do not contain sufficient readily-available nutrients to stimulate active bacterial growth. A raw humus-maker is transformed into a matured humus-maker by composting — a process which produces humus.

Common examples are well-rotted animal manure, properly-made garden compost and Bio Humus. The warming effect on the soil is lost, but this is outweighed by the advantages. Matured humus-makers cannot damage tender roots and the nitrogen content of the soil remains available rather than being partly locked up in bacterial bodies.

All matured compost-makers contain the colloidal gums released by dead bacteria during the composting process. Unlike the fibrous humus-makers listed below, they do more than improve aeration and water-holding capacity by physical means — they also immediately provide the agents to produce soil crumbs and so improve friability.

FIBROUS HUMUS-MAKERS

These organic materials are rich in cellulose, but the lack of sugars and simple starches means that little bacterial activity is stimulated. Soil improvement by these humus-makers is basically a physical effect — bark opens up the soil and peat improves aeration and water-holding capacity.

Common examples are peat, pulverised bark and sawdust. Peat is the most inactive material — it is clean and easy to handle but it is hardly a humus-maker in the true sense of the word. It resists breakdown and so crumb-forming gums are not produced.

Sawdust and some bark products are slowly broken down by bacteria. This bacterial activity requires nitrogen, and the soil's supply will be robbed if you don't add a nitrogen-rich fertilizer — choose from the list on page 19.

An A–Z of Humus-makers

Humus-maker	Nitrogen % N	Phosphates % P_2O_5	Potash % K_2O	Application rate	Notes
BARK	¼	★	★	1 in. layer over soil surface — dig in or use as a surface mulch	Bark chippings, variously described as pulverised, shredded, granular etc, are now offered under various brand names as a peat substitute. Very useful for mulching (see page 76) because bark is a dense material, but less useful for digging-in as it does not have the water- or nutrient-holding capacity of moss peat. Fresh bark needs 1 oz of nitrogen per 1 cubic ft when used for soil incorporation.
BIO HUMUS	½	★	★	¼ lb per yd of seed drill before sowing or ¼ lb–2 lb under roots before planting	A proprietary matured humus-maker, produced by stacking vegetable matter, seaweed extract, chalk and nutrients in giant heaps until bacterial digestion comes to an end.
COMPOST	1½	2	½	1 bucket per sq. yd — dig in or use as a surface mulch	More nonsense has been written about compost-making than any other gardening subject. We still read about helpful lime, harmful soil, the need to turn, the need for nitrogen and so on. Whether your heap is a useful source of humus or an evil-smelling rubbish dump depends on one simple rule — look after the bacteria and they will look after the compost. Their needs are simple — just provide a way to keep the water out and the heat in, ensure the right balance between carbon and nitrogen, and add some soil to mop up water and harmful gases. (1) Pick the right container. Forget the advertisements — go for maximum insulation. A pit in the ground is best of all — next comes a brick or wooden-sided compost bin. A plastic bag or wire netting gives little or no insulation. (2) Get the carbon/nitrogen balance right. You don't have to be a chemist. If you are using soft greenstuff (grass, weeds etc), the nitrogen is too high. Mix in straw, sawdust, leaves or a *carbon*-rich additive. If you are using woody or strawy stuff, the carbon is too high. Add grass cuttings or a *nitrogen*-rich additive — any of the popular ones. (3) Build up the layers — 6 in. of organic matter and then a 1 in. layer of soil. Finish off with a layer of soil. (4) Cover to keep out rain — an absolutely vital step. (5) Leave it alone. Don't drive in holes. Don't add water. Don't turn. Use after 4 months.
FARMYARD MANURE	½	¼	½	1 bucket per sq. yd — dig in or use as a surface mulch	The great gardens of the past testify to the value of farmyard manure properly applied, but both the quantity and quality have declined in recent years. Use farmyard manure (FYM) rather than stable manure when the soil is sandy. Before use, stack it under some form of roofing, cover with several inches of soil and leave to decay. It is ready when the unpleasant smell has disappeared and the straw is no longer recognisable.
GREEN MANURE	2	¼	¾	Dig in during summer/autumn	Green manure is a crop grown for the purpose of digging-in and providing humus for chalky or sandy soil. Apply a fertilizer and sow rape or mustard in April–July. Dig in 2 months after germination. Some plant parts are available as 'green manure' — examples are grass cuttings, fallen leaves and weeds. Use them as ingredients for making compost.
LEAFMOULD	½	¼	¼	1 bucket per sq. yd — dig in or use as a surface mulch	Collect leaves in autumn (Oak and Beech are the favourites) and build a heap — 6 in. layers of leaves between 1 in. layers of soil. Composting is slow — leave for a year and use in the following autumn/winter. Leafmould is usually acidic.

★ = less than ¼ %

An A–Z of Humus-makers continued

Humus-maker	Nitrogen % N	Phosphates % P_2O_5	Potash % K_2O	Application rate	Notes
MUSHROOM COMPOST	½	¼	½	1 bucket per sq. yd — dig in before planting	Spent mushroom compost used to be stable manure plus soil, straw and chalk — nowadays it is composted straw. A useful material for enriching sandy soil — but remember the lime content. Do not use if you intend to grow lime haters such as Rhododendrons.
PEAT	¾	★	★	1 in. layer over soil surface — dig in or use as a surface mulch	Peat has superseded animal manure as the most popular humus-maker. It is consistent in quality, sterile and pleasant to handle. There are two types — both are basically useful but possess rather different properties. Sedge peat is the residue from sedges and grasses. It is a little richer in nitrogen and breaks down more quickly in the soil. Moss peat is obtained from sphagnum moss and holds more air and water. Moss peat is especially important for mixing with the soil before planting lime-hating plants.
POULTRY MANURE	2	1½	1	Compost before use	Fresh poultry manure is rich in nutrients — unfortunately it is also rich in materials which can be toxic to young roots. The best plan is to add poultry manure to the compost heap — it is an excellent activator.
SAWDUST	¼	★	★	Compost before use or apply 1 in. layer over soil surface — dig in before planting	Cheap, but use with care. It will rob the soil of nitrogen, so add 1 oz of nitrogen per cubic ft of sawdust before digging into the soil. Another problem is that some woods contain resins which can be toxic to plant growth.
SEAWEED	¼	¼	½	1 bucket per sq. yd — dig in before planting	An excellent manure-maker — free for the taking if you live near the sea. Dig in without composting — both the humus and trace element content of the soil will be enriched. A word of warning — wash off the salt before use.
SEWAGE SLUDGE (DRIED)	5	4	2	2–3 lb per sq. yd — dig in during autumn/winter	Never use raw sewage — buy dried material. Dried material is of two types — 'digested' and 'activated'. Use activated sludge — it is richer and safer. Not much organic matter is applied per sq. yd but it is a fairly effective source of plant nutrients.
SHODDY	10	★	★	2 lb per sq. yd — dig in during autumn/winter	This waste from woollen mills used to be popular with Northern gardeners, but it is rarely seen nowadays. Not very effective as a humus-maker, but the nitrogen is released steadily over a period of years.
SPENT HOPS	1	½	★	1 bucket per sq. yd — dig in during autumn/winter	After flavour extraction, hops are disposed of by breweries and for the gardener provide a useful peat substitute. Let the spent hops weather for a few months before use. Spent hops are bought and mixed with nutrients by some manufacturers — the resulting products are really fertilizers and add only small amounts of organic matter to the soil.
STABLE MANURE	¾	¼	½	1 bucket per sq. yd — dig in or use as a surface mulch	The best type of manure for clayey soils is obtained from horses, and the best type of stable manure contains plenty of straw rather than wood shavings. Do not use it immediately. Stack it under cover for several months — see farmyard manure (page 23) for details.
STRAW	½	★	¾	Compost before use	Straw is an active humus-maker when plenty of nitrogen is present, but it is not a good idea to add it directly to the soil. If often contains hormone weedkillers, and so it should be composted before use. Mix with plenty of greenstuff or use a standard activator when building the compost heap.

★ = less than ¼%

CHAPTER 3
CLIMATE & WEATHER

Weather is the combination of rainfall, temperature, wind, sunshine and air humidity which affects your garden at a particular point in time. **Climate** is the summary of the weather which is likely to affect your garden throughout the year. The climatic maps of your area should be used as rough guides only. They provide averages over many years rather than telling you the extremes of weather conditions which you are likely to enjoy (or suffer) during a particular year. In addition, the general climate of your region will be much modified by the factors around the garden (the local climate) and the factors around each plant (the microclimate).

The Seasons

DECEMBER	
JANUARY	Winter
FEBRUARY	
MARCH	
APRIL	Spring
MAY	
JUNE	
JULY	Summer
AUGUST	
SEPTEMBER	
OCTOBER	Autumn
NOVEMBER	

The Growing Season

STARTS when the soil temperature reaches 43°F

The **Growing Season** is the period of the year when most plants (including grass) are in growth. This growth may be slow at the start and finish of the growing season, and may cease altogether if there is an unseasonal frost.

FINISHES when the soil temperature falls below 43°F

Growing Season in Britain	
Average	250 days
Longest (Extreme S.W.)	330–360 days
Shortest (Scottish Highlands)	150–180 days

General Climate

The general climate provides a rough guide to the weather you can expect in your garden. In Britain it varies from nearly sub-tropical (S.W. coastal areas) to nearly sub-arctic (N. Scottish highlands). The general climate is controlled by the latitude, altitude, direction of the prevailing wind and the closeness to the sea. The effect of latitude is obvious to everyone — southern gardens are warmer than northern ones. The effect of being close to the sea is equally well known — western coastal gardens are kept virtually frost-free by the Gulf Stream. Less well known is the effect of small increases in altitude (page 26) and the plant-damaging effect of salt in coastal areas for as much as 5 miles inland.

Local Climate

The local climate is the modified form of general climate. It is controlled by
- Slope — a south-facing sloping site starts its growing season about 1 week before a level plot.
- Openness — nearby trees and bushes will cast shade and reduce solar energy, but they will also reduce the damaging effect of high winds.
- Proximity of buildings — town gardens are affected in many ways by the closeness of walls, houses etc. Walls cast shadows and so reduce solar energy — they can also cast rain shadows and so reduce rainfall. Walls affect the temperature — heat is released at night and south-facing walls can form a sun-trap.
- Soil type — frosts are more likely to occur over sandy soils than over heavy ones.
- Proximity to water — a nearby large lake can have a cooling effect on hot summer days.

Microclimate

The microclimate is the modified form of local climate in the immediate vicinity of a plant. Large variations can occur from one part of a garden to another. Nearby walls and hedges or overhanging plants will of course result in less light and less rainfall than in the open garden — the effect of this rain shadow can be to cut the water supply to only 25 per cent of the rainfall in the open garden. On the credit side the effect of nearby walls and plants is to cut the risk of frosts on clear, still nights and to reduce the harmful effect of wind. The general climate cannot, of course, be changed. The local climate is usually impossible to alter but the microclimate can often be changed by moving nearby plants or features, or by introducing cloches or windbreaks.

Frost

THE FIRST FROST is likely to occur —

- after November 1
- mid October – November 1
- October 1 – mid October
- before October 1

THE LAST FROST is likely to occur —

- before April 1
- April 1 – mid April
- mid April – mid May
- mid May – 3rd week May
- after 3rd week May

Hardy Plants will survive in the garden during the period between the first frosts in autumn and the last frosts in spring. **Half-hardy Plants** are killed during this period if left unprotected outdoors.

A frost occurs when the temperature falls below 32°F (0°C). It is damaging to plants in two ways — water is rendered unavailable to plant roots and the cells of sensitive plants are ruptured. These dangers are linked with the severity and duration of the frost as well as the constitution of the plant — in Britain we leave our Roses unprotected over winter whereas in some parts of Scandinavia and N. America straw or sacking protection is essential.

Late spring frosts which occur after growth has started are the most damaging of all. The danger signs are clear skies in the evening, a northerly wind which decreases at dusk and a settled dry period during the previous few days. The risk to a plant is reduced if there are overhanging branches above, other plants around, heavy soil below and the coast nearby.

In frost-prone areas avoid planting fruit trees and delicate shrubs. Provide some form of winter protection for choice specimens.

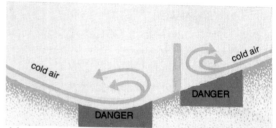

A frost pocket is an area which is abnormally prone to early autumn and late spring frosts. It occurs where a solid barrier is present on a sloping site — replace with an open barrier which allows air drainage. A frost pocket is also formed in the hollow at the bottom of a sloping site.

Wind

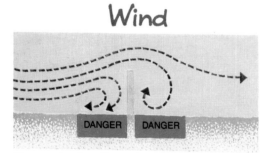

The spectacular effects of a gale are well known — broken branches, knocked-over pots etc. But the effects of persistent winds are less well known — lop-sided development due to the death of buds on the windward side, and stunted growth due to the cooling and drying effect on the growing point. On exposed sites a windbreak may be necessary, but never use a solid screen. A wall or closed fence will create down-draughts on either side (see above) and plants will be harmed. A hedge, on the other hand, will gently reduce wind speed for a distance of 15–30 times its height.

Rainfall

The average annual rainfall is 34 in. in England (41 in. in the British Isles). Unlike some other areas of the globe there is no distinct rainy season, but October–January is usually the wettest period. The driest region is the Thames Estuary (20 in.) — the wettest spots are the mountains of Wales and Scotland (175 in.). The U.K. record, however, belongs in the Lake District — 257 in. in 1954 at Sprinkling Tarn.

A drought is a period of 15 consecutive days without measurable rainfall, and droughts do occur at fairly regular intervals in Britain. Thorough watering is necessary at such times, otherwise plants will suffer or die. Snow is a mixed blessing — a blanket of snow can protect plants which would otherwise be damaged by arctic-like winds, but heavy snowfalls can damage or break the branches of evergreens.

Altitude

The height of your garden has an effect on the general climate. For every 600 ft increase in altitude, the average annual temperature falls by 2°F and the start of the growing season is delayed by 3 days. Solar energy decreases whereas both rainfall and wind speed increase.

Temperature

- Temperatures of 10°F occur occasionally during still, clear nights in winter — prolonged spells of abnormally cold weather can lead to the death of some plants normally regarded as hardy.

- High summer temperatures are necessary for the satisfactory ripening of Tomatoes, Sweet Corn and many fruits which originated in warmer climates. Hot weather (80°F and above) has its drawbacks — soils dry out quickly, bloom life is shortened, transplanting is made difficult and the germination of some seeds (e.g Lettuce) is impaired.

CHAPTER 4

PLANTS

The purpose of the soil in your garden is to grow plants. You may wish to be utterly conventional, with turf grasses forming a central lawn which is edged with borders and spotted with beds. These beds and borders are filled with shrubs, herbaceous perennials and bedding plants. You will almost certainly find room for some Rose bushes and a woody climber or two for the walls of the house. For many the lure of home-grown vegetables is irresistible. This standard pattern of the suburban garden is slowly changing — flowering shrubs, evergreen ground covers and small trees are becoming more popular and the classical herbaceous border is losing its appeal.

You may wish to depart from the routine pattern. There are people who devote their front gardens to alpines and bulbs — others create Rose gardens, some produce natural gardens with shrubs and wild flowers, and there is the organised chaos of the cottage garden with its herbs, annuals and old-fashioned perennials.

The range of plants you can choose from is quite staggering. The catalogue of a seed nurseryman contains many hundreds of varieties — the list of a general nurseryman is even more bewildering with all its shrubs, trees, climbers, herbaceous border plants, alpines, and so forth. A stroll around a modern garden centre is a most enjoyable experience which was denied to our ancestors, but it is also a perplexing job when the object is to pick a number of plants which will be right for the garden.

Still, you might think, the choice is up to you. It is just a matter of liking the picture in the catalogue or the specimen at the garden centre. No it isn't — there are a number of factors which must be considered if you are not going to waste a lot of time and money, and some of these factors are outside your control. Follow the step-by-step guide below in order to make sure that the plants you want to grow will thrive in your garden. You need the right plant from the right supplier.

STEP 1

CHOOSE THE RIGHT PLANT TYPE — see page 28

Do I want a permanent feature or a temporary display? Trees and shrubs are used to form the permanent living skeleton of the garden. Hardy perennials will live in the garden for years, but die down in the winter. Annuals are for temporary display only. **Do I want a labour-saving plant?** Herbaceous perennials and 'hobby plants' such as Dahlias and Chrysanthemums involve a lot of work — staking, feeding, dead-heading, dividing etc. Most shrubs and trees involve little annual maintenance, but well-timed pruning may be a requirement. **Do I want the leaves to stay on over winter?** Choose an evergreen, but it is not always the best plant to grow. A garden filled with evergreens can look dull and unchanging — deciduous plants add an extra dimension with fresh leaves opening in the spring and changing colours in autumn.

STEP 2

CHOOSE THE RIGHT EXAMPLE OF THIS PLANT TYPE — see pages 29–57

What shape and size would be suitable? One of the commonest mistakes in gardening is to buy a plant which at maturity is far too large for the space available. Chopping back every year means that both natural beauty and floral display can be lost. Always check the expected height before buying. **What will the growing conditions be like?** Check if the plant has clear-cut requirements with regard to sunshine, temperature, soil texture, lime tolerance, drainage and soil moisture. Some plants are remarkably tolerant of climatic and soil conditions — others are not. Nearly all annuals need full sun, rockery perennials demand good drainage and Pieris, Rhododendron, Camellia, Calluna and Pernettya hate lime.

STEP 3

CHOOSE THE MOST SUITABLE PLANT MATERIAL OF THIS SPECIES OR VARIETY — see pages 58–64

Is money the main consideration? Seed bought in packets or saved from your own plants is inexpensive, but it may take years to raise a shrub or herbaceous perennial by this method. Rooted cuttings taken from plants in the garden are another inexpensive source of plant material. **Is simplicity the main consideration?** Containers have revolutionised planting out. Just choose a container-grown specimen at any time of the year, dig a hole in the garden and pop it in. Containers are not *quite* that easy (page 64), but they are the most convenient and 'instant' of all plant materials.

STEP 4

BUY FROM THE RIGHT SOURCE OF SUPPLY — see pages 65–66

As a general rule you get what you pay for, but this does not mean that there is a 'best' supplier for all situations. A 'bargain offer' from a mail order nursery may be the right choice if you are short of money and have a large space to fill with common-or-garden shrubs, but in most cases it is preferable to see what you are buying and it is always wise to seek out a supplier with a good reputation.

Plant Types

ROSES

Deciduous Shrubs and Trees of the genus Rosa, usually listed separately in the catalogues because of their importance and great popularity

A **Half Standard** is a Rose Tree with a 2½ ft stem

A **Full Standard** is a Rose Tree with a 3½ ft stem

WOODY PLANTS

Perennial plants with woody stems which survive the winter

A **Shrub** bears several woody stems at ground level

A **Tree** bears only one woody stem at ground level

A **Climber** has the ability when established to attach itself to or twine around an upright structure. Some weak-stemmed plants which require tying to stakes (e.g Climbing Roses) are included here

A **Hedge** is a continuous line of Shrubs or Trees in which the individuality of each plant is partly or wholly lost

EVERGREEN SHRUBS & TREES

Woody plants which retain their leaves during winter

Conifers bear cones and nearly all are Evergreens

Semi-evergreens (e.g Privet) retain most of their leaves in a mild winter

A **Ground Cover** is a low-growing and spreading plant which forms a dense, leafy mat

DECIDUOUS SHRUBS & TREES

Woody plants which shed their leaves in winter

Top Fruit are Trees which produce edible fruit (e.g Apple, Pear, Peach, Plum)

Soft Fruit are Shrubs and Climbers which produce edible fruit (e.g Blackcurrant, Gooseberry). A few are Herbaceous Plants (e.g Strawberry)

TURF PLANTS

Low-growing carpeting plants, nearly always members of the Grass Family, which can be regularly sheared and walked upon

HERBACEOUS PLANTS

Plants with non-woody stems which generally die down in winter

VEGETABLES

Plants which are grown for their edible roots, stems or leaves. A few are grown for their fruits (e.g Tomato, Cucumber, Marrow, Capsicum)

HERBS

Plants which are grown for their medicinal value, their culinary value as garnishes or flavourings, or their cosmetic value as sweet-smelling flowers or leaves

BULBS

Bulbs (more correctly Bulbous Plants) produce underground fleshy organs which are offered for sale for planting indoors or outdoors. Included here are the **True Bulbs, Corms, Rhizomes** and **Tubers**

BIENNIALS

Plants which complete their life span, from seed to death, in two seasons

A **Hardy Biennial** (HB) is sown outdoors in summer, producing stems and leaves in the first season and flowering in the next

Some Perennials are treated as Biennials (e.g Wallflower, Daisy)

A **Bedding Plant** is an Annual or Biennial set out in quantity in autumn or spring to provide a temporary display

PERENNIALS

Plants which complete their life span, from seed to death, in three or more seasons

A **Hardy Perennial** (HP) will live for years in the garden — the basic plant of the herbaceous border

A **Half-hardy Perennial** (HHP) is not fully hardy and needs to spend its winter in a frost-free place (e.g Fuchsia, Geranium)

A **Greenhouse Perennial** (GP) is not suitable for outdoor cultivation

A **Rockery Perennial** (RP) is a dwarf Hardy Perennial suitable for growing in a rockery. **Alpine** is an alternative name, although some originated on the shore rather than on mountains, and some delicate True Alpines need to be grown indoors

ANNUALS

Plants which complete their life span, from seed to death, in a single season

A **Hardy Annual** (HA) is sown outdoors in spring

A **Half-hardy Annual** (HHA) cannot withstand frost, and so they are raised under glass and planted outdoors when the danger of frost is past

A **Greenhouse** (or **Tender**) **Annual** (GA) is too susceptible to cold weather for outdoor cultivation, but may be planted out for a short time in summer

Plant Types Climbers

Latin name	Common name	Site & soil	Deciduous (D) or Evergreen (E)	Pruning	Propagation	Notes
ACTINIDIA	Actinidia	Sunny site — ordinary soil	D	Not necessary	Cuttings — summer	A. kolomikta is the usual one — green, pink and cream leaves
ARISTOLOCHIA	Dutchman's Pipe	Sun or light shade — fertile soil	D	Not necessary	Cuttings — summer	A. macrophylla is hardy outdoors — rarely seen in Britain
CAMPSIS	Trumpet Vine	Sunny site — fertile soil	D	Cut back old stems — winter	Layer stems — summer	Self-clinging climber with red blooms. Not very hardy
CELASTRUS	Bittersweet	Sun or light shade — ordinary soil	D	Shorten stems — spring	Layer stems — summer	C. orbiculatus grown for its bright seeds and seed pods
CLEMATIS HYBRIDS	Virgin's Bower	Fussy. Sun on stems — fertile soil	D or E or semi E	Complicated. Depends on variety	Cuttings — summer	The large-flowered hybrids are the ones usually grown
CLEMATIS SPECIES	Virgin's Bower	Sunny site — fertile soil	D	Complicated. Depends on variety	Cuttings — summer	Small flowers — easier to grow than hybrids
HEDERA	Ivy	Shady site — ordinary soil	E	Not necessary	Plant rooted runners	Many colourful varieties are available — yellow, white and golden
HYDRANGEA	Climbing Hydrangea	Sun or shade — well-drained soil	D	Not necessary	Side growths — summer	H. petiolaris is a self-clinging climber
JASMINUM	Jasmine	Sunny site — ordinary soil	D	Not necessary	Cuttings — summer	J. officinale and J. o. Grandiflorum are the usual ones
LONICERA	Honeysuckle	Sun or light shade — fertile soil	D or semi E	Cut back some stems — after flowering	Cuttings — summer	Most varieties have fragrant blooms — June – August
PARTHENOCISSUS	Virginia Creeper	Sun or light shade — fertile soil	D	Remove unwanted growth — spring	Layer stems — autumn	Leaves turn red in autumn. Popular one is P. tricuspidata
PASSIFLORA	Passion Flower	Sunny site — well-drained soil	D	Remove unwanted growth — spring	Cuttings — summer	P. caerulea is the species grown — not very hardy
POLYGONUM	Russian Vine	Sun or light shade — ordinary soil	D	Remove unwanted growth — spring	Cuttings — summer	Fast-growing, twining climber. Popular one is P. baldschuanicum
SOLANUM	Perennial Nightshade	Sunny site — ordinary soil	Semi E	Remove unwanted growth — spring	Layer stems — summer	S. crispum Glasnevin is the variety to choose
VITIS	Ornamental Vine	Sun or light shade — well-drained soil	D	Remove unwanted growth — summer	Cuttings — summer	Tendril-bearing climber grown for autumn foliage colour
WISTERIA	Wistaria	Sunny site — fertile soil	D	Cut back current side growths — July	Layer stems — summer	W. sinensis is the popular one — W. floribunda Macrobotrys is more spectacular

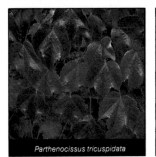

Parthenocissus tricuspidata

Clematis jackmanii

Passiflora caerulea

Wisteria sinensis

Lonicera tellmanniana

Hedera helix Goldheart

See
THE TREE & SHRUB EXPERT
for a more complete list
together with full details
and photographs

Plant Types Shrubs

Latin name	Common name	Site & soil	Deciduous (D) or Evergreen (E)	Pruning	Propagation	Notes
ACER	Japanese Maple	Partial shade — acid soil	D	Not necessary	Buy from garden centre	Varieties of A. palmatum grown for leaf shape and colour
ARUNDINARIA	Bamboo	Partial shade — ordinary soil	E	Not necessary	Divide clumps	Varieties range from 3–20 ft tall
AUCUBA	Aucuba	Sun or shade — ordinary soil	E	Not necessary	Cuttings — summer	Popular — planted where little else will grow
BERBERIS	Barberry	Sun or light shade — ordinary soil	D or E	Not necessary	Cuttings — summer	Popular and easy — range from 2–9 ft tall
BUDDLEIA	Butterfly Bush	Sunny site — well-drained soil	D or semi E	Popular varieties — cut back in March	Cuttings — autumn	Types bearing floral cones need annual pruning
BUXUS	Box	Sun or light shade — ordinary soil	E	Not necessary	Cuttings — summer	An excellent hedging or tub plant. Small glossy leaves
CALLUNA	Heather	Sunny site — acid soil	E	Lightly trim — March	Cuttings — summer	Hundreds of named varieties — 9–24 in. high
CAMELLIA	Camellia	Sun or light shade — acid soil	E	Not necessary	Cuttings — summer	Should be more popular — large blooms in March–May
CEANOTHUS	Californian Lilac	Sunny site — well-drained soil	D or E	D types — cut back in March	Cuttings — summer	Evergreen varieties are not fully hardy. Plant in spring
CHAENOMELES	Japonica	Sun or light shade — ordinary soil	D	Not necessary	Plant rooted suckers	Old favourite, grown for spring flowers and autumn fruits
CHIMONANTHUS	Winter Sweet	Sunny site — well-drained soil	D	Not necessary	Layer stems — summer	Fragrant flowers appear before leaves in winter
CHOISYA	Mexican Orange Blossom	Sunny site — ordinary soil	E	Not necessary	Cuttings — summer	Fragrant plant — white, starry flowers in May
CISTUS	Rock Rose	Sunny site — well-drained soil	E	Not necessary	Cuttings — summer	Succession of papery flowers throughout June and July
CORNUS	Dogwood	Sun or light shade — ordinary soil	D	Bark types — cut back in March	Cuttings — autumn	Varieties chosen for coloured bark or floral display
CORYLUS	Hazel	Sun or light shade — well-drained soil	D	Cut back old stems — March	Plant rooted suckers	Varieties chosen for twisted stems or coloured leaves
COTINUS	Smoke Bush	Sunny site — ordinary soil	D	Remove unwanted growth — spring	Plant rooted suckers	Feathery flower-heads — sold under old name Rhus cotinus
COTONEASTER	Cotoneaster	Sun or light shade — ordinary soil	D or E or semi E	Not necessary	Cuttings — summer	All shapes and sizes from ground covers to 20 ft bushes
CYTISUS	Broom	Sunny site — sandy soil	D or E or semi E	Trim back — after flowering	Cuttings — summer	Flowers clothe long whippy branches in May or June
DAPHNE	Daphne	Sunny site — humus-rich soil	D or E or semi E	Not necessary	Seed or summer cuttings	Popular species is D. mezereum — purplish flowers in February
DEUTZIA	Deutzia	Sun or light shade — ordinary soil	D	Cut back — after flowering	Cuttings — autumn	White or pink flowers borne freely in June
ELAEAGNUS	Oleaster	Sun or light shade — ordinary soil	D or E	Not necessary	Plant rooted suckers	Popular variety is E. pungens Maculata — glossy, yellow-splashed leaves
ERICA	Heather	Sun or light shade — well-drained soil	E	Lightly trim — after flowering	Cuttings — summer	Varieties available for flowering at any season and for chalky soil
ESCALLONIA	Escallonia	Sun or light shade — ordinary soil	E	Cut back — autumn	Cuttings — summer	Useful as a hedge, especially in coastal areas

Berberis darwinii

Buddleia davidii

Camellia Lady Clare

Elaeagnus pungens Maculata

Latin name	Common name	Site & soil	Deciduous (D) or Evergreen (E)	Pruning	Propagation	Notes
EUONYMUS	Euonymus	Sun or light shade — ordinary soil	D or E	Not necessary	Cuttings — summer	The popular ones are the evergreens — excellent ground covers
FATSIA	Castor Oil Plant	Partial shade — ordinary soil	E	Not necessary	Cuttings — summer	Not just a house plant — grows up to 10 ft outdoors
FORSYTHIA	Golden Bells	Sun or light shade — ordinary soil	D	Cut back shoots with faded blooms	Cuttings — autumn	Very popular — yellow flowers in March and April
FUCHSIA	Fuchsia	Sun or light shade — fertile soil	D	Cut back — March	Cuttings — summer	Choose a hardy variety. Pendent bells July – October
GARRYA	Silk Tassel Bush	Sun or light shade — ordinary soil	E	Not necessary	Cuttings — summer	Long and slender catkins drape bushes January – February
GENISTA	Broom	Sunny site — avoid heavy soil	D	Cut back shoots with faded blooms	Seed	Pea-like yellow flowers in June. Avoid feeding
HAMAMELIS	Witch Hazel	Sun or light shade — well-drained soil	D	Not necessary	Buy from garden centre	Fragrant flowers appear before leaves in winter
HEBE	Veronica	Sun or light shade — well-drained soil	E	Not necessary	Cuttings — summer	Small varieties, such as Autumn Glory, are completely hardy
HELIANTHEMUM	Rock Rose	Sunny site — well-drained soil	E	Cut back — after flowering	Cuttings — summer	Succession of flowers May – July. Avoid feeding
HIBISCUS	Tree Hollyhock	Sunny site — well-drained soil	D	Not necessary	Buy from garden centre	Bush grows 6 – 8 ft high. Not suitable for clayey or cold sites
HYDRANGEA	Hydrangea	Partial shade — well-drained soil	D	Remove flower-heads — March	Cuttings — summer	Many Lacecap and Mophead varieties are available
HYPERICUM	St. John's Wort	Sun or shade — ordinary soil	E or semi E	Cut back — March	Cuttings — summer	Excellent yellow-flowered shrubs — usually grown as ground cover
ILEX	Holly	Sun or shade — ordinary soil	E	Trim back — spring or summer	Cuttings — autumn	Wide range of leaf and berry colours. Always buy small plants
JASMINUM	Winter Jasmine	Sun or light shade — ordinary soil	D	Cut back shoots with faded blooms	Cuttings — summer	J. nudiflorum is an old favourite — yellow flowers November – February
KALMIA	Calico Bush	Partial shade — acid soil	E	Not necessary	Cuttings — summer	Rhododendron-like bush — pink flowers in June
KERRIA	Jew's Mallow	Sun or light shade — ordinary soil	D	Cut back shoots with faded blooms	Plant rooted suckers	Popular and easy — yellow flowers in April and May
LAURUS	Bay Laurel	Sun or light shade — ordinary soil	E	Trim back — spring	Cuttings — summer	L. nobilis grows up to 20 ft — leaves scorched by frost
LAVANDULA	Lavender	Sun or light shade — well-drained soil	E	Trim back — spring	Cuttings — autumn	Flowers appear in July – September — white, pink, blue or lavender
LIGUSTRUM	Privet	Sun or shade — ordinary soil	E or semi E	Trim back — May and August	Cuttings — autumn	Often regarded with contempt, but there are colourful varieties
MAGNOLIA	Magnolia	Sun or light shade — humus-rich soil	D or E	Not necessary	Layer stems — summer	Beautiful flowers (white, pink or red) on 4 – 20 ft plants
MAHONIA	Mahonia	Partial shade — ordinary soil	E	Not necessary	Plant rooted suckers	Useful yellow-flowered shrubs — popular under trees as ground cover
PERNETTYA	Prickly Heath	Sun or light shade — acid soil	E	Trim back — summer	Plant rooted suckers	Large, porcelain-like berries throughout the winter
PHILADELPHUS	Mock Orange	Sun or light shade — ordinary soil	D	Cut back some shoots with faded blooms	Cuttings — autumn	White fragrant flowers in June and July. Wrongly called Syringa
PIERIS	Andromeda	Partial shade — acid soil	E	Not necessary	Layer stems — summer	Bright red new growth in spring. White floral sprays
POTENTILLA	Shrubby Cinquefoil	Sun or light shade — well-drained soil	D	Cut back old stems — March	Cuttings — summer	Noted for length of flowering season — May – September

Hydrangea macrophylla

Potentilla fruticosa

Euonymus alatus

Ilex aquifolium Bacciflava

Latin name	Common name	Site & soil	Deciduous (D) or Evergreen (E)	Pruning	Propagation	Notes
PRUNUS	Prunus	Sun or light shade — ordinary soil	D or E	Trim — late spring (E), late summer (D)	Cuttings (E) — summer	Evergreens include Cherry Laurel and Portugal Laurel. Useful hedging plants
PYRACANTHA	Firethorn	Sun or light shade — ordinary soil	E	Cut back unwanted stems — after flowering	Cuttings — summer	Grown for massed display of red or yellow berries in autumn
RHODODENDRON	Azalea	Partial shade — acid soil	D or E	Remove dead flowers	Layer stems — summer	Daintier than Rhododendron. Deciduous types taller than evergreens
RHODODENDRON	Rhododendron	Partial shade — acid soil	E	Remove dead flowers	Buy from garden centre	Very popular — usual height 4–6 ft, usual flowering month May
RHUS	Sumach	Sunny site — ordinary soil	D	Cut stems to 1 ft — February	Plant rooted suckers	Grown for their brilliant foliage colours in autumn. Large flower spikes
RIBES	Flowering Currant	Sun or light shade — ordinary soil	D or semi E	Cut back shoots with faded blooms	Cuttings — autumn	R. sanguineum is seen everywhere. Pink or red flowers in pendent heads
ROSMARINUS	Rosemary	Sunny site — well-drained soil	E	Lightly trim — after flowering	Cuttings — summer	R. officinalis makes a 5 ft high hedge — greyish leaves, pale blue flowers
RUBUS	Ornamental Bramble	Sun or light shade — ordinary soil	D	Bark types — cut back in March	Cuttings — summer	Varieties chosen for coloured bark or floral display
SALIX	Willow	Sun or light shade — moist soil	D	Cut back coloured bark types — March	Cuttings — autumn	Grown mainly for coloured bark — red or yellow
SANTOLINA	Lavender Cotton	Sunny site — well-drained soil	E	Trim back — after flowering	Cuttings — summer	Yellow, button-like flowers (June–August) and silvery foliage
SENECIO	Senecio	Sunny site — well-drained soil	E	Not necessary	Cuttings — summer	Yellow, Daisy-like flowers (June) and leathery foliage
SKIMMIA	Skimmia	Partial shade — acid soil	E	Not necessary	Cuttings — summer	You will need male and female plants of S. japonica for red berries
SPARTIUM	Spanish Broom	Sunny site — well-drained soil	D	Trim back last year's growth — March	Cuttings — summer	Yellow flowers, rush-like stems. Keep in check by regular pruning
SPIRAEA	Spiraea	Sun or light shade — fertile soil	D	Cut back summer-flowering types — March	Cuttings — autumn	Spring-flowering varieties white — summer-flowering ones pink or red
SYMPHORICARPOS	Snowberry	Sun or shade — ordinary soil	D	Trim back — summer	Plant rooted suckers	Rampant grower — marble-like berries in October
SYRINGA	Lilac	Sunny site — non-acid soil	D	Cut back old stems — after flowering	Buy from garden centre	Fragrant blooms in May and early June
TAMARIX	Tamarisk	Sunny site — well-drained soil	D	Cut back summer-flowering types — March	Cuttings — autumn	Spring-flowering varieties pale pink — summer-flowering ones deep pink or red
ULEX	Gorse	Sunny site — ordinary soil	E	Trim back — May	Cuttings — summer	Yellow flowers (April–May) on spiny stems. Poor on fertile sites
VIBURNUM	Viburnum	Sunny site — humus-rich soil	D or E	Not necessary	Cuttings — summer	Many varieties — year-round colour is possible by growing several types
VINCA	Periwinkle	Sun or shade — well-drained soil	E	Not necessary	Plant rooted suckers	An excellent ground cover under trees. White or blue flowers — May–September
WEIGELA	Weigela	Sun or light shade — ordinary soil	D	Cut back shoots with faded blooms	Cuttings — summer	An old favourite — arching stems bear pink or red flowers in May and June
YUCCA	Yucca	Sun or light shade — well-drained soil	E	Not necessary	Plant rooted offsets	A spectacular plant — sword-like leaves and a tall flower-head

Rhododendron Britannia

Viburnum opulus

See
THE TREE & SHRUB EXPERT
for a more complete list
together with full details
and photographs

Plant Types **Conifers**

Latin name	Common name	Notes	Species & Varieties			
			Latin name	Ultimate height	Height after 10 years	Notes
ABIES	Silver Fir	Most firs are giants — choose with care	A. balsamea Hudsonia	DWARF	1 ft	Ideal for rock gardens
			A. koreana	MEDIUM	6 ft	Dark green foliage
ARAUCARIA	Monkey Puzzle	Once very popular — reaches 70 ft in time	A. araucana	TALL	5 ft	Branches like curved ropes
CEDRUS	Cedar	A tree for parkland rather than a suburban garden	C. atlantica Glauca	TALL	10 ft	Very popular — blue-green
			C. deodara	TALL	10 ft	Drooping growth habit
			C. libani	TALL	10 ft	Flat-topped with age
CHAMAECYPARIS	False Cypress	The most popular evergreen trees in Britain. Scores of varieties are available, ranging from rockery dwarfs to stately trees	C. lawsoniana Allumii	MEDIUM	6 ft	Conical — blue-grey foliage
			C. l. Ellwoodii	DWARF	5 ft	Very popular — grey-green
			C. l. Ellwood's Gold	DWARF	4 ft	Branchlet tips golden-yellow
			C. l. Minima Aurea	DWARF	1 ft	Compact pyramid — bright yellow
			C. l. Minima Glauca	DWARF	1 ft	Rounded — sea green foliage
			C. obtusa Nana Gracilis	DWARF	2 ft	Rounded sprays — dark foliage
			C. pisifera Boulevard	DWARF	3 ft	Silver-blue feathery sprays
CRYPTOMERIA	Japanese Cedar	Slow-growing — needs acid soil	C. japonica Elegans	MEDIUM	6 ft	Brown-green feathery sprays
CUPRESSO-CYPARIS	Leyland Cypress	The fastest growing conifer in Britain	C. leylandii	TALL	30 ft	Most popular conifer hedge
			C. l. Castlewellan	TALL	30 ft	Yellow foliage in spring
CUPRESSUS	Cypress	More difficult than Chamaecyparis	C. arizonica	MEDIUM	7 ft	Conical — blue-grey foliage
			C. macrocarpa Goldcrest	MEDIUM	8 ft	Conical — golden foliage
GINKGO	Maidenhair Tree	Unusual — leaves are wide and deciduous	G. biloba	TALL	10 ft	Pale green fan-like foliage
JUNIPERUS	Juniper	Most popular Junipers are either dwarfs or spreading ground covers. All are easy to grow, withstanding cold and poor soil conditions	J. chinensis	DWARF	5 ft	Conical — blue-green foliage
			J. communis Compressa	DWARF	1 ft	Columnar — grey-green foliage
			J. c. Depressa Aurea	DWARF	1 ft	Spreading — golden foliage
			J. horizontalis Glauca	PROSTRATE	1 ft	9 ft wide blue carpet
			J. media Pfitzerana	DWARF	4 ft	Popular — wide-spreading
			J. squamata Meyeri	DWARF	4 ft	Erect — blue-grey foliage
			J. virginiana Skyrocket	MEDIUM	6 ft	Blue-grey narrow column
LARIX	Larch	Deciduous — too tall for average garden	L. decidua	TALL	15 ft	Needs space and acid soil
METASEQUOIA	Dawn Redwood	Deciduous — discovered in 1941	M. glyptostroboides	TALL	15 ft	Orange foliage in autumn
PICEA	Spruce	Most (but not all) Piceas look like Christmas Trees. Dislike dry and chalky soils	P. albertiana Conica	DWARF	2 ft	Popular rockery conifer
			P. brewerana	TALL	5 ft	Excellent weeping conifer
			P. omorika	TALL	10 ft	Best Christmas Tree
			P. pungens Koster	MEDIUM	6 ft	Most popular Blue Spruce
PINUS	Pine	Pines are usually too tall for the average garden, but dwarf varieties are available	P. mugo Gnom	DWARF	2 ft	Globular rockery Pine
			P. nigra	TALL	10 ft	Dark green foliage
			P. strobus Nana	DWARF	2 ft	Spreading — silvery foliage
			P. sylvestris	TALL	12 ft	Familiar Scots Pine
TAXODIUM	Swamp Cypress	Deciduous — thrives in swampy soil	T. distichum	TALL	15 ft	Large tree — ferny foliage
TAXUS	Yew	Yews are generally slow-growing. Suitable for shade	T. baccata	MEDIUM	6 ft	Dark green tree or hedge
			T. b. Fastigiata	MEDIUM	5 ft	Columnar Irish Yew
			T. b. Semperaurea	DWARF	2 ft	Spreading — golden foliage
THUJA	Arbor-vitae	Similar to the much more popular Chamaecyparis. Many make excellent hedges	T. occidentalis Rheingold	DWARF	3 ft	Conical — bronzy foliage
			T. orientalis Aurea Nana	DWARF	2 ft	Globular — golden foliage
			T. o. Rosedalis	DWARF	2 ft	Globular — purple in autumn
			T. plicata	TALL	16 ft	Pyramid — specimen tree
TSUGA	Hemlock	Most types too tall for gardens	T. canadensis Pendula	DWARF	2 ft	Spreading — weeping branches

See
THE TREE & SHRUB EXPERT
for a more complete list
together with full details
and photographs

PROSTRATE: under 1½ ft
DWARF: 1½ – 15 ft
MEDIUM: 15 – 50 ft
TALL: Over 50 ft

Plant Types Trees

Latin name	Common name	Site & soil	Deciduous (D) or Evergreen (E)	Pruning	Notes
ACER	Maple	Sunny site — ordinary soil	D	Not necessary	Choose a variety with colourful foliage (yellow, purple or variegated) or with decorative bark
AESCULUS	Horse Chestnut	Sunny site — ordinary soil	D	Not necessary	Select a garden variety, such as A. parviflora or A. carnea Briotii
AILANTHUS	Tree of Heaven	Sun or light shade — ordinary soil	D	Cut back — spring	An exotic common name for an ordinary tree — A. altissima is the only common species
ALNUS	Alder	Sun or light shade — damp soil	D	Not necessary	Best garden variety is A. glutinosa Aurea — new foliage pale yellow
BETULA	Birch	Sun or light shade — ordinary soil	D	Remove dead wood — spring	B. pendula (Silver Birch) is the popular one — many varieties available
CARAGANA	Pea Tree	Sun or light shade — ordinary soil	D	Not necessary	Yellow, pea-like flowers. C. arborescens is the basic species. Not common
CARPINUS	Hornbeam	Sun or light shade — ordinary soil	D	Not necessary	Best garden variety is C. betulus Fastigiata — erect, columnar
CASTANEA	Sweet Chestnut	Sun or light shade — ordinary soil	D	Not necessary	Brown Chestnuts in spiny coats. Too large for the average garden
CATALPA	Indian Bean Tree	Sun or light shade — well-drained soil	D	Not necessary	Best garden variety is C. bignonioides Aurea — yellow foliage
CERCIS	Judas Tree	Sunny site — well-drained soil	D	Not necessary	Pink, pea-like flowers appear in May before the leaves
CORYLUS	Hazel	Sunny site — ordinary soil	D	Remove some old wood — spring	Choose a variety with colourful foliage (yellow or purple) or with corkscrew-like branches
CRATAEGUS	Hawthorn	Sun or light shade — ordinary soil	D	Not necessary	White, red or pink flowers in May — red or orange berries in autumn
DAVIDIA	Handkerchief Tree	Sun or light shade — fertile soil	D	Not necessary	Large white flowers in May. D. involucrata has Lime-like foliage
EUCALYPTUS	Gum Tree	Sunny site — avoid sandy soil	E	Cut back — spring	Regular pruning maintains round and waxy blue foliage
FAGUS	Beech	Sun or light shade — avoid heavy soil	D	Trim back — summer	Choose a variety of F. sylvatica. Purple, copper and yellow foliage available
FRAXINUS	Ash	Sun or light shade — ordinary soil	D	Not necessary	Choose F. excelsior Jaspidea (yellow) or F. excelsior Pendula (weeping)
GLEDITSIA	Honey Locust	Sun or light shade — well-drained soil	D	Not necessary	The one to pick is G. triacanthos Sunburst — golden foliage in spring
JUGLANS	Walnut	Sunny site — well-drained soil	D	Remove dead wood — autumn	J. regia Laciniata is the most attractive — drooping branches and deeply-cut leaves
LABURNUM	Golden Rain	Sun or light shade — ordinary soil	D	Remove dead wood — summer	Long sprays of flowers in May or June. L. watereri Vossii is the one to buy
LIQUIDAMBAR	Sweet Gum	Sun or light shade — ordinary soil	D	Not necessary	L. styraciflua is the popular one. Grown for beautiful autumn colours
LIRIODENDRON	Tulip Tree	Sunny site — ordinary soil	D	Not necessary	Choose a compact variety such as L. tulipifera Aureomarginatum
MALUS	Flowering Crab	Sunny site — well-drained soil	D	Remove dead wood — winter	White, red or pink flowers in April or May — colourful fruits in autumn
MORUS	Mulberry	Sun or light shade — ordinary soil	D	Remove dead wood — winter	M. nigra is the usual species — heart-shaped leaves and Blackberry-like fruits

Acer Brilliantissimum

Aesculus parviflora

Cercis siliquastrum

Corylus avellana Contorta

Latin name	Common name	Site & soil	Deciduous (D) or Evergreen (E)	Pruning	Notes
NOTHOFAGUS	Antarctic Beech	Sunny site — lime-free soil	D	Not necessary	N. antarctica is the one you will see — small, dark green leaves
NYSSA	Tupelo	Sun or light shade — lime-free soil	D	Not necessary	For most of the year an ordinary-looking tree — but brilliant colouring in autumn
PLATANUS	Plane	Sun or light shade — ordinary soil	D	Not necessary	Creamy patches beneath grey bark. Too large for the average garden
POPULUS	Poplar	Sun or light shade — ordinary soil	D	Remove dead wood — summer	Very quick growing — not for . small gardens or close-to-house planting
PRUNUS	Ornamental Almond	Sunny site — ordinary soil	D	Remove dead wood — summer	P. dulcis is the common one — P. amygdalo-persica Pollardii the most attractive
PRUNUS	Ornamental Cherry	Sunny site — ordinary soil	D	Remove dead wood — summer	Very popular — large number of varieties available. Usual choice is a Japanese Cherry
PRUNUS	Ornamental Peach	Sunny site — ordinary soil	D	Remove dead wood — summer	Has drawbacks — short-lived and suffers from disease. P. persica Klara Meyer is the usual choice
PRUNUS	Ornamental Plum	Sunny site — ordinary soil	D·	Remove dead wood — summer	P. cerasifera Nigra is a popular one — pink flowers and almost black leaves
PYRUS	Ornamental Pear	Sunny site — ordinary soil	D	Remove dead wood — winter	P. salicifolia Pendula is an attractive weeping tree — white flowers in April
QUERCUS	Oak	Sunny site — deep soil	D or E	Remove dead wood — winter	Most species are too large for ordinary gardens — evergreen Q. ilex used for hedging
ROBINIA	False Acacia	Sun or light shade — ordinary soil	D	Remove dead wood — summer	R. pseudoacacia Frisia is outstanding — layers of golden foliage all season long
SALIX	Willow	Sun or light shade — deep soil	D	Not necessary	Ordinary Weeping Willow too large for average gardens — choose instead S. caprea Pendula
SORBUS	Mountain Ash	Sun or light shade — ordinary soil	D	Not necessary	Feathery leaves — white flowers in May and red or yellow berries in autumn
SORBUS	Whitebeam	Sun or light shade — ordinary soil	D	Not necessary	Simple oval leaves — white flowers in May and red berries in autumn
TILIA	Lime	Sun or light shade — well-drained soil	D	Not necessary	Choose an aphid-resistant variety — T. petiolaris or T. euchlora
TRACHYCARPUS	Windmill Palm	Sunny site — well-drained soil	E	Remove dead leaves	The hardiest Palm for outdoors — still a gamble in most areas
ULMUS	Elm	Sun or light shade — deep soil	D	Remove dead wood when seen	Most disease-resistant is U. parvifolia (40 ft, glossy leaves)

Crataegus oxyacantha Paul's Scarlet

Davidia involucrata vilmoriniana

Laburnum watereri Vossii

Prunus persica Klara Meyer

Robinia pseudoacacia Frisia

Sorbus aucuparia

**See
THE TREE & SHRUB EXPERT
for a more complete list
together with full details
and photographs**

Plant Types Roses

Part of the fun (and frustration) of this group of plants is the vast assortment from which you have to choose. Each Rose can be placed in one or other of five classes, and each class contains a bewildering array. So choice is difficult and the pitfalls can be costly — some varieties are now well past their prime and others have not yet proved their worth. Each year the members of the Royal National Rose Society vote on the best and most popular Roses — the result of the latest poll is listed on these two pages. If your search is for reliability rather than novelty, this Rose Analysis is an excellent guide.

HYBRID TEA ROSES
new name: LARGE FLOWERED ROSES

The most popular class, available in both bush and standard form. The flower stems are long and the blooms are shapely. The typical Hybrid Tea bears blooms which are medium-sized or large, with many petals forming a distinct central cone. The blooms are borne singly or with several side buds.

Position	Name	Colour	Height (ft)	Petals	Growth habit	Fragrance	Year of introduction
1	SILVER JUBILEE	Peach pink & cream	2½	25	Bushy	Slight	1978
2	GRANDPA DICKSON	Lemon yellow	2¾	35	Upright	Slight	1966
3	RED DEVIL	Pale scarlet; lighter reverse	3½	70	Upright	Strong	1967
4	PEACE	Yellow, flushed pink	4½	45	Bushy	Slight	1942
5	FRAGRANT CLOUD	Coral red	3	30	Bushy	Strong	1963
6	WENDY CUSSONS	Rose red	3¼	35	Bushy	Strong	1959
7	PINK FAVORITE	Deep pink	2¾	30	Upright	Slight	1956
8	TROIKA	Orange-bronze, flushed red	3	30	Upright	Moderate	1972
9	JUST JOEY	Coppery pink & buff	2½	30	Bushy	Moderate	1973
10	ERNEST H MORSE	Rich red	3	30	Upright	Moderate	1965
11	ADMIRAL RODNEY	Rose pink	3½	45	Bushy	Strong	1973
12	KEEPSAKE	Rosy carmine	2½	30	Upright	Slight	1981
13	PICCADILLY	Scarlet; yellow reverse	2½	25	Upright	Slight	1960
14	NATIONAL TRUST	Crimson	2¼	60	Bushy	Nil	1970
15	ROYAL HIGHNESS	Flesh pink	3¼	40	Upright	Strong	1962
16	FRED GIBSON	Amber yellow	3¼	30	Upright	Slight	1968
17	PRECIOUS PLATINUM	Bright crimson	3	35	Bushy	Slight	1974
18	ALEXANDER	Bright vermilion	5	25	Upright	Slight	1971

FLORIBUNDA ROSES
new name: CLUSTER FLOWERED ROSES

Second only to Hybrid Teas in popularity. The Floribunda bears its flowers in clusters or trusses, and several blooms open at one time in each truss. This class is unrivalled for providing a colourful, reliable and long-lasting bedding display, but in general the flower form is inferior to that of the Hybrid Tea.

Position	Name	Colour	Height (ft)	Petals	Growth habit	Fragrance	Year of introduction
1	ICEBERG	White	4	25	Bushy	Slight	1958
2	ANNE HARKNESS	Apricot yellow	5	25	Upright	Slight	1980
3	SOUTHAMPTON	Apricot orange, flushed red	3½	25	Upright	Moderate	1972
4	EVELYN FISON	Bright scarlet	2½	30	Bushy	Slight	1962
5	LIVERPOOL ECHO	Pale pink	3½	25	Bushy	Slight	1971
6	QUEEN ELIZABETH	Pink	5	30	Upright	Slight	1954
7	MATANGI	Vermilion; white eye	2¾	25	Upright	Slight	1974
8	KORRESIA	Bright yellow	2½	35	Bushy	Strong	1975
9	MARGARET MERRIL	Pearly white	3	25	Bushy	Strong	1977
10	CITY OF LEEDS	Salmon pink	2½	25	Bushy	Nil	1966
11	TRUMPETER	Orange-red	2	35	Bushy	Slight	1978
12	ELIZABETH OF GLAMIS	Orange-salmon	3	35	Upright	Strong	1964
13	GLENFIDDICH	Golden amber	2¾	25	Upright	Slight	1976
14	ESCAPADE	Rosy lilac; white eye	3	15	Upright	Strong	1967
15	ARTHUR BELL	Bright yellow	3¼	20	Bushy	Strong	1965
16	PINK PARFAIT	Pink; cream base	3	25	Bushy	Slight	1960
17	KORBELL	Salmon	2¾	25	Upright	Slight	1972
18	MOLLY McGREDY	Cherry red; silver reverse	2¾	35	Upright	Nil	1969

MINIATURE ROSES

A class which is increasing in popularity due to its novelty and versatility. Miniatures can be used for edging beds, growing in tubs and rockeries or taking indoors as temporary pot plants. Both leaves and flowers are small, and under normal conditions the maximum height does not exceed 18 in. Many varieties are considerably shorter.

Position	Name	Colour	Height (in.)	Petals	Bloom size (in.)	Fragrance	Year of introduction
1	STARINA	Orange-red	18	35	2¼	Slight	1965
2	DARLING FLAME	Orange-vermilion	12	25	1½	Nil	1971
3	MAGIC CARROUSEL	White, edged red	15	25	1½	Slight	1972
4	ANGELA RIPPON	Coral pink	12	45	1½	Moderate	1978
5	RED ACE	Dark crimson	12	20	1¼	Slight	1982
6	RISE 'N SHINE	Yellow	15	30	2	Slight	1977
7	BABY MASQUERADE	Yellow & red	15	30	1¼	Nil	1956
8	STACEY SUE	Pale pink	15	45	1¼	Slight	1976
9	POUR TOI	Creamy white	15	20	1¼	Slight	1946
10	JUDY FISCHER	Pink	12	25	1¼	Slight	1946

CLIMBERS & RAMBLERS

A class of Roses which if tied to a support can be made to climb. There are two groups: Ramblers with long pliable stems, bearing large trusses of small flowers as a single summer flush, and Climbers with stiff stems, bearing flowers which are larger than Rambler blooms and may be repeat flowering.

Position	Name	Colour	Height (ft)	Type	Blooms	Fragrance	Year of introduction
1	HANDEL	Cream, edged pink	10	Climber	Double	Slight	1965
2	COMPASSION	Pink, flushed apricot	8	Climber	Double	Strong	1973
3	DANSE DU FEU	Orange-scarlet	8	Climber	Double	Nil	1953
4	PINK PERPETUE	Pink; carmine reverse	8	Climber	Double	Slight	1965
5	MAIGOLD	Apricot yellow	10	Climber	Semi-D	Strong	1953
6	GOLDEN SHOWERS	Golden-yellow	7	Climber	Double	Moderate	1956
7	ALBERTINE	Pale pink	15	Rambler	Double	Strong	1921
8	ZEPHIRINE DROUHIN	Dark pink	10	Climber	Semi-D	Strong	1868
9	MERMAID	Primrose yellow	25	Climber	Single	Moderate	1918
10	NEW DAWN	Pearly pink	12	Rambler	Semi-D	Strong	1930

SHRUB ROSES

A large class of bush Roses with only one feature in common — they are neither Hybrid Teas nor Floribundas. The typical Shrub is taller than a bedding Rose, and is a Species variety (related to a wild Rose), an Old-fashioned variety (dating back to pre-Hybrid Tea days) or a Modern Shrub Rose.

Position	Name	Colour	Height (ft)	Blooms	Growth habit	Fragrance	Year of introduction
1	FRED LOADS	Vermilion-orange	5	Semi-D	Upright	Moderate	1967
2	BALLERINA	Pale pink; white eye	3½	Single	Bushy	Slight	1937
3	CHINATOWN	Yellow, edged pink	5	Double	Bushy	Strong	1963
4	CANARY BIRD	Yellow	6	Single	Arching	Strong	pre 1939
5	SALLY HOLMES	Ivory	4	Single	Bushy	Moderate	1976
6	NEVADA	Creamy white	7	Semi-D	Arching	Moderate	1927
7	PENELOPE	Shell pink	6	Semi-D	Bushy	Strong	1924
8	DOROTHY WHEATCROFT	Orange-red	5	Semi-D	Bushy	Slight	1960
9	FOUNTAIN	Crimson	5	Double	Bushy	Moderate	1970
10	ROSERAIE DE L'HAY	Wine red	7	Double	Bushy	Strong	1902

See
THE ROSE EXPERT
for a more complete list
together with full details
and photographs

Plant Types Top Fruit

There is no exact definition of top fruit. Included in this group are all the fruit-bearing woody plants which grow as trees in their natural state, but a few (e.g Quince) are shrubs. Remember that the trees will be with you for many years, so pick the site with care and prepare the soil properly.

APPLE

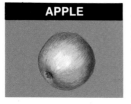

Apples are the most popular of all top fruit trees — attractive in bloom and rewarding at cropping time. Most areas of Britain are quite suitable for Apple cultivation, but some people with small gardens are put off by the thought of large standards. Standard trees are not for the average plot — these days you can buy dwarf bushes which will not reach your height in their lifetime, or you can train cordons to clothe a garden fence or wall.

Size

The size of the tree will depend on many factors — soil, situation, vigour of variety etc, but the main controlling factor is the type of rootstock on which the variety has been grafted. Some rootstocks produce dwarf trees, others create 20 ft giants. Never buy an Apple tree if the nature of the rootstock (the M or MM number) is not provided.

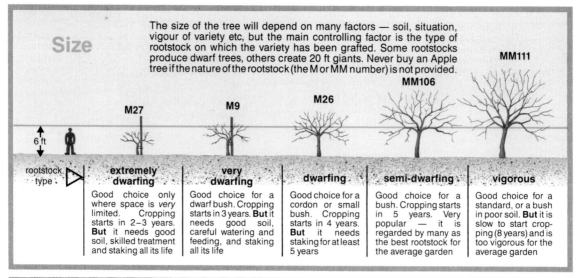

extremely dwarfing	very dwarfing	dwarfing	semi-dwarfing	vigorous
Good choice only where space is *very* limited. Cropping starts in 2–3 years. **But** it needs good soil, skilled treatment and staking all its life	Good choice for a dwarf bush. Cropping starts in 3 years. **But** it needs good soil, careful watering and feeding, and staking all its life	Good choice for a cordon or small bush. Cropping starts in 4 years. **But** it needs staking for at least 5 years	Good choice for a bush. Cropping starts in 5 years. Very popular — it is regarded by many as the best rootstock for the average garden	Good choice for a standard, or a bush in poor soil. **But** it is slow to start cropping (8 years) and is too vigorous for the average garden

Shape

Apple trees can be trained in various ways — the correct choice depends on the needs of the gardener. Free-standing trees (bushes and standards) are the usual form — maintenance is usually straightforward once the framework has been established. A restricted form is used where space is limited. Such forms (cordons, espaliers and fans) are grown against a fence or wall and are pruned in summer. They require more work than bushes and the yields are lower.

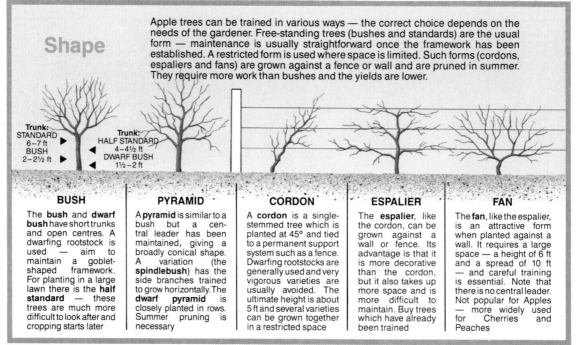

Trunk:
STANDARD 6–7 ft
BUSH 2–2½ ft

Trunk:
HALF STANDARD 4–4½ ft
DWARF BUSH 1½–2 ft

BUSH	PYRAMID	CORDON	ESPALIER	FAN
The **bush** and **dwarf bush** have short trunks and open centres. A dwarfing rootstock is used — aim to maintain a goblet-shaped framework. For planting in a large lawn there is the **half standard** — these trees are much more difficult to look after and cropping starts later	A **pyramid** is similar to a bush but a central leader has been maintained, giving a broadly conical shape. A variation (the **spindlebush**) has the side branches trained to grow horizontally. The **dwarf pyramid** is closely planted in rows. Summer pruning is necessary	A **cordon** is a single-stemmed tree which is planted at 45° and tied to a permanent support system such as a fence. Dwarfing rootstocks are generally used and very vigorous varieties are usually avoided. The ultimate height is about 5 ft and several varieties can be grown together in a restricted space	The **espalier**, like the cordon, can be grown against a wall or fence. Its advantage is that it is more decorative than the cordon, but it also takes up more space and is more difficult to maintain. Buy trees which have already been trained	The **fan**, like the espalier, is an attractive form when planted against a wall. It requires a large space — a height of 6 ft and a spread of 10 ft — and careful training is essential. Note that there is no central leader. Not popular for Apples — more widely used for Cherries and Peaches

Site & Soil

Apples will thrive in most situations, but growth and cropping suffer in chalky soils, poorly-drained sites and gardens close to the sea. The choice of variety is completely up to you if conditions are fully satisfactory for Apples, but site and soil should govern your selection if there are problems. For northern gardens, shaded sites and land which is more than 500 ft above sea level, choose cooking and/or early-ripening dessert varieties.

Planting

Follow the general rules for planting trees and shrubs — see pages 63–64. October-March is the planting period. Cut back any damaged or broken roots — ensure that the remaining roots are spread out without bending in the planting hole. For bushes and standards firm staking is essential — drive in a short stake *before* planting. Plant to the old soil mark — the graft must not be buried. Make sure that the soil is kept moist after planting. Do not grass over the soil above the planting hole for at least 2–3 years.

Buying

Go to a reputable supplier (see pages 65–66) who can give you the information you require about the plants. If you have the skill and time, buy 1 year old maidens and train them from scratch.

1 year old 'maiden'	Untrained. You will have to prune for about 3 years to produce a satisfactory framework of branches
2 year old	Partly trained. You will have to continue training to produce a satisfactory framework
3–4 year old	Trained. Purpose of pruning will be to maintain balance between growth and fruitfulness
Over 4 year old	Generally too old for planting. Establishment may be very slow

Spacing

Two and a half ft apart or 30 ft — it all depends on the shape you have chosen and the rootstock. The space may seem excessive, but do not be tempted to plant more closely.

Shape	Between trees (ft)	Between rows (ft)
Standard	30	30
Half standard	24	24
Fan	20	—
Bush	15	15
Espalier	14	6
Dwarf bush	9	15
Dwarf pyramid	4	8
Cordon	2½	6

Feeding

A starved tree cannot support a large crop — lack of nutrients can also affect next year's harvest. The traditional recommendation is to use Growmore in the spring — a better plan is to spike the soil with a garden fork in several places and then use a balanced liquid fertilizer around the base of the trees.

Picking

Much damage is caused at picking time. An Apple is ready for picking when it comes away easily with stalk attached after being lifted and gently twisted. Tugging can cause serious fruiting spur damage. Store sound fruit by wrapping in newspaper, placing in wooden trays and keeping at about 40°F.

Pruning

Between November and February it is necessary to prune bushes and standards. The first job is to cut out dead and diseased branches — look carefully for mildewed, cankered and broken stems. Remove crowded branches so as to maintain an open growth habit. There are several pruning systems — see page 78.

Spraying

The usual plan is to spray when a pest or disease attacks — see pages 92-95. The *really* keen fruit grower, however, follows a regular routine — a spray programme to automatically protect the trees against major troubles.

THE MIXTURE

Supercarb + Fenitrothion. Tip the contents of one Supercarb sachet into about a teaspoonful of water in a small container. Stir to form a thin cream. Wash this into a bucket and make up to one gallon with water. Add 20 ml of pbi Fenitrothion and stir well. You are now ready to spray.

A medium-sized fruit tree will require about 1–2 gallons of spray. Make sure you cover the foliage and shoots thoroughly. After spraying pour away any mixture left over; do not keep it for use next time you spray.

APPLE & PEAR TROUBLES CONTROLLED OR REDUCED

Apple blossom weevil	Capsid bug	Mildew
Apple sawfly	Caterpillar	Scab
Blossom wilt	Codling moth	Sucker
Canker	Greenfly	Tortrix moth

BUD BURST	◀ SPRAY
MOUSE EAR	NO NEED TO SPRAY
GREEN CLUSTER	◀ SPRAY
PINK BUD (Apples) **WHITE BUD (Pears)**	◀ SPRAY
BLOSSOM TIME	DO NOT SPRAY
PETAL FALL **When nearly all petals have fallen**	◀ SPRAY
FRUITLET **Mid June**	◀ SPRAY
FRUITLET **Early July**	◀ SPRAY

Varieties

Nearly all Apples require a pollination partner nearby — a different variety which flowers at the same time. The Triploid varieties are even more difficult — they need pollen from two different compatible varieties. If neither you nor your neighbours grow Apples then it is necessary to plant at least 2 compatible varieties rather than a single tree. Where space is limited you can plant a Family Tree — a bush grafted with several compatible varieties.

Name	Flowering season	Skin colour	Season of use	Dessert (D) or Cooking (C)	Notes
ALLINGTON PIPPIN	Mid-season	Greenish-yellow, flushed red	Nov-Jan	D or C	Hardy tree. Crisp flesh
ARTHUR TURNER	Mid-season	Green, flushed orange	Aug-Oct	C	Heavy yield. Acid flesh
ASHMEAD'S KERNEL	Mid-season	Greenish-yellow	Dec-Feb	D	Light yield. Small fruit
BLENHEIM ORANGE	Mid-season	Orange, flushed red	Oct-Dec	D or C	Triploid. Excellent nutty flavour
BRAMLEY'S SEEDLING	Mid-season	Green	Oct-Mar	C	Triploid. Excellent cooker
CHARLES ROSS	Mid-season	Yellowish, flushed red	Oct-Dec	D or C	Regular cropper. Tender flesh
COX'S ORANGE PIPPIN	Mid-season	Dull brownish-red	Nov-Jan	D	Temperamental. Excellent flavour
CRAWLEY BEAUTY	Late	Green, flushed red	Dec-Mar	C	Heavy yield. Suitable for cordons
CRIMSON BRAMLEY	Mid-season	Bright red	Oct-Mar	C	Triploid. Excellent cooker
CRISPIN	Mid-season	Yellow	Oct-Feb	D	Triploid. Vigorous — heavy yield
DISCOVERY	Mid-season	Bright red	Aug-Sept	D	Moderate yield. Acid flesh
EARLY VICTORIA	Mid-season	Greenish-yellow	July-Aug	C	Best early cooker
EGREMONT RUSSET	Early	Dull brown, russetted	Oct-Nov	D	Rather small fruit. Good flavour
ELLISON'S ORANGE	Mid-season	Greenish-yellow, striped red	Sept-Oct	D	Hardy tree. Crisp flesh
FORTUNE	Mid-season	Greenish-yellow, flushed red	Sept-Oct	D	Upright growth. Aromatic fruit
GEORGE CAVE	Early	Yellow, marked red	Aug	D	Heavy yield. Crisp flesh
GEORGE NEAL	Early	Greenish-yellow, flushed pink	Aug-Sept	C	Heavy yield. Regular cropper
GOLDEN DELICIOUS	Late	Greenish-yellow	Nov-Feb	D	Stores well. Crisp flesh
GRENADIER	Mid-season	Pale green	Aug-Oct	C	Hardy tree. Heavy yield
HOWGATE WONDER	Late	Green, flushed red	Oct-Jan	C	Heavy yield. Large fruit
IDARED	Early	Yellow, flushed red	Dec-Apr	D	Hardy tree. Stores well
JAMES GRIEVE	Early	Yellow, flushed orange	Sept-Oct	D	Hardy tree. Slightly acid flesh
JUPITER	Mid-season	Dull brown	Oct-Mar	D	Triploid. Easier than Cox
KIDD'S ORANGE RED	Mid-season	Dark red, russetted	Nov-Jan	D	Regular cropper. Good flavour
LANE'S PRINCE ALBERT	Mid-season	Green, striped red	Nov-Mar	C	Large fruit. Stores well
LAXTON'S EPICURE	Early	Yellow, striped red	Sept	D	Small fruit. Heavy yield
LAXTON'S SUPERB	Late	Greenish-yellow, flushed red	Nov-Feb	D	Upright growth. Biennial cropper
LORD DERBY	Late	Dark green	Oct-Dec	C	Upright growth. Heavy yield
LORD LAMBOURNE	Early	Greenish-yellow, flushed red	Oct-Nov	D	Regular cropper. Good flavour
MONARCH	Mid-season	Green, flushed pink	Dec-Apr	C	Large fruit. Stores well
NEWTON WONDER	Late	Yellow, striped red	Nov-Mar	C	Good flavour. Stores well
ORLEANS REINETTE	Late	Yellow, marked red	Nov-Jan	D	Moderate yield. Good flavour
REV W WILKS	Early	Creamy yellow	Sept-Nov	C	Moderate yield. Good baker
RIBSTON PIPPIN	Early	Greenish-yellow, russetted	Nov-Jan	D	Triploid. Moderate yield
SPARTAN	Mid-season	Dark red	Nov-Jan	D	Stores well. Crisp flesh
SUNSET	Early	Golden-yellow, flushed red	Nov-Dec	D	Good flavour. Easier than Cox
TYDEMAN'S LATE ORANGE	Mid-season	Orange-red	Jan-Apr	D	Crisp flesh. Poor in store
WAGENER	Mid-season	Greenish-yellow, marked red	Dec-Apr	D or C	Healthy. Flavour only fair
WINSTON	Late	Orange & red	Jan-Apr	D	Hardy tree. Stores well
WORCESTER PEARMAIN	Mid-season	Yellow, flushed bright red	Sept-Oct	D	Heavy yield. Crisp flesh

Causes of poor yields

- POOR LOCATION Upland or exposed sites, poor soil and waterlogging can all lead to disappointing yields.
- PESTS & DISEASES See pages 92-95.
- FROST See page 26.
- OVERCROPPING A heavy crop of Apples should be thinned in June or the resulting fruit will be small and next year's crop will be very light. Failure to thin is one of the main causes of biennial bearing — crop one year and none the next.

Remove the king Apple (large, central Apple). Use scissors

Remove small and damaged fruit. Leave 2 Apples on the truss

- POOR PRUNING & CARELESS PICKING
- STARVATION
- BLOSSOM DROP & FRUIT DROP See page 92.
- OVERVIGOROUS GROWTH Too much nitrogen can result in vigorous growth with no blossom. Don't manure; water with Bio Tomato Food. If trouble persists try ring barking on Apples and Pears, but never on stone fruit.

4 in.

¼ in. wide strip of bark removed. Paint with Arbrex

- IMPATIENCE A cordon may bear fruit the season after planting, but a bush may take 3–5 years. Do not allow a fruit tree to bear more than one or two fruit in the first season.

PEAR

Pears are a little more temperamental than Apples. They detest cold easterly winds — young foliage is blackened and torn on exposed sites. Flowers open earlier than Apple blossom — late spring frosts can be very damaging. Catalogues and large garden centres offer numerous varieties, but choose Conference if you live in the north of Britain — no other Pear is quite as dependable under cool conditions.

Rootstocks

Most Pears offered for sale are grafted on to Quince A rootstocks. The resulting bushes grow about 15 ft tall and come into fruit in about 4–8 years. Quince C produces rather smaller trees and is sometimes used for cordon Pears, but Quince C trees are less tolerant of poor conditions than Quince A ones. Do not buy plants which are on Pear rootstocks — the standard trees produced are too large.

Shape & Spacing

Pears can be grown as bushes, dwarf pyramids, cordons, espaliers and fans in the same way as Apples. For details and planting distances see pages 38–39. The usual practice is to buy bushes as 2 year old trees and restricted types such as fans and espaliers as 3 year olds. Do not plant standard or half standard Pear trees in an average-sized garden — they are far too vigorous and after a few years spraying, pruning and picking become difficult operations.

Site & Soil

Pears dislike shallow soils, chalk around the roots and salt-laden air. They are more sensitive to cold winds and late frosts than Apples, as noted above, but they do have the distinct advantage of thriving in heavier land than is suitable for their more popular rival. In general, the site for Pears should be chosen with a little more care than for Apples — some shelter from cold winds is essential and try to choose the warmest spot in the garden.

Picking

One of the surprises of gardening is the skill required to pick Pears properly. The early-ripening varieties should be harvested when they are full-sized but before they are fully ripe. Cut the stalks and leave the fruit at room temperature for a few days for the full flavour to develop. Eat as they ripen — do not attempt to store. The late varieties are ripened in store. Pick when they come away from the tree quite easily and place them unwrapped in wooden trays. Keep at about 40°F.

Planting Feeding Pruning Spraying

See page 39

Varieties

Pears, like Apples, require a pollination partner nearby — a few (the Triploid varieties) need two different pollination partners. For more details see the Apple varieties section (page 40). Two of the varieties listed below (Conference and Dr Jules Guyot) will set some fruit even when a mate is absent. All the listed Pears are dessert varieties. For cooking, cut the fruit when it is near its maximum size but before it is ripe.

Name	Flowering season	Skin colour	Season of use	Notes
BEURRE HARDY	Late	Greenish-yellow, flushed red	Oct	Good disease resistance. Very juicy
BEURRE SUPERFIN	Mid-season	Yellow, russetted	Oct	Excellent flavour. Poor in store
CONFERENCE	Mid-season	Green, russetted	Oct-Nov	Most reliable variety. Heavy yield
DOYENNE DU COMICE	Late	Yellow, flushed brown	Nov	Excellent flavour. Needs good conditions
DR JULES GUYOT	Mid-season	Yellow, flushed pink	Sept	Better flavour than Conference. Upright growth
EMILE D'HEYST	Early	Yellow, russetted	Oct-Nov	Compact growth. Good for North
FERTILITY	Late	Yellow, russetted	Oct	Hardy, reliable but flavour only fair
JARGONELLE	Mid-season	Greenish-yellow	Aug	Triploid. Reliable old favourite
LOUISE BONNE OF JERSEY	Early	Green, flushed red	Oct	Excellent flavour. Good for North
MERTON PRIDE	Mid-season	Green	Sept-Oct	Triploid. Excellent flavour. Upright growth
ONWARD	Late	Green	Oct	Outstanding juiciness and sweetness
THOMPSON'S	Mid-season	Greenish-gold, russetted	Oct-Nov	Spreading growth. Needs good conditions
WILLIAM'S BON CHRETIEN	Mid-season	Yellow, spotted red	Sept	Reliable — the familiar Bartlett Pear
WINTER NELIS	Late	Green, russetted	Nov-Jan	Arching growth. Fruit not large

PLUM

There are ordinary Plum varieties for eating fresh and for cooking, and sour Damsons for cooking and bottling. The yellow or green Gages are generally regarded as sweeter than ordinary Plums, but they are also more difficult to grow. Begin by picking one of the self-fertile varieties listed below — a pollinating partner is not needed. Grow a dwarf pyramid or fan (see page 38) and choose a tree which has St Julien A as its rootstock. Plant in a warm, sheltered spot and fruiting should start when the tree is about 5 years old. Net to keep out bullfinches, and if the crop is a heavy one you must thin out the fruits in June and provide support for the branches. Harvest carefully — careless picking can lead to wounding which allows the entry of silver leaf (page 92). There are detailed pruning systems for Plums but in practice trees require little pruning in the ordinary garden once the framework has been established.

Name	Skin colour	Season of use	Dessert (D) or Cooking (C)	Notes
CZAR	Dark purple	Aug	Plum C	Heavy yield. Easiest to grow
DENNISTON'S SUPERB	Green, flushed red	Aug	Gage D	Upright growth. Good flavour
EARLY TRANSPARENT GAGE	Yellow, spotted red	Aug	Gage D	Very sweet. Small fruit
MARJORIE'S SEEDLING	Purple	Sept-Oct	Plum C or D	Vigorous — heavy yield. Large fruit
MERRYWEATHER	Purple	Sept	Damson C	Large fruit. Best garden Damson
OULLIN'S GOLDEN GAGE	Yellow, spotted red	Aug	Gage D	Vigorous — heavy yield. Large fruit
VICTORIA	Pink, spotted red	Aug	Plum C or D	Large fruit. Reliable. Most popular Plum
YELLOW EGG	Yellow	Aug	Plum C	Small fruit. Popular for jam-making

CHERRY

Both sweet dessert and sour cooking varieties are available. The sour types are much easier to grow — they are self-fertile, much less vigorous and come to fruit more quickly than their sweet counterparts. Morello is the variety to choose and it should be trained as a bush, espalier or fan. Plant it in a sunny, protected spot and mulch established trees in May. Until recently sweet varieties were out of the question for the small garden — 40 ft high trees and the need for a nearby pollinating partner made pruning, picking and protection against birds quite impractical. Recently the dwarfing rootstock Colt has been introduced and the variety Stella has appeared — a self-fertile sweet Cherry which does not need a pollinating partner. It does, however, need netting or birds may well remove the crop. Harvest the fruit as soon as it is ripe. The stalks of sour Cherries should be cut with scissors — pulling may break the fruiting spurs. Cherry trees require little pruning once the framework has been established.

Name	Skin colour	Season of use	Self-fertile	Sweet or Sour	Notes
EARLY RIVERS	Dark red	June	No	Sweet	Weeping growth. Large fruit
MERTON GLORY	Yellow, flushed red	July	No	Sweet	Upright growth. Large fruit
MORELLO	Dark red	Aug-Sept	Yes	Sour	Best sour Cherry for garden use
STELLA	Black	July	Yes	Sweet	Best sweet Cherry for garden use
VAN	Dark red	July	No	Sweet	Excellent flavour. Large fruit
WATERLOO	Black	June-July	No	Sweet	Biennial cropper. Rich flavour

PEACH NECTARINE APRICOT

You will often find this trio listed in the larger catalogues, but they are far too much of a gamble for the average garden. Peach is the easiest, but even here you will require a south-facing wall in a sheltered garden in Southern England. Bushes require frost protection and artificial pollination and fans require complex training and pruning. If you wish to take up the challenge, choose a reliable Peach variety, such as Rochester, Peregrine or Hale's Early. Thin the fruitlets to about 4 in. apart when they are the size of a Walnut.

Plant Types Soft Fruit

The increase in shop prices and the interest in home freezing have combined to make soft fruit growing much more popular than ever before. Unlike vegetables you can crop the plants year after year once they are established, and unlike top fruit there is a place for at least one example in every garden. Plant Gooseberry bushes and Raspberry canes where space permits, or plant Strawberries in a tub or window box where the garden is tiny. The attraction of luscious soft fruit from one's own garden is obvious, but beginners do run into all sorts of problems because they ignore two basic points:

- **Soft fruit needs skilled attention.** You cannot neglect the plants during the year and still expect long-living and high-yielding bushes and canes. This does not mean that soft fruit care is difficult, but you must pay attention to feeding, pruning and spraying. Soft fruit is prey to all sorts of pests and problems — keep careful watch and take remedial action at the first sign of trouble. Birds are the big problem, attacking flowers at the start of the season and fruit at the end of the soft fruit year. Netting is essential — the most satisfactory way of growing these plants is inside a permanent fruit cage.

- **There are few general rules.** A small number of rules apply to all types. Enrich the soil with well-rotted manure or compost before planting and feed each year after planting. Make sure there is ample water around the roots both at planting time and when the fruits are swelling. But the differences in looking after the various types of soft fruit far outweigh the similarities. Study the planting and pruning instructions for each type — even Blackcurrant and Red Currant are treated quite differently.

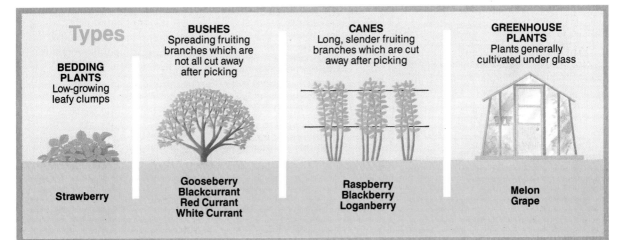

Types

BEDDING PLANTS
Low-growing leafy clumps

Strawberry

BUSHES
Spreading fruiting branches which are not all cut away after picking

**Gooseberry
Blackcurrant
Red Currant
White Currant**

CANES
Long, slender fruiting branches which are cut away after picking

**Raspberry
Blackberry
Loganberry**

GREENHOUSE PLANTS
Plants generally cultivated under glass

**Melon
Grape**

Causes of poor yields

- POOR LOCATION Too much shade, poor soil, waterlogging and cold winds can all result in disappointing crops.
- PESTS & DISEASES There are unfortunately a large number of soft fruit enemies, ranging from large birds to tiny eelworms. Viruses are especially important as they get steadily worse as time passes.
- OLD AGE Soft fruit has a limited life span in the garden, after which yields are disappointing. The normal economic expectancy is 10 years for bushes and canes, 3 years for Strawberries.
- FROST A serious problem of soft fruit, see pages 96–97.
- IMPATIENCE Fruiting is light, and is often undesirable, in the first season after planting. Autumn fruiting Raspberries may not fruit properly for 3 years after planting.
- DRYNESS AT THE ROOTS
- POOR PRUNING
- CARELESS PICKING Pulling away fruit rather than snipping the stalks cleanly can break fruiting spurs and damage stems. Remaining fruit may not ripen.
- POOR WEATHER AT BLOSSOM TIME Blossom drop, see page 97.
- SHORTAGE OF POTASH A common cause of poor yields. Feed regularly. See leaf scorch, page 96.

Site & Soil

Pick a sunny spot. Prepare the ground thoroughly — enrich with organic matter and remove roots of perennial weeds. Check on any special needs for the type of soft fruit to be planted — some fail miserably in limy land, others will fail in exposed gardens subject to heavy frosts.

Feeding

A spring dressing has 2 functions — it promotes a good crop later in the season and also encourages the production of new growth which will bear next year's crop. Use either a solid fertilizer such as Growmore or a potash-rich liquid feed such as Tree & Shrub Fertilizer or Instant Bio.

STRAWBERRY

If you have the space and choose the varieties with care, it is possible to pick Strawberries for six months of the year — from May until the arrival of the first frosts. By covering the plants with cloches in early spring it is possible to extend this harvesting season by bringing cropping forward to late April. The first step is to buy young, healthy plants in late summer or early autumn — make sure that they are certified as virus-free. A recent introduction is the Perpetual variety Sweetheart which can be raised from seed sown under glass in February.

Planting & Pruning

Planting	**Summer Fruiting varieties:** August-September **Perpetual varieties:** Autumn or spring Note: container-grown specimens can be planted at any time of the year when the weather is suitable. small mound — crown level with surface
Spacing	Rows 2½ ft apart. Plants 1½ ft apart. Plant Alpine varieties 1 ft apart.
Pruning immediately after planting	None required.
Pruning established plants	Immediately after picking cut off leaves to about 3 in. above the crown.

Site & Soil

A sunny, sheltered site is required — a little shade during the day is acceptable. The area chosen for the Strawberry bed should not be in a frost pocket and ideally the land should not have been used for growing Potatoes, Tomatoes, Chrysanthemums nor Strawberries for several years. Good drainage is essential and light soil will ensure early crops. Incorporate a bucketful of compost or manure per sq. yd when preparing the bed.

Caring for the crop

- Cover with newspaper if frost is expected when the plants are in flower.
- Weeds can be a problem. Strawberries are shallow-rooted so hoe very carefully.
- Once the fruits have begun to swell apply a mulch around the plants. Use straw, black polythene or Strawberry mats. Guard against squirrels and birds and protect from slugs by scattering Slug Pellets around the plants.

Picking

Harvest every few days during the cropping season — do not remove fruits until they are fully ripe.

Raising new plants

In June or July peg down the little plants which appear at the ends of runners, using a small wire hoop. Sever the plantlet by cutting the runner 4–6 weeks later and transplant about a week later.

Varieties

The most popular Strawberries are the Summer Fruiting varieties which are cropped for about 2–3 weeks. The Early and 2nd Early types are in fruit between late May and mid June — the Mid-season ones range from mid June to the end of July and the Late types are not ready for picking until August. The Perpetual (or Remontant) varieties have a long fruiting season, first in June and then from August or September until the frosts arrive. Alpine varieties bear tiny fruits.

Name	Type	Size of fruit	Season of use	Notes
AROMEL	Perpetual	Medium	June; Sept-Nov	Best-flavoured Perpetual. Reliable
BARON SOLEMACHER	Alpine	Small	June-Oct	Heavy yield. Runners not produced
CAMBRIDGE FAVOURITE	Summer Fruiting	Large	June-July	Heavy yield. Popular. Orange-red fruit
DOMANIL	Summer Fruiting	Large	Aug	Heavy yield. Orange-red fruit
GENTO	Perpetual	Medium	June; Aug-Oct	Heavy yield. Somewhat unreliable
GRANDEE	Summer Fruiting	Very large	June	Moderate flavour. Dark red fruit
HAPIL	Summer Fruiting	Large	June-July	Good flavour. Heavy yield
PANTAGRUELLA	Summer Fruiting	Medium-large	May-June	Very early — ideal for cloches
RED GAUNTLET	Summer Fruiting	Large	June-July	Second crop appears Sept-Oct
RED RICH	Perpetual	Medium	June; Sept-Nov	Moderate yield. Dark red fruit
ROYAL SOVEREIGN	Summer Fruiting	Large	June	Good flavour. Moderate yield
SWEETHEART	Perpetual	Medium	June; Aug-Oct	Can be grown from spring-sown seed
TAMELLA	Summer Fruiting	Large	June	Heavy yield. Dark red fruit

RASPBERRY BLACKBERRY LOGANBERRY

Cane fruits often play a dual role in the garden, providing a screen to hide the vegetable plot or unsightly objects during the summer and then an abundance of succulent fruit later in the season. The basic types are the Blackberry (used mainly for pies, jam-making and other culinary purposes) and the Raspberry (used mainly for dessert purposes — either immediately or frozen for later use). Then there are the hybrid berries — Loganberry, Youngberry, Tayberry, Boysenberry etc. The cane fruits require strong supports — 6–8 ft posts with horizontal wires or nylon cords stretched between them. Raspberries produce erect canes, but Blackberries bear long, arching branches which are trained along the horizontal wires. Always buy stock which is certified virus-free and follow the pruning instructions exactly.

Planting & Pruning

Planting

Raspberries: October-December
Other cane fruits: October-March

Note: container-grown specimens can be planted at any time of the year when the weather is suitable.

old soil mark level with surface

3 in. deep trench

Spacing

Raspberries: Rows 6 ft apart, plants 1½ ft apart.
Other cane fruits: Rows 7–10 ft apart, plants 7–12 ft apart.

Pruning immediately after planting

Lifted plants: Cut down all shoots to a bud 9–12 in. above soil level.
Container-grown plants: Not necessary. Treat as established plants.

Pruning established plants

Summer Fruiting Raspberries: Immediately after picking cut out all the canes which have fruited. Retain best 8–10 young unfruited canes and tie to wires 3–4 in. apart. Remove tips in February.
Autumn Fruiting Raspberries: Cut all canes down to ground level in February. Support new growth in summer.
Other cane fruits: Immediately after picking cut out all the canes which have fruited. Tie unfruited canes to the wires.

Site & Soil

Cane fruits can thrive in heavier soil and shadier conditions than Strawberries, but they do need shelter from stormy winds and good drainage is essential for Raspberries. Late frosts are rarely a problem.

Caring for the crop

- Mulch around the plants in spring with well-rotted farmyard manure or compost. Peat or bark can be used, but are less effective.
- Weeds can be a problem. Do not hoe deeply or roots will be damaged.
- Pull up suckers whilst they are still small.

Picking

Do not allow the plants to bear fruit too early — remove flowers during the first summer after planting. Gather fruit from established plants when it is fully ripe.

Varieties

Raspberries are by far the most popular cane fruit cultivated in British gardens — they are easier to care for than Blackberries and hybrids, and the fruit is less tart. Not all Raspberries are red and not all fruit in midsummer. The Summer Fruiting varieties (June-August) are the usual ones, but you can buy Autumn Fruiting varieties to extend the cropping season. These bear fruit from August until October or November.

Name	Type	Size of fruit	Season of use	Notes
BEDFORD GIANT	Blackberry	Large	July-Aug	Thorny variety. Moderate yield
FALLGOLD	Autumn Fruiting Raspberry	Medium	Sept-Oct	Moderate yield. Golden fruit
GLEN CLOVA	Summer Fruiting Raspberry	Medium	July	Heavy yield. Easy to grow
HIMALAYA GIANT	Blackberry	Large	Aug-Sept	Thorny variety. Very vigorous
JOHN INNES BERRY	Hybrid Berry	Large	Aug-Sept	Sweet flavour. Jet black fruit
LY 59	Loganberry	Very large	July-Aug	Thorny variety. Dark red fruit
LY 654	Loganberry	Very large	July-Aug	Thornless variety. Weaker than LY 59
MALLING ADMIRAL	Summer Fruiting Raspberry	Medium	July-Aug	Good flavour. Recommended for freezing
MALLING DELIGHT	Summer Fruiting Raspberry	Very large	June-July	Heavy yield. Vigorous growth
MALLING JEWEL	Summer Fruiting Raspberry	Medium	July	Excellent flavour. Bright red fruit
MALLING PROMISE	Summer Fruiting Raspberry	Large	June-July	Heavy yield. Good flavour
OREGON THORNLESS	Blackberry	Large	Aug-Oct	Thornless variety. Needs warmth
SEPTEMBER	Autumn Fruiting Raspberry	Medium	Sept-Oct	Moderate yield. Short stems
TAYBERRY	Hybrid Berry	Very large	July-Aug	Sweet flavour. Fruit like Loganberry
ZEVA	Autumn Fruiting Raspberry	Large	Sept-Nov	Good flavour. Dark red fruit

GOOSEBERRY RED CURRANT WHITE CURRANT

The bush fruits are divided into two basic groups which differ in their pruning and feeding requirements. The compact, easy-to-grow section is made up of Gooseberry, Red Currant and White Currant — the more demanding and space-consuming section is represented by Blackcurrant. Here we deal with the first section — hardy plants with a long fruiting season. Green Gooseberries for cooking in late May, the Currants in midsummer and the dessert Gooseberries up to August. These fruits are usually grown as bushes — hence the name, but they can also be grown as half standards, cordons and fans. Buy 2 year old specimens for bushes — for cordons obtain 3 year olds.

Planting & Pruning

Planting	November–February. Plant in November if possible. Note: container-grown specimens can be planted at any time of the year when the weather is suitable.
	old soil mark level with surface
Spacing	**Bushes:** 5 ft apart. **Cordons:** 1½ ft apart.
Pruning immediately after planting	**Lifted plants:** If not already pruned, cut back branches to half their length. **Container-grown plants:** Not necessary. Treat as established plants.
Pruning established plants	For first 4 years build up framework — cut back new growth by half each winter. Keep centre of bush open. Later, prune by removing thin and overcrowded branches each year. Lightly prune remaining branches — shorten side growths.

Site & Soil

Gooseberries, Red Currants and White Currants will thrive in a wide range of soil types, but they do require good drainage and shelter from strong winds. Avoid frost pockets and dig in compost or rotted manure when preparing the soil prior to planting.

Caring for the crop

- If a late spring frost is expected, drape sacking over the bushes.
- Mulch around the plants with straw or compost each May.
- Weeds can be a problem. Do not hoe deeper than ½ in. or the shallow root system may be damaged.
- Thin dessert Gooseberries to 1 in. apart if you want maximum-sized fruits.

Picking

Begin picking Gooseberries in late May for cooking — for eating fresh, delay picking until the fruits have softened and developed their mature colour. Gather Currants as bunches, not as single berries.

Varieties

Most Gooseberries can be used for cooking or eating fresh, depending on the time of picking. However, there are varieties noted for their culinary qualities (e.g Careless) and others which are more suitable for dessert purposes (e.g Whinham's Industry). The choice of Red Currants and White Currants is more limited, often restricted to Red Lake and White Versailles at the garden centre.

Name	Type	Colour of fruit	Season of dessert use	Notes
CARELESS	Gooseberry	Creamy-white	June–July	Large, oval fruit. Smooth skin
GOLDEN DROP	Gooseberry	Greenish-yellow	June–July	Good flavour. Upright growth
JONKHEER VAN TETS	Red Currant	Dark red	July	Heavy yield. Earlier than others
KEEPSAKE	Gooseberry	Pale green	July	Large fruit. Protect from frost
LANCASHIRE LAD	Gooseberry	Dark red	July	Heavy yield. Upright growth
LAXTON'S NO. 1	Red Currant	Bright red	July	Large fruit in long bunches
LEVELLER	Gooseberry	Greenish-yellow	July	Large fruit. Popular. Smooth skin
MAY DUKE	Gooseberry	Dark red	June–July	Usually picked green for cooking
RED LAKE	Red Currant	Dark red	July	Good flavour. Upright growth
RIVERS' LATE RED	Red Currant	Bright red	Aug	Long bunches. Spreading growth
WHINHAM'S INDUSTRY	Gooseberry	Dark red	July	Spreading growth. Hairy skin
WHITE GRAPE	White Currant	Creamy-white	July	Excellent flavour. Moderate yield
WHITE LION	Gooseberry	White	Aug	Good flavour. Upright growth
WHITE VERSAILLES	White Currant	Pale yellow	July	Sweet flavour. Heavy yield
WHITESMITH	Gooseberry	Yellowish-white	July	Good flavour. Downy skin

BLACKCURRANT

Unlike with other popular bush types (see page 46) most of the fruit is borne on branches produced in the previous season rather than on old wood. Not all areas are suitable for Blackcurrants — they bloom in early April and so crops in frost-prone areas are disappointing. They will tolerate poor drainage better than other soft fruits but they do need rich soil and thorough watering in times of drought. Plant 2 year old certified bushes in a site which is protected from cold winds. Full sun is preferred but light shade is not a problem. Prune according to instructions and the bushes should remain productive for 10–20 years — if the dreaded big bud mite stays away.

Planting & Pruning

Planting	January-February Do not plant in a frost pocket. Note: container-grown specimens can be planted at any time of the year when the weather is suitable. old soil mark 2 in. below surface
Spacing	5 ft apart.
Pruning immediately after planting	If not already pruned, cut back all shoots to 2 in. above soil level.
Pruning established plants	Immediately after picking cut about one-third of the fruiting branches right out. Leave all the strong young shoots unpruned. No wood should be retained which is more than 4 years old.

Caring for the crop

- If a late spring frost is expected, drape sacking over the bushes.
- Mulch around the plants with straw or compost each May. Do not remove the mulch in autumn.
- Never hoe more deeply than ½ in. or the shallow root system may be damaged.

Picking

Harvest fruit when it is firm and dry. Wait until the currants are fully ripe, which is several days after they have turned black. Be careful with early varieties — they soon drop their fruit if not gathered in time.

Varieties

Name	Notes
BALDWIN	Late July. Acid flavour. Upright growth
BEN LOMOND	Early July. Late flowering. Some mildew resistance
BLACKDOWN	Mid July. Heavy yield. Some mildew resistance
BOSKOOP GIANT	Early July. Sweet flavour. Spreading growth
MALLING JET	August. Long fruit sprigs. Late flowering
SEABROOK'S BLACK	Mid July. Acid flavour. Compact growth
TENAH	Late July. Small fruit. Heavy yield
WELLINGTON XXX	Mid July. Good flavour. Spreading growth

MELON GRAPE

Melons and Grapes are generally regarded as exotic fruits in Britain, requiring the protection of a greenhouse. It is true that the best crops are obtained under such conditions, but there are Vine varieties which will grow and ripen in sheltered gardens in the southern counties of England, and Melons can be grown in a cold frame.

For outdoor Grapes you will need a suitable site and variety. A sunny wall protected from strong winds is the right place — reliable varieties include Brandt, Seyve-Villard 5–276 and Noir Hâtif de Marseille. Plant a 1 year old specimen and train as an espalier (page 38). Pruning is quite complex for the beginner. Cut back side shoots in winter to 3 buds from the main stem. In summer remove tips at 2 leaves beyond the developing bunches.

Melons are usually found in the vegetable rather than the fruit section of gardening books. Their requirements are rather similar to the greenhouse Cucumber, but Melons prefer drier air. For cold frame cultivation pick a small fruited and easy-to-grow variety such as Ogen or Sweetheart. Sow under glass in early April and plant out in late May–early June on a 3 in. high mound of soil. Train side shoots to corners of the cold frame. Partly open the lights on sunny days during flowering to allow pollinating insects to enter.

Plant Types Annuals & Biennials

Latin name	Common name	Site & soil	Type (see page 28)	Spacing	Flowering period	Height
AGERATUM	Floss Flower	Sun or light shade — ordinary soil	HHA	8 in.	June–October	8 in.
ALTHAEA	Hollyhock	Sunny site — ordinary soil	HA or HB or HP	15 in.–2 ft	July–September	3–9 ft
ALYSSUM	Sweet Alyssum	Sunny site — well-drained soil	HA	9 in.	June–September	3–6 in.
AMARANTHUS	Love-lies-bleeding	Sunny site — well-drained soil	HHA	2 ft	July–October	3 ft
ANTIRRHINUM	Snapdragon	Sunny site — well-drained soil	HHA	9 in.–1½ ft	July–October	6 in.–4 ft
BEGONIA	Bedding Begonia	Partial shade — humus-rich soil	HHA	5–15 in.	June–September	6 in.–1½ ft
BELLIS	Daisy	Sun or light shade — ordinary soil	HB	6 in.	March–July	3–6 in.
CALENDULA	Pot Marigold	Sun or light shade — poor soil	HA	1 ft	June–October	1–2 ft
CALLISTEPHUS	China Aster	Sunny site — well-drained soil	HHA	9 in.–1½ ft	August–October	9 in.–2½ ft
CAMPANULA	Canterbury Bell	Sunny site — well-drained soil	HB	1 ft	May–July	1½–2½ ft
CENTAUREA	Cornflower	Sun or light shade — well-drained soil	HA	9 in.–1 ft	June–September	1–2½ ft
CHEIRANTHUS	Wallflower	Sunny site — non-acid soil	HB	8 in.–1 ft	March–May	9 in.–2 ft
CHRYSANTHEMUM	Annual Chrysanthemum	Sunny site — non-acid soil	HA	1 ft	July–September	1½–2 ft
CLARKIA	Clarkia	Sunny site — avoid heavy soil	HA	1 ft	July–October	1½–2 ft
COREOPSIS	Tickseed	Sunny site — avoid heavy soil	HA	1 ft	July–September	1–2 ft
COSMOS	Cosmea	Sunny site — well-drained soil	HHA	1½ ft	July–October	1–3 ft
DAHLIA	Bedding Dahlia	Sunny site — avoid light soil	HHA	1 ft	July–November	1–2 ft
DELPHINIUM	Larkspur	Sun or light shade — well-drained soil	HA	1½ ft	June–August	1–4 ft
DIANTHUS	Annual Carnation	Sunny site — non-acid soil	HHA	1 ft	July–October	1½ ft
DIANTHUS	Indian Pink	Sunny site — non-acid soil	HHA	6 in.	July–October	6 in.–1½ ft
DIANTHUS	Sweet William	Sunny site — non-acid soil	HB	9 in.	June–July	1–2 ft
DIGITALIS	Foxglove	Partial shade — humus-rich soil	HB	1½ ft	June–August	3–5 ft
DIMORPHOTHECA	Star of the Veldt	Sunny site — well-drained soil	HA	9 in.	June–August	1 ft
ESCHSCHOLZIA	Californian Poppy	Sunny site — well-drained soil	HA	6 in.	June–September	6 in.–1½ ft
GAZANIA	Gazania	Sunny site — well-drained soil	HHA	1 ft	June–October	9–15 in.
GODETIA	Godetia	Sunny site — well-drained soil	HA	9 in.–1 ft	June–September	9 in.–2 ft
GYPSOPHILA	Baby's Breath	Sunny site — non-acid soil	HA	1 ft	June–September	1–1½ ft
HELIANTHUS	Sunflower	Sunny site — ordinary soil	HA	1–2½ ft	July–September	2–10 ft
HELICHRYSUM	Straw Flower	Sunny site — well-drained soil	HA	1 ft	July–September	1–3 ft
IBERIS	Candytuft	Sunny site — well-drained soil	HA	9 in.	May–August	9 in.–1½ ft

Latin name	Common name	Site & soil	Type (see page 28)	Spacing	Flowering period	Height
IMPATIENS	Busy Lizzie	Sun or shade — well-drained soil	HHA	6–9 in.	June–October	6 in.–1 ft
IPOMOEA	Morning Glory	Sunny site — well-drained soil	HHA	1½ ft	July–September	6–12 ft
LATHYRUS	Sweet Pea	Sunny site — well-drained soil	HA	6 in.–1 ft	June–October	1–8 ft
LAVATERA	Annual Mallow	Sun or light shade — ordinary soil	HA	2 ft	July–September	2–4 ft
LOBELIA	Lobelia	Sun or light shade — ordinary soil	HHA	6 in.	June–September	4–8 in.
MALCOLMIA	Virginia Stock	Sun or light shade — ordinary soil	HA	4 in.	1–2 months after sowing	6–9 in.
MATTHIOLA	Brompton Stock	Sun or light shade — well-drained soil	HB	9 in.–1 ft	March–May	1–2 ft
MATTHIOLA	Ten Week Stock	Sun or light shade — well-drained soil	HHA	9 in.–1 ft	June–August	1–2½ ft
MIMULUS	Monkey Flower	Partial shade — moist soil	HHA	9 in.	June–September	9 in.
MYOSOTIS	Forget-me-not	Light shade — well-drained soil	HB	8 in.	April–May	6 in.–1 ft
NEMESIA	Nemesia	Sun or light shade — ordinary soil	HHA	6 in.	June–September	9 in.–1½ ft
NICOTIANA	Tobacco Plant	Sun or light shade — well-drained soil	HHA	9 in.–1 ft	June–October	9 in.–3 ft
NIGELLA	Love-in-a-mist	Sun or light shade — well-drained soil	HA	9 in.	July–September	1½ ft
PAPAVER	Poppy	Sun or light shade — ordinary soil	HA or HB	9 in.–1 ft	May–September	6 in.–3 ft
PETUNIA	Petunia	Sunny site — ordinary soil	HHA	6 in.–1 ft	June–October	6 in.–1½ ft
PHLOX	Annual Phlox	Sunny site — well-drained soil	HHA	8 in.	June–September	6 in.–1½ ft
RUDBECKIA	Rudbeckia	Sun or light shade — ordinary soil	HHA	1–2 ft	August–October	1–3 ft
SALPIGLOSSIS	Painted Tongue	Sunny site — well-drained soil	HHA	1 ft	July–September	1½–2½ ft
SALVIA	Sage	Sunny site — ordinary soil	HA or HB or HHA	1 ft	June–October	9 in.–1½ ft
TAGETES	African Marigold	Sunny site — ordinary soil	HHA	1–1½ ft	June–October	1–3 ft
TAGETES	French Marigold	Sunny site — ordinary soil	HHA	6–9 in.	June–October	6 in.–1 ft
TAGETES	Tagetes	Sunny site — ordinary soil	HHA	6–9 in.	June–October	6–9 in.
TROPAEOLUM	Nasturtium	Sun or light shade — poor soil	HA	6 in.–1½ ft	June–October	6 in.–6 ft
VERBENA	Verbena	Sunny site — ordinary soil	HHA	1 ft	July–September	6 in.–1 ft
VIOLA	Pansy, Viola	Sun or light shade — ordinary soil	HA or HB	9 in.–1 ft	Varieties for all seasons	6–9 in.
VISCARIA	Viscaria	Sun or light shade — ordinary soil	HA	6 in.	June–August	6 in.–1 ft
ZINNIA	Youth and Old Age	Sunny site — humus-rich soil	HHA	6 in.–1 ft	July–October	6 in.–2½ ft

See
THE FLOWER EXPERT
for a more complete list
together with full details
and photographs

Plant Types Rockery Perennials

Latin name	Common name	Site & soil	Propagation	Notes
ACHILLEA	Alpine Yarrow	Sunny site — sandy soil	Divide clumps — spring	The Yarrow in rockeries is A. tomentosa — height 6 in., spread 1 ft, flowers July–September. Yellow blooms are tiny
AETHIONEMA	Aethionema	Sunny site — non-acid soil	Cuttings — early summer	The popular one is A. Warley Rose — height 6 in., spread 1 ft, flowers April–May. Colour rosy red
ALYSSUM	Alyssum	Sunny site — ordinary soil	Cuttings — early summer	A. saxatile is seen everywhere — height 9–12 in., spread 1½ ft, flowers April–June. Yellow flowers cover plant
ANDROSACE	Rock Jasmine	Sun or light shade — well-drained soil	Cuttings — early summer	Some are too delicate to grow outdoors. Choose A. sarmentosa chumbyi — height 4 in., spread 2 ft, flowers April–June
ANTENNARIA	Cat's Ear	Sunny site — well-drained soil	Divide clumps — spring	A. dioica is an unspectacular ground cover — height 2–6 in., spread 1½ ft, flowers May–June
ARABIS	White Rock Cress	Sun or light shade — ordinary soil	Divide clumps — autumn	Very popular — height 9 in., spread 2 ft, flowers March–April. White, pink and red varieties available
ARENARIA	Sandwort	Sun or light shade — moist soil	Divide clumps — autumn	Mat-forming plant useful for covering rocks. Small white flowers (March–July) above moss-like leaves
ARMERIA	Thrift	Sunny site — well-drained soil	Cuttings — summer	Popular — hummocks of grass-like leaves. Globular flower-heads appear in May–July — choose from white, pink or red
AUBRIETA	Rock Cress	Sunny site — well-drained soil	Divide clumps — autumn	Very popular — height 3 in., spread 2 ft, flowers March–June. Many varieties available — pink, mauve, blue and red
CAMPANULA	Bellflower	Sun or light shade — well-drained soil	Divide clumps — spring	Several species available. One of the most popular is C. carpatica — height 10 in., spread 1 ft, flowers June–September
CERASTIUM	Snow-in-summer	Sun or light shade — ordinary soil	Divide clumps — spring	C. tomentosum is a common sight in rockeries — height 6 in., spread 2 ft, flowers May–July. Take care — very invasive
DIANTHUS	Rockery Pink	Sun or light shade — sandy soil	Cuttings — summer	D. deltoides is an old favourite — height 6 in., spread 9 in., flowers June–September. D. alpinus bears larger blooms
DODECATHEON	Shooting Star	Light shade — moist soil	Divide clumps — spring	Cyclamen-like flowers on long stalks. Usual one is D. media — height 1½ ft, spread 1 ft, flowers June–July
DRABA	Whitlow Grass	Sunny site — well-drained soil	Sow seeds — spring	Useful for growing in crevices. Largest species is D. aizoides — height 4 in., spread 6 in., flowers April
DRYAS	Mountain Avens	Sunny site — non-acid soil	Cuttings — summer	Useful ground cover with blooms like small single Roses. Height 4 in., spread 2 ft, flowers May–June
ERIGERON	Fleabane	Sunny site — sandy soil	Sow seeds — spring	Daisy-like flowers darken from white to deep pink with age. Height 8 in., spread 2 ft, flowers June–September
ERINUS	Summer Starwort	Sun or light shade — sandy soil	Sow seeds — spring	The one you will find is E. alpinus — height 3 in., spread 6 in., flowers April–August. Choose from white, pink or red
GENTIANA	Gentian	Sun or light shade — well-drained soil	Divide clumps — spring or summer	Indispensable in the rockery. Many varieties available. Grow G. acaulis for large trumpet-like flowers in May and June
GERANIUM	Rock Geranium	Sunny site — well-drained soil	Divide clumps — spring	The usual one is G. cinereum — height 6 in., spread 1 ft, flowers May–September. Pink blooms are prominently veined
GYPSOPHILA	Baby's Breath	Sunny site — well-drained soil	Cuttings — early summer	G. repens is an attractive trailing plant — height 6 in., spread 2 ft, flowers June–August. Colour white or pink
HABERLEA	Haberlea	Partial shade — acid soil	Divide clumps — autumn	A difficult-to-grow crevice plant. Plant sideways in north-facing rockery. Lilac flowers appear in May
HELIANTHEMUM	Rock Rose	Sunny site — well-drained soil	Cuttings — summer	Usual one is a small shrub — see page 31. True alpine species are H. alpestre (height 4 in., spread 1 ft) and H. lunulatum
HELICHRYSUM	Everlasting Flower	Sunny site — well-drained soil	Divide clumps — summer	The alpine Helichrysum is H. bellidioides — height 3 in., spread 1½ ft, flowers June–August. White is the only colour
HEPATICA	Hepatica	Sun or light shade — damp soil	Divide clumps — autumn	H. nobilis is the one you will find — height 3 in., spread 1 ft, flowers February–April. Starry blooms — white, pink, red or blue
IBERIS	Perennial Candytuft	Sunny site — well-drained soil	Cuttings — summer	I. sempervirens is the evergreen Candytuft seen in rockeries — height 9 in., spread 1½ ft, flowers May–June. White is the only colour
LEONTOPODIUM	Edelweiss	Sunny site — well-drained soil	Sow seeds — spring	The symbol of alpine flowers, but not very attractive. Woolly leaves, furry flowers — height 6 in., spread 9 in., flowers June–July
LEWISIA	Lewisia	Sunny site — well-drained soil	Cuttings — early summer	Not easy to keep alive. The easiest is L. cotyledon — height 1 ft, spread 9 in., flowers May–June. Many colours available
LINNAEA	Twin Flower	Partial shade — moist soil	Layer stems — summer	L. borealis is the basic species — height 2 in., spread 2 ft, flowers May–July. Bell-like pink blooms
LITHOSPERMUM	Gromwell	Sunny site — humus-rich soil	Cuttings — summer	A ground cover plant with funnel-shaped blue flowers — height 6 in., spread 2 ft, flowers June–September
LYCHNIS	Alpine Campion	Sunny site — lime-free soil	Sow seeds — spring	White or pink blooms on short stalks. A tiny plant — height 4 in., spread 4 in., flowers May–July

Latin name	Common name	Site & soil	Propagation	Notes
LYSIMACHIA	Creeping Jenny	Partial shade — humus-rich soil	Divide clumps — autumn	L. nummularia is an old favourite — a vigorous ground cover with yellow flowers. Height 2 in., spread 1½ ft, flowers June–July
MIMULUS	Monkey Flower	Light shade — moist soil	Divide clumps — spring	The rockery Mimulus to grow is M. primuloides — height 4 in., spread 9 in., flowers May–August. Trumpet-shaped yellow blooms
OXALIS	Oxalis	Sunny site — well-drained soil	Divide clumps — autumn	The most popular rockery Oxalis is O. adenophylla — height 3 in., spread 6 in., flowers June–July. Pink-edged white blooms
PHLOX	Dwarf Phlox	Sunny site — well-drained soil	Cuttings — summer	The Moss Phlox is an attractive carpeter — height 3 in., spread 1½ ft, flowers April–May. Pink or mauve blooms cover leaves
POLYGONUM	Rock Polygonum	Sunny site — well-drained soil	Divide clumps — autumn	P. vaccinifolium is the common rockery type — height 6 in., spread 3 ft, flowers September–December. Upright floral spikes
POTENTILLA	Rock Cinquefoil	Sunny site — ordinary soil	Divide clumps — autumn	The popular rockery Potentilla is P. nitida — height 3 in., spread 1 ft, flowers July–September. Silvery leaves, pink blooms
PRIMULA	Rockery Primrose	Light shade — humus-rich soil	Divide clumps — after flowering	Many types available, including the old favourite Auricula. P. Wanda is popular — height 3 in., spread 6 in., flowers March–May
PULSATILLA	Pasque Flower	Sunny site — well-drained soil	Sow seeds — summer	Large flowers (3 in. across) followed by ferny leaves. Usual species is P. vulgaris — height 9 in., spread 1 ft, flowers April–May
RAOULIA	Raoulia	Sunny site — sandy soil	Divide mats — autumn	A silvery mat with pale yellow minute flowers. R. australis is the best known species — height ½ in., spread 1 ft, flowers May
SANGUINARIA	Bloodroot	Sun or light shade — humus-rich soil	Divide clumps — spring	Large flowers (1½ in. across) amongst greyish leaves. Buy the double form — height 6 in., spread 1½ ft, flowers April–May
SAPONARIA	Rock Soapwort	Sunny site — well-drained soil	Cuttings — summer	S. ocymoides is a carpeting plant — height 3 in., spread 1½ ft, flowers July–September. Star-shaped blooms in pink or red
SAXIFRAGA	Saxifrage	Sun or light shade — well-drained soil	Offsets — summer	Many varieties available — usual form is a low-growing group of rosettes or mossy sheets. Flowers starry or saucer-shaped
SEDUM	Stonecrop	Sunny site — well-drained soil	Divide clumps — autumn	Many varieties available — usual form is low-growing stems, fleshy leaves and star-shaped flowers in June
SEMPERVIVUM	Houseleek	Sunny site — well-drained soil	Offsets — autumn	Ball-like rosettes of green or coloured fleshy leaves. Thick flower stems appear in July. Ideal for dry spots
SHORTIA	Shortia	Partial shade — humus-rich soil	Divide clumps — early summer	S. galacifolia is the usual one — height 6 in., spread 1 ft, flowers April–May. Shiny, red-tinged leaves and pale pink blooms
SILENE	Moss Campion	Sunny site — well-drained soil	Cuttings — summer	Carpeting plants for planting in crevices. Narrow leaves — star-faced tubular flowers appear in summer. Do not disturb
THYMUS	Thyme	Sunny site — well-drained soil	Divide clumps — spring	T. serpyllum is the basic species — height 2 in., spread 2 ft, flowers June–July. Starry blooms in white, pink or red

Aethionema Warley Rose

Alyssum saxatile

Campanula carpatica

Dodecatheon meadia

Gentiana acaulis

Pulsatilla vulgaris

See
THE FLOWER EXPERT
for a more complete list
together with full details
and photographs

Plant Types Bulbs

Latin name	Common name	Site & soil	Planting time	Planting depth	Spacing	Flowering period	Height
ACIDANTHERA	Acidanthera	Sunny site — well-drained soil	April	4 in.	9 in.	September	3 ft
ALLIUM	Flowering Garlic	Sunny site — well-drained soil	September –October	4–6 in.	6 in.–1 ft	June–July	9 in.–4 ft
ANEMONE BLANDA	Daisy-flowered Windflower	Sun or light shade — well-drained soil	September	2 in.	4 in.	February –April	6 in.
ANEMONE CORONARIA	Poppy-flowered Windflower	Warm and sheltered — well-drained soil	November –April	2 in.	4 in.	February –October	6–9 in.
BEGONIA	Tuberous Begonia	Light shade — moist, acid soil	June	Plant sprouted tubers	1 ft	July– September	1–1½ ft
CAMASSIA	Quamash	Sun or light shade — damp soil	September –October	4 in.	6 in.	June– July	2½–3½ ft
CANNA	Indian Shot	Sunny site — humus-rich soil	June	2 in.	1½ ft	August– October	3–4 ft
CHIONODOXA	Glory of the Snow	Sun or light shade — well-drained soil	September	3 in.	4 in.	February –March	6 in.
COLCHICUM	Autumn Crocus	Sun or light shade — well-drained soil	July– August	4 in.	9 in.	September –November	6–9 in.
CONVALLARIA	Lily of the Valley	Partial shade — damp soil	October –March	1 in.	4 in.	April –May	8 in.
CRINUM	Crinum	Sunny site — well-drained soil	April –May	10 in.	1½ ft	August– September	2–3 ft
CROCOSMIA	Montbretia	Sunny site — well-drained soil	March	3 in.	6 in.	August– September	2–3 ft
CROCUS	Crocus	Sun or light shade — well-drained soil	September –October	3 in.	4 in.	February –April	3–5 in.
CROCUS SPECIOSUS	Crocus	Sun or light shade — well-drained soil	July	3 in.	4 in.	August– October	3–5 in.
CYCLAMEN	Cyclamen	Partial shade — damp soil	July– September	2 in.	6 in.	Species for all seasons	3–6 in.
DAHLIA	Dahlia	Sunny site — humus-rich soil	April –May	3 in. to top of tuber	1½–3 ft	August– October	2–5 ft
ERANTHIS	Winter Aconite	Sun or light shade — well-drained soil	August– September	2 in.	3 in.	January –March	3–4 in.
ERYTHRONIUM	Dog's-tooth Violet	Partial shade — damp soil	August– October	4 in.	4 in.	March –April	6 in.
FREESIA	Outdoor Freesia	Sunny site — light soil	April	2 in.	4 in.	August– October	1 ft
FRITILLARIA IMPERIALIS	Crown Imperial	Light shade — well-drained soil	September –November	8 in.	1½ ft	April	1–3 ft
FRITILLARIA MELEAGRIS	Snake's Head Fritillary	Light shade — well-drained soil	September –November	5 in.	6 in.	April	1–3 ft
GALANTHUS	Snowdrop	Light shade — moist soil	September –October	4 in.	3 in.	January –March	5–10 in.
GALTONIA	Summer Hyacinth	Sunny site — well-drained soil	March– April	6–8 in.	1 ft	August– September	3–4 ft
GLADIOLUS	Gladiolus Hybrid	Sunny site — well-drained soil	March –May	4–5 in.	4–6 in.	July– September	1–4 ft
GLADIOLUS COLVILLII	Species Gladiolus	Sunny site — well-drained soil	October	4–5 in.	4–6 in.	April– June	2 ft
HYACINTHUS ORIENTALIS	Dutch Hyacinth	Sun or light shade — well-drained soil	September –October	6 in.	8 in.	April –May	6 in.–1 ft
HYACINTHUS O. ALBULUS	Roman Hyacinth	Sun or light shade — well-drained soil	September –October	6 in.	8 in.	March– April	6 in.–1 ft
IPHEION	Spring Starflower	Sun or light shade — well-drained soil	September –October	2 in.	4 in.	April –May	6 in.
IRIS-RETICULATA group	Dwarf Iris	Sunny site — light soil	September –October	2 in.	4 in.	January –March	4–6 in.

Latin name	Common name	Site & soil	Planting time	Planting depth	Spacing	Flowering period	Height
IRIS-XIPHIUM group	Iris	Sunny site — light soil	September–October	4–6 in.	6 in.	June–July	1–2 ft
IXIA	Corn Lily	Sunny site — light soil	March	3 in.	4 in.	June–July	1–1½ ft
LEUCOJUM AESTIVUM	Summer Snowflake	Sun or light shade — well-drained soil	August–September	4 in.	8 in.	April–May	2 ft
LEUCOJUM VERNUM	Spring Snowflake	Sun or light shade — well-drained soil	August–September	4 in.	4 in.	February–March	8 in.
LILIUM	Lily	Sun or light shade — well-drained soil	October	2–6 in. to top of bulb	6 in.–1½ ft	June–October	1–8 ft
MUSCARI	Grape Hyacinth	Sunny site — well-drained soil	September–October	3 in.	4 in.	April–May	6 in.–1 ft
NARCISSUS	Narcissus, Daffodil	Sun or light shade — well-drained soil	August–September	4–7 in.	4–8 in.	March–April	3 in.–2 ft
NERINE	Nerine	Sunny site — well-drained soil	April–May	4 in.	6 in.	September–October	2 ft
ORNITHOGALUM	Star of Bethlehem	Sun or light shade — well-drained soil	October	2 in.	4–6 in.	April–May	6 in.–1 ft
PUSCHKINIA	Striped Squill	Sun or light shade — well-drained soil	September–October	2 in.	3 in.	March–April	4 in.
RANUNCULUS	Turban Buttercup	Sunny site — well-drained soil	March–April	2 in.	6 in.	June–July	1 ft
SCILLA NONSCRIPTA	Bluebell	Sun or light shade — damp soil	August–September	4 in.	4 in.	April–June	9 in.
SCILLA SIBERICA	Siberian Squill	Sun or light shade — damp soil	August–September	4 in.	4 in.	March–April	6 in.
SPARAXIS	Harlequin Flower	Sunny site — well-drained soil	November	3 in.	4 in.	May–June	1 ft
TIGRIDIA	Tiger Flower	Sunny site — well-drained soil	April	4 in.	6 in.	July–September	1½ ft
TRITONIA	Blazing Star	Sunny site — well-drained soil	September	2 in.	6 in.	May–June	1½ ft
TULIPA	Tulip	Sunny site — well-drained soil	November–December	6 in.	5–8 in.	April–May	9 in.–2½ ft
TULIPA SPECIES	Species Tulip	Sunny site — well-drained soil	November–December	4 in.	4–6 in.	March–May	6 in.–1½ ft

Acidanthera murielae

Chionodoxa luciliae

Eranthis tubergenii

Gladiolus Red Cascade

Leucojum vernum

Tigridia pavonia

See
THE FLOWER EXPERT
for a more complete
list together with full
details and photographs

The
FLOWER
EXPERT
Dr.D.G.Hessayon

Plant Types   Herbaceous Perennials

Latin name	Common name	Site & soil	Propagation	Notes
ACANTHUS	Bear's Breeches	Sun or light shade — well-drained soil	Divide clumps — autumn	A. spinosus is the usual one — height 4 ft, spacing 2½ ft, flowers July–September. Blooms are white lipped and purple hooded
ACHILLEA	Yarrow	Sunny site — well-drained soil	Divide clumps — autumn	A. filipendulina Gold Plate bears flat-topped yellow flower-heads — height 4½ ft, spacing 2 ft, flowers June–September
AGAPANTHUS	African Lily	Sunny site — humus-rich soil	Divide clumps — spring	Large head of blue flowers above strap-like leaves. Height 2½ ft, spacing 2 ft, flowers July–September. Not fully hardy
AJUGA	Bugle	Sun or light shade — ordinary soil	Divide clumps — autumn	A creeping plant — grow a variety with coloured leaves — bronze, purple, cream etc. Height 4 in., spacing 15 in., flowers May–August
ALCHEMILLA	Lady's Mantle	Sun or light shade — well-drained soil	Divide clumps — spring	A. mollis is an old favourite — height 1½ ft, spacing 1½ ft, flowers June–August. Blooms small, greenish-yellow
ALSTROEMERIA	Peruvian Lily	Sunny site — fertile soil	Sow seeds — spring	Large trumpets (2 in. across) in loose clusters. Many hybrids available — height 2 ft, spacing 1½ ft, flowers June–August
ANCHUSA	Alkanet	Sunny site — well-drained soil	Divide clumps — spring	Grown for its vivid blue flowers — a straggly short-lived plant. Choose an A. azurea variety — height 1½–5 ft, flowers June–August
ANEMONE	Japanese Anemone	Sun or light shade — well-drained soil	Divide clumps — spring	Saucer-shaped blooms (2 in. across) and deeply-lobed leaves. Height 2–4 ft, spacing 1–1½ ft, flowers August–October
AQUILEGIA	Columbine	Partial shade — well-drained soil	Divide clumps — autumn	Old cottage-garden favourite. Choose a modern hybrid — height 1½–3 ft, spacing 1 ft, flowers May–June
ASTER	Michaelmas Daisy	Sunny site — well-drained soil	Divide clumps — spring	Scores of varieties available — white, red, blue, pink and mauve. Height 2–5ft, spacing 1½ ft, flowers August–October
ASTILBE	Astilbe	Light shade — moist soil	Divide clumps — spring	Feathery plumes of tiny flowers. Many varieties of A. arendsii can be bought — height 2–3 ft, spacing 1½ ft, flowers June–August
BERGENIA	Large-leaved Saxifrage	Sun or light shade — well-drained soil	Divide clumps — autumn	Easy-to-grow ground cover. Fleshy leaves, Hyacinth-like flower-spikes. Height 1½ ft, spacing 1½ ft, flowers March–April
BRUNNERA	Perennial Forget-me-not	Partial shade — well-drained soil	Divide clumps — autumn	Easy-to-grow ground cover. Heart-shaped leaves, Myosotis-like blooms. Height 1½ ft, spacing 1½ ft, flowers April–June
CALTHA	Marsh Marigold	Sun or light shade — moist soil	Divide clumps — after flowering	Golden flowers (1–2 in. across) above dark green leaves. Height 1 ft, spacing 1 ft, flowers April–June
CAMPANULA	Bellflower	Sun or light shade — well-drained soil	Cuttings — spring	Blooms bell-like or star-shaped — white or blue. Several species available — height 2–5 ft, spacing 1–1½ ft, flowers June–August
CHRYSANTHEMUM	Chrysanthemum	Sunny site — well-drained soil	Cuttings — spring	Raised afresh each year from cuttings. Hundreds of varieties available — all colours except blue. See The Flower Expert for details
CHRYSANTHEMUM	Shasta Daisy	Sunny site — non-acid soil	Divide clumps — spring	C. maximum is the hardy Chrysanthemum. Many named varieties available — height 2½–3 ft, spacing 1½ ft, flowers June–August
COREOPSIS	Tickseed	Sun or light shade — well-drained soil	Sow seeds — spring	Yellow Daisy-like flowers on slender stalks. C. grandiflora is the usual species — height 1½ ft, spacing 1½ ft, flowers June–September
CORTADERIA	Pampas Grass	Sun or light shade — well-drained soil	Buy from garden centre	Silvery plumes about 1½ ft long on tall stalks. Grow a variety of C. selloana — height 4–10 ft, flowers October
DELPHINIUM	Delphinium	Sunny site — well-drained soil	Divide clumps — spring	Dwarfs and giants available in white, blue, pink, mauve and purple. Height 3–8 ft, spacing 1½–2½ ft, flowers June–July
DIANTHUS	Border Carnation	Sunny site — non-acid soil	Cuttings — summer	Enormous list of varieties — all sorts of colours. Height 2–3 ft, spacing 1½ ft, flowers July–August. Petals smooth-edged
DIANTHUS	Pinks	Sunny site — non-acid soil	Cuttings — summer	Old-fashioned and modern varieties available — smaller and daintier than Carnations. Height 1–1½ ft, spacing 1 ft, flowers June–July
DICENTRA	Bleeding Heart	Light shade — well-drained soil	Divide clumps — autumn	Most popular Dicentra is also the largest — D. spectabilis. Height 2–3 ft, spacing 1½ ft, flowers May–June
DORONICUM	Leopard's Bane	Sun or light shade — well-drained soil	Divide clumps — autumn	Varieties of D. plantagineum are usually chosen — height 2–3 ft, spacing 1½ ft, flowers April–June. Large Daisy-like blooms
ECHINACEA	Purple Coneflower	Sunny site — well-drained soil	Divide clumps — spring	E. purpurea is the species to grow — height 3–4 ft, spacing 2 ft, flowers July–October. Pink or purple petals
ECHINOPS	Globe Thistle	Sunny site — well-drained soil	Divide clumps — spring	Globular flower-heads above Thistle-like leaves. For the back of the border — height 3–5 ft, spacing 2 ft, flowers July–September
ERIGERON	Fleabane	Sun or light shade — well-drained soil	Divide clumps — spring	Looks like a small Michaelmas Daisy — height 1–2 ft, spacing 1 ft, flowers June–August. Pink, blue and lilac available
ERYNGIUM	Sea Holly	Sunny site — well-drained soil	Divide clumps — spring	Thimble-shaped blue flowers above Thistle-like leaves. Several species available — height 1½–3 ft, spacing 1–1½ ft, flowers July–September
EUPHORBIA	Spurge	Sun or light shade — well-drained soil	Cuttings — spring	Flower colour is nearly always yellow or green, but there is a bright orange one. Height 2½ ft, spacing 1½ ft, flowers May
FUCHSIA	Fuchsia	Sun or light shade — well-drained soil	Cuttings — summer	Hundreds of named hybrids are available — a few are hardy but most are treated as summer bedding plants. Flowers 2–4 in. long

Latin name	Common name	Site & soil	Propagation	Notes
GAILLARDIA	Blanket Flower	Sunny site — avoid heavy soil	Divide clumps — spring	Popular — large Daisy-like blooms (2–4 in. across) in yellow and red. Height 1½–2½ ft, spacing 1½ ft, flowers June–September
GERANIUM	Crane's-bill	Sun or light shade — well-drained soil	Divide clumps — spring	Useful ground cover — saucer-shaped flowers in white, pink, blue or red. Height 1–2 ft, spacing 1½ ft, flowers May–August
GEUM	Avens	Sun or light shade — well-drained soil	Divide clumps — spring	An old favourite — bright, bowl-shaped blooms on top of wiry stems. Height 1–2 ft, spacing 1½ ft, flowers May–September
GYPSOPHILA	Baby's Breath	Sun or light shade — non-acid soil	Cuttings — summer	Tiny white or pale pink flowers form a billowy cloud above thin stems. Height 3 ft, spacing 3 ft, flowers June–August
HELENIUM	Sneezewort	Sun or light shade — well-drained soil	Divide clumps — autumn	Bronze-red H. autumnale Moerheim Beauty is the popular one — height 3 ft, spacing 2 ft, flowers July–September. Yellow varieties available
HELLEBORUS	Christmas Rose	Partial shade — moist soil	Buy from garden centre	H. niger bears large, saucer-shaped blooms — white with golden stamens. Height 1–1½ ft, spacing 1½ ft, flowers January–March
HELLEBORUS	Lenten Rose	Partial shade — moist soil	Buy from garden centre	H. orientalis bears large, saucer-shaped blooms —white, pink or purple. Height 1–1½ ft, spacing 1½ ft, flowers February–April
HEMEROCALLIS	Day Lily	Sun or light shade — ordinary soil	Divide clumps — autumn	Large Lily-like trumpets in shades from pale yellow to rich red. Many varieties — height 3 ft, spacing 2 ft, flowers June–August
HEUCHERA	Coral Flower	Sun or light shade — well-drained soil	Divide clumps — autumn	Tiny bell-shaped blooms on top of slender stems. Height 1½–2½ ft, spacing 1½ ft, flowers June–August. White, pink or red
HOSTA	Plantain Lily	Partial shade — ordinary soil	Divide clumps — spring	Useful ground cover grown for its spikes of flowers and its attractive foliage. Height 1½–3 ft, spacing 2 ft, flowers July–August
INCARVILLEA	Chinese Trumpet Flower	Sunny site — well-drained soil	Sow seeds — spring	Large trumpets in clusters appear before the leaves. Height 1–2 ft, spacing 1 ft, flowers May–June. Pale or deep pink
IRIS	Iris	Sunny site — well-drained soil	Divide rhizomes — late summer	Bearded types (fleshy hairs on petals) dominate the catalogue lists. Height 9 in.–3ft, spacing 1 ft, flowers April–June, depending on variety
KNIPHOFIA	Red Hot Poker	Sunny site — well-drained soil	Divide clumps — spring	Usual choice is a variety or hybrid of K. uvaria — height 2½–5 ft, spacing 3 ft, flowers July–September. Various colour combinations
LIATRIS	Gayfeather	Sun or light shade — moist soil	Divide clumps — spring	Unusual flower-spike feature — blooms open from top downwards. Height 1½ ft, spacing 1½ ft, flowers August–September
LIGULARIA	Ligularia	Partial shade — moist soil	Divide clumps — autumn	Useful ground cover with large leaves and yellow or orange Daisy-like blooms. Height 3–4 ft, spacing 2½ ft, flowers July–September
LINUM	Perennial Flax	Sunny site — well-drained soil	Sow seeds — spring	Short-lived blooms on wiry stems — blue is the most popular colour. Height 1–2 ft, spacing 1 ft, flowers June–August
LUPINUS	Lupin	Sun or light shade — well-drained soil	Sow seeds — spring	Russell hybrids provide stately spires of blooms in a vast range of colours — height 3–4 ft, spacing 2 ft, flowers June–July
LYCHNIS	Campion	Sunny site — well-drained soil	Divide clumps — autumn	L. chalcedonica (Jerusalem Cross) is the one to grow — large heads of red blooms. Height 3 ft, spacing 1½ ft, flowers June–August
LYTHRUM	Purple Loosestrife	Sun or light shade — moist soil	Divide clumps — autumn	Long and narrow flower-spikes, pink or red. Basic species is L. salicaria — height 2½–5 ft, spacing 1½ ft, flowers June–September
MACLEAYA	Plume Poppy	Sun or light shade — ordinary soil	Divide clumps — autumn	Space is needed for the bronzy leaves and tall plumes of pinkish flowers. Height 6–8 ft, spacing 3 ft, flowers July–August
MECONOPSIS	Meconopsis	Light shade — humus-rich soil	Sow seeds — spring	Both the blue Himalayan Poppy (3 ft) and yellow Welsh Poppy (1 ft) belong here. Flowering period June–August
MONARDA	Bergamot	Sun or light shade — moist soil	Divide clumps — spring	Grow one of the named hybrids of M. didyma — height 2–3 ft, spacing 2 ft, flowers June–September
NEPETA	Catmint	Sunny site — ordinary soil	Divide clumps — spring	Popular edging plant — small lavender flowers and aromatic greyish leaves. Height 1–3 ft, spacing 1½ ft, flowers May-September
OENOTHERA	Evening Primrose	Sunny site — well-drained soil	Divide clumps — spring	Yellow Poppy-like blooms — O. missouriensis bears the largest. Height 6 in.–1½ ft, spacing 1–1½ ft, flowers July–September

Oenothera Fireworks

Hemerocallis Pink Prelude

Aquilegia McKana Hybrid

Kniphofia Royal Standard

Latin name	Common name	Site & soil	Propagation	Notes
PAEONIA	Paeony	Sunny site — well-drained soil	Buy from garden centre	Vast bowls of petals up to 7 in. across — single, double or Anemone-flowered. Height 1½–3 ft, spacing 1½–2 ft, flowers April–July
PAPAVER	Oriental Poppy	Sunny site — well-drained soil	Divide clumps — spring	Bowl-shaped flowers up to 6 in. across. Many named varieties available — height 3 ft, spacing 1½ ft, flowers May–June
PELARGONIUM	Geranium	Sunny site — well-drained soil	Cuttings — summer	Height 1–2 ft, spacing 1 ft. Two basic types — Bedding Geraniums (flowers ½–1 in. across) and Regal Geraniums (frilled flowers 1½–2 in. across)
PENSTEMON	Beard Tongue	Sunny site — well-drained soil	Cuttings — summer	Grow a named hybrid — height 1½–2 ft, spacing 1 ft, flowers June–September. Red is the usual colour. Not fully hardy
PHLOX	Phlox	Sun or light shade — moist soil	Divide clumps — spring	Large trusses of flat-faced flowers. The most popular Phlox is P. paniculata — height 2–4 ft, spacing 1½ ft, flowers July–October
PHYSALIS	Chinese Lantern	Sun or light shade — ordinary soil	Divide clumps — spring	Grown for 2 in. long 'lanterns' — useful for drying. Height 2 ft, spacing 3 ft, fruits September–October. Gold- or flame-coloured
PLATYCODON	Balloon Flower	Sun or light shade — well-drained soil	Buy from garden centre	Unusual flower feature — buds swell into large, angular balloons before opening. Height 1–2 ft, spacing 1 ft, flowers June–September
POLEMONIUM	Jacob's Ladder	Sun or light shade — well-drained soil	Divide clumps — autumn	An old cottage-garden plant — choose a modern variety if space is limited. Height 1–3 ft, spacing 1 ft, flowers June–August
POLYGONATUM	Solomon's Seal	Shade — ordinary soil	Divide clumps — autumn	Thrives under trees and shrubs — green-tipped white blooms in pendent clusters. Height 2–3 ft, spacing 2 ft, flowers May–June
POLYGONUM	Knotweed	Sun or light shade — ordinary soil	Divide clumps — autumn	Evergreen ground cover — pokers of pink flowers. Chose a P. affine variety — height 1 ft, spacing 2 ft, flowers June–October
POTENTILLA	Cinquefoil	Sunny site — well-drained soil	Divide clumps — spring	Bright saucer-shaped flowers in reds and yellows. Several named hybrids — height 1–2 ft, spacing 1½ ft, flowers June–September
PRIMULA	Primrose	Partial shade — humus-rich soil	Divide clumps — spring	Many species and hybrids are available — Pacific Strain of Polyanthus most popular. Height 1 ft, spacing 1 ft, flowers March–May
PYRETHRUM	Feverfew	Sunny site — well-drained soil	Divide clumps — spring	Single or double Daisy-like blooms 2 in. across — usual colours pink and red. Height 2–3 ft, spacing 1½ ft, flowers May–June
RUDBECKIA	Coneflower	Sun or light shade — ordinary soil	Divide clumps — spring	Dark-centred, star-shaped blooms. Popular variety is R. fulgida Goldsturm — height 2 ft, spacing 2 ft, flowers July–September
SALVIA	Perennial Sage	Sun or light shade — well-drained soil	Divide clumps — autumn	Blue — not red like the Annual Salvia. Usual species is S. superba — height 3 ft, spacing 1½ ft, flowers July–September
SAXIFRAGA	Saxifrage	Partial shade — humus-rich soil	Divide clumps — spring	Starry flowers above rosettes or clumps of leaves. Popular one is London Pride — height 1 ft, spacing 1½ ft, flowers May–July
SCABIOSA	Scabious	Sunny site — non-acid soil	Divide clumps — spring	Flowers are frilly-edged pincushions up to 4 in. across. Basic species is S. caucasica — height 2–3 ft, spacing 1½ ft, flowers June–October
SEDUM	Stonecrop	Sunny site — well-drained soil	Divide clumps — spring	The popular Ice Plant is S. spectabile — height 1–2 ft, spacing 1 ft, flowers August–October. Flower-heads 4–6 in. across
SOLIDAGO	Golden Rod	Sun or light shade — well-drained soil	Divide clumps — spring	Feathery flower-heads above narrow leaves. Choose a named hybrid — height 1–7 ft, spacing 1–2 ft, flowers July–September
STACHYS	Lamb's Ears	Sun or light shade — well-drained soil	Divide clumps — autumn	The popular Stachys is Lamb's Ears (S. lanata) — height 1½ ft, spacing 1 ft, flowers July–August. Woolly foliage, pale purple blooms
TRADESCANTIA	Spiderwort	Sun or light shade — ordinary soil	Divide clumps — spring	Silky three-petalled blooms above sword-like leaves. The species is T. virginiana — height 1½–2 ft, spacing 1½ ft, flowers June–September
TROLLIUS	Globe Flower	Sun or light shade — moist soil	Divide clumps — autumn	Buttercup-like blooms 2 in. across. Hybrids range from pale cream to dark orange — height 1½–2½ ft, spacing 1½ ft, flowers May–June
VERBASCUM	Mullein	Sunny site — well-drained soil	Root cuttings — winter	Branched flower-spikes above woolly leaves. Choose a named variety — many colours available. Height 3–6 ft, spacing 2 ft, flowers June–August
VERONICA	Speedwell	Sun or light shade — well-drained soil	Divide clumps — autumn	Narrow spikes of blue or white blooms. Size of varieties covers a wide range — height 1–5 ft, spacing 1–2 ft, flowers May–June

Rudbeckia Goldsturm

Verbascum hybridum

See THE FLOWER EXPERT for a more complete list together with full details and photographs

Plant Types — Vegetables

Crop	Sow	Plant	Harvest	Yield	Time taken (weeks)	Easy to grow	Easy to store
ASPARAGUS	Apr	Apr	May-June	25 spears/P	120 P→H	X	X
AUBERGINE	Feb ⌂	Apr ⌂	Aug-Sept	4 lb/P	20 S→H	X	X
BEANS, BROAD	Feb-Apr	—	July-Aug	10 lb/R	14 S→H	✓	X
BEANS, FRENCH	May-June	—	July-Sept	8 lb/R	10 S→H	✓	X
BEANS, RUNNER	May-June	—	Aug-Oct	30 lb/R	13 S→H	(✓)	X
	Apr ⌂	May-June	Aug-Oct	30 lb/R	14 S→H	(✓)	X
BEET, LEAF	Apr	—	Aug-Nov	7 lb/R	12 S→H	✓	X
BEETROOT	Apr-June	—	June-Oct	10 lb/R	11 S→H	✓	✓
BROCCOLI	Apr-May	June-July	Feb-May	1½ lb/P	44 S→H	(✓)	X
BRUSSELS SPROUTS	Mar-Apr	May-June	Oct-Feb	2 lb/P	30 S→H	(✓)	X
CABBAGE, SPRING	July-Aug	Sept-Oct	Apr-May	¾ lb/P	35 S→H	(✓)	X
CABBAGE, SUMMER	Apr	May-June	Aug-Sept	1½ lb/P	20 S→H	(✓)	X
CABBAGE, WINTER	Apr-May	July	Nov-Feb	2½ lb/P	35 S→H	(✓)	✓
CABBAGE, CHINESE	July-Aug	—	Oct	1½ lb/P	10 S→H	✓	X
CALABRESE	Apr-May	June-July	Aug-Oct	1½ lb/P	12 S→H	(✓)	X
CAPSICUM	Feb ⌂	Apr ⌂	Aug-Sept	8 fruits/P	18 S→H	X	X
CARROT, EARLY	Mar-Apr	—	July	8 lb/R	12 S→H	(✓)	X
CARROT, MAINCROP	Apr-June	—	Sept-Oct	10 lb/R	16 S→H	(✓)	✓
CAULIFLOWER, SUMMER	Apr	June	Aug-Sept	1 lb/P	18 S→H	X	X
CAULIFLOWER, AUTUMN	Apr-May	June	Oct-Nov	2 lb/P	24 S→H	X	X
CAULIFLOWER, WINTER	May	July	Mar-May	2 lb/P	45 S→H	X	X
CELERIAC	Mar ⌂	May-June	Oct-Nov	7 lb/R	33 S→H	X	✓
CELERY, TRENCH	Mar-Apr ⌂	June	Oct-Feb	12 lb/R	40 S→H	X	X
CELERY, SELF-BLANCHING	Mar-Apr ⌂	June	Aug-Oct	12 lb/R	25 S→H	X	X
CHICORY	May	—	Dec-Mar	6 lb/R	25 S→H	X	X
COURGETTE	May-June	—	July-Sept	16 fruits/P	10 S→H	(✓)	X
CUCUMBER, GREENHOUSE	Apr ⌂	May ⌂	July-Sept	25 fruits/P	12 S→H	X	X
CUCUMBER, OUTDOOR	May-June	—	Aug-Sept	10 fruits/P	12 S→H	X	X
ENDIVE	Apr-Aug	—	Sept-Feb	10 heads/R	18 S→H	X	X
KALE	May	July	Dec-Mar	2 lb/P	33 S→H	✓	X
KOHL RABI	Apr-June	—	Aug-Oct	20 globes/R	10 S→H	✓	X
LEEK	Mar-Apr	June	Nov-Mar	10 lb/R	45 S→H	(✓)	X
LETTUCE	Mar-July	—	June-Oct	15 heads/R	10 S→H	✓	X
MARROW	May-June	—	Aug-Oct	4 fruits/P	14 S→H	(✓)	✓
	Apr ⌂	June	Aug-Oct	4 fruits/P	14 S→H	X	✓
ONION, SETS	—	Mar-Apr	Aug	7 lb/R	20 P→H	✓	✓
ONION, SEED	Mar-Apr	—	Aug-Sept	8 lb/R	22 S→H	✓	✓
PARSNIP	Mar	—	Nov-Feb	8 lb/R	34 S→H	✓	✓
PEA	Mar-July	—	May-Oct	10 lb/R	12–32 S→H	X	X
POTATO, EARLY	—	Mar-Apr	June-Aug	12 lb/R	13 P→H	✓	✓
POTATO, MAINCROP	—	Apr	Sept-Oct	20 lb/R	22 P→H	✓	✓
RADISH	Mar-June	—	May-Sept	4 lb/R	6 S→H	✓	✓
RHUBARB	—	Feb-Mar	Apr-July	5 lb/P	65 P→H	✓	X
SALSIFY	Apr	—	Nov-Jan	4 lb/R	25 S→H	✓	✓
SHALLOT	—	Feb-Mar	Aug	7 lb/R	20 P→H	✓	✓
SPINACH	Mar-May	—	June-Oct	6 lb/R	10 S→H	(✓)	X
SWEDE	May-June	—	Nov-Feb	30 lb/R	22 S→H	✓	✓
SWEET CORN	May	—	Aug-Sept	10 cobs/R	14 S→H	X	X
TOMATO, GREENHOUSE	Feb ⌂	Apr ⌂	July-Oct	8 lb/P	16 S→H	X	X
TOMATO, OUTDOOR	Mar-Apr ⌂	June	Aug-Sept	4 lb/P	20 S→H	X	X
TURNIP, EARLY	Mar-June	—	May-Sept	7 lb/R	8 S→H	✓	X
TURNIP, MAINCROP	July-Aug	—	Oct-Dec	12 lb/R	12 S→H	✓	✓

⌂ — under glass

P — per plant	S — sowing
R — per 10 ft row	P — planting
	H — harvesting

✓ — easy
(✓) — not really easy
X — difficult

✓ — can be stored for months
X — cannot be stored

See
THE VEGETABLE EXPERT
for a more complete list
together with full details
and photographs

Plant Material & Planting Methods   Seeds

Looking through seed catalogues during the winter is one of the pleasures of the gardening year. From mail order nurseries, High St shops and garden centres about 85 million packets are bought each year — half are vegetables and half are flowers. Many gardeners gained their first horticultural experience with a packet of Radishes, Nasturtiums or other hardy annual. Perhaps we move too quickly from sowing seeds to buying bedding plants and container-grown specimens. A much wider range of annuals and biennials can be raised from seed and some perennials can readily be obtained in this way. Poor storage greatly reduces germination capacity. If you wish to save leftover seed tightly close the package and place in a jar with a screw top. Close the top securely and state the variety and date on the label. Store in a dark and cool place. Do not store opened packets of pelleted or dressed seed. Starter kits are widely available — plastic trays filled with pre-sown seed compost. They are useful if you are short of time, but the range of plants offered is limited and the cost is understandably higher than starting from scratch.

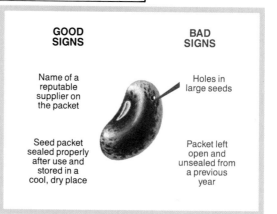

GOOD SIGNS — Name of a reputable supplier on the packet. Seed packet sealed properly after use and stored in a cool, dry place.

BAD SIGNS — Holes in large seeds. Packet left open and unsealed from a previous year.

Sowing seeds indoors

Some popular flowers are too tender to be grown outdoors until the end of spring. The seeds are sown in compost in March or April and the trays or pots kept in a greenhouse, garden frame or on the windowsill. The seedlings are set out in the garden in late May or early June. Some half-hardy vegetables (Tomato, Cucumber, Aubergine, Capsicum etc) are also sown indoors in early spring for greenhouse culture or for planting outside when the danger of frost is past. Indoor sowing is not restricted to half-hardy subjects. It is also used for raising hardy types of flowers and vegetables when early blooms or early crops are required. Transplanting indoor-sown plants rather than sowing on site is useful for wet and cold areas.

1 **CONTAINERS** Use a seed tray, pan or ordinary flower pot. Drainage holes or cracks are necessary. Wash used containers before filling — soak clay pots overnight.

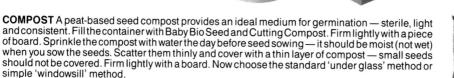

2 **COMPOST** A peat-based seed compost provides an ideal medium for germination — sterile, light and consistent. Fill the container with Baby Bio Seed and Cutting Compost. Firm lightly with a piece of board. Sprinkle the compost with water the day before seed sowing — it should be moist (not wet) when you sow the seeds. Scatter them thinly and cover with a thin layer of compost — small seeds should not be covered. Firm lightly with a board. Now choose the standard 'under glass' method or simple 'windowsill' method.

STANDARD 'UNDER GLASS' METHOD

3 **COVER** Place a sheet of glass over the tray or pot and put brown paper on top. Keep at 60°–70°F and wipe and turn the glass every day.

4 **LIGHT** As soon as the seedlings break through the surface, remove the paper and prop up the sheet of glass. After a few days the glass should be removed and the container moved close to the light. Keep the compost moist but not wet.

SIMPLE 'WINDOWSILL' METHOD

3 **COVER** Place a transparent polythene bag over the pot as shown. Fit with a rubber band. Keep at 60°–70°F in a shady spot.

4 **LIGHT** As soon as the seedlings break through the surface, remove the polythene bag and move the pot to a windowsill which does not receive direct sunlight. Turn the pot regularly to avoid lop-sided growth — keep the compost moist but not wet.

5 **PRICK OUT** As soon as the first set of true leaves have opened the seedlings should be pricked out into trays, pans or small pots filled with potting compost. Handle the plants by the seed leaves — not the stems. The seedlings should be set about 1½ in. apart. Keep the container in the shade for a day or two after pricking out.

Correct stage for pricking out

6 **HARDEN OFF** When the seedlings have recovered from the pricking out move, they must be hardened off to prepare them for the life outdoors. Increase the ventilation and move the container to a cool room or to a cold frame. Then move outdoors during daylight hours; finally leaving them outdoors all the time for about 7 days before planting out.

Sowing seeds outdoors

In order to germinate a seed must have warmth, air and moisture. March and April are the usual months for sowing hardy annuals, when the soil is warm enough for germination and dry enough to allow you to make a seed bed. The weather is more important than the calendar — hold up operations if the weather is cold and wet, even though it may mean being a couple of weeks late. Some annuals (e.g Larkspur, Cornflower and Pot Marigold) can be sown in September — these autumn-sown annuals bloom earlier than their spring-sown counterparts. Half-hardy annuals can be sown outdoors in late spring when the danger of frost is past — these outdoor-sown plants bloom later than bedded-out ones. It is quite impossible to generalise about the correct time to sow vegetables — it depends on the type grown and you should consult the seed packet or a guide such as The Vegetable Expert.

1   **PREPARE SOIL** Careful soil preparation is necessary to ensure that the seeds will have enough air and water, and that the tiny roots will secure a proper foothold. Choose a day when the soil is moist under the surface and quite dry on top. Lightly tread over and then rake until the surface is even and crumbly.

2   **PREPARE SEED AREAS**

Mark out zones for each variety with a pointed stick — make sure the zones overlap slightly. You can scatter seed over each allotted area but this will make thinning and weeding difficult. It is better to sow the seeds in drills.

or

PREPARE SEED DRILLS

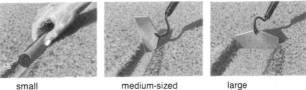

small seeds   medium-sized seeds   large seeds

The depth of the drill depends upon the size of the seeds. A general rule is to ensure that the seeds will be covered with soil to about twice their size. Never water the seed bed after sowing — if the soil is dry it should be gently watered before sowing.

3   **SOW SEED** Seed must be sown thinly. Do not sow directly from the packet — place some seed in the palm of your hand and gently sprinkle between thumb and forefinger. Fine seed should be mixed with sand before sowing. After sowing, carefully rake the soil back into the drill and then firm with the back of the rake. If you are not skilled at this operation it is better to forget the textbook and push the soil back with your fingers. Do not water — if the weather is dry then cover the surface with newspaper. Some seeds need protection from birds — cover the surface with wire guards or twigs.

4   **THIN OUT** When seedlings reach the stage illustrated on page 58, it is time to start thinning. At this first stage reduce the stand to one seedling every 1–2 in. Repeat this thinning about 10 days later so that the plants are at the distance recommended for them.

VARIATIONS

★ Using a nursery bed

Some seeds are sown in a special plot of ground (a nursery bed) set aside for raising seedlings. The drills should be 6–12 in. apart. As soon as the seedlings reach the stage shown on page 58 they should be thinned to about 2 in. apart — firm the soil around the seedlings. The next stage depends on the type of plant.

Hardy Biennials: Sow in May-July. In autumn lift each plant with a trowel from the nursery bed and transfer to the bed or border where it is to flower.

Hardy Perennials: Sow in May-July. In autumn lift each plant with a trowel from the nursery bed and transfer to a small pot filled with potting compost.

Greens (Cabbage, Cauliflower, Broccoli, Brussels Sprouts and Kale): Sow at the appropriate time (see The Vegetable Expert). Lift the seedlings with a trowel from the nursery bed when they have 5–6 leaves — transplant to the vegetable plot, planting at the recommended spacing distance.

★ Fluid sowing

This technique is becoming increasingly popular for vegetable seeds — the plants get off to an early start. The seeds are germinated indoors on moistened paper and then they are mixed with a jelly-like material. The usual base is a fungicide-free wallpaper paste, and the sticky mixture is poured into a plastic squeezy bottle and the nozzle replaced. If the nozzle is too small use a small plastic bag with one small corner cut off to form a 'nozzle'. Squeeze out the jelly/seed mixture along the drill and cover with soil in the usual way.

★ Station sowing

Very large seeds such as Sweet Corn, Marrow or Broad Bean are usually sown in holes dug with a trowel or dibber at the stations where they are to grow. It is usual to sow 2 or 3 seeds at each station, thinning all but the strongest seedling after germination.

Seed types

Open-pollinated seed Most of the varieties in the catalogues are of this 'conventional' or 'standard' type. No specialist hybridisation has been carried out and so it is generally the most economic. Remember, however, that new varieties cost more than old favourites.

F₁ hybrid seed A variety produced by the careful crossing of two pure-bred parents. Increased vigour and uniformity of height, shape etc are the major characteristics and so an F_1 hybrid is often a good buy despite the higher price. One major drawback — the plants all tend to mature at the same time, which is good for the professional but bad for the amateur.

Pelleted seed Seed coated with clay or other material to make handling easier. Useful for tiny seeds as you can sow them at wide enough intervals so as to cut down or eliminate the need for thinning. Results are often disappointing as the soil around the seeds must be kept uniformly moist — if kept too dry or too wet germination will be poor.

Dressed seed Seed which has been coated with a fungicide or fungicide/insecticide before packing by the nurseryman.

Vacuum-packed seed Seed which has been packed into vacuum-sealed foil sachets before being placed in the package. Such seeds maintain their viability longer than seeds packed in the ordinary way.

Chitted seed Seed which has been germinated by the grower and sent out in waterproof sachets. Such seed must be planted immediately.

Saved seed Some seed is usually left over after sowing. Nearly all varieties can be saved for next year — see below.

Home-grown seed It is tempting to save seed from vegetables which have been left to form pods or seed-heads. In most cases it is not advisable. F_1 hybrids will not breed true and brassicas may well have been cross-bred and so produce worthless plants. Exceptions are Peas, Beans and Onions — many champion Onion growers insist on using their own seed.

Plant Material & Planting Methods   Bulbs

Bulbs are one of the most popular types of planting material. If the soil is reasonable and the bulbs healthy and large enough then hardly anything can go wrong. The general practice is to plant in autumn for flowers to brighten up the spring garden, but this basic pattern can be greatly extended. By careful selection you can have bulbous plants in bloom all year round.

True bulbs (e.g Hyacinth, Tulip) have fleshy or scale-like leaves or leaf bases arising from a basal plate. Corms (e.g Crocus, Gladiolus) are thickened stem bases, and tubers (e.g Dahlia, Tuberous Begonia) are swollen roots or stems. Don't regard bulbous plants as planting material which like seeds can be stored for months before planting. A few of the popular ones can be kept in a cool shed for a while after purchase, but as a rule they should be planted as soon as possible. This is especially important for soft-textured types such as Lilies. The largest bulbs produce the largest flowers, but the best buy if you have a large area to fill are medium-sized specimens. Bulbous varieties come in all shapes and sizes — see the summary on pages 52–53 or consult The Flower Expert for full details.

Aftercare is important. When flowering is over, the leaves must be left on the plant. This is the stage when food is produced for next year's bulbs — feed with a liquid fertilizer and do not tie Daffodil foliage into a knot. If the land is required, lift the plants and transfer to a shallow trench elsewhere in the garden.

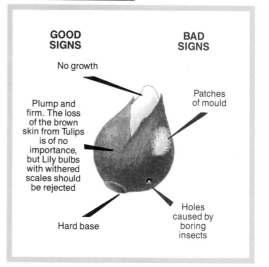

GOOD SIGNS

No growth

Plump and firm. The loss of the brown skin from Tulips is of no importance, but Lily bulbs with withered scales should be rejected

Hard base

BAD SIGNS

Patches of mould

Holes caused by boring insects

Planting

Plant to the recommended depth in well-drained soil — this distance is measured from the soil surface to the bottom of the bulb. Reduce the depth slightly in heavy soil — increase it slightly in sandy ground. Dig a hole with a trowel or bulb planter — make sure that the hole is deeper than the recommended depth. Add sand to the hole and set the bulb firmly on this bed. Return the soil and press down firmly. If a large area is to be planted, dig out the soil to the required depth and cover the base of this planting area with sand. Space out the bulbs and press them firmly into the sand. Return the soil and tread down lightly.

DANGER
air pocket below bulb

Bulbs and corms generally spread to form clumps in the garden. Every few years lift these clumps when the foliage has died down and separate them with the fingers. Replant large specimens at once but move the bulblets or cormlets to an out-of-the-way spot. Plant them 2–4 in. deep and leave until they reach flowering size in 2–3 years.

Plant Material & Planting Methods — Cuttings

A cutting is a small piece removed from a plant which with proper treatment can be induced to form roots and then grow into a specimen which is identical to the parent plant. You cannot guess the best type of cutting to take nor the best time to propagate it — consult The Flower Expert and The Tree & Shrub Expert. There are, however, a few general rules. Plant the cutting as soon as possible after severing it from the parent plant and make sure that the compost is in close contact with the inserted part. Do not keep pulling at the cutting to see if it has rooted — the appearance of new growth is the best guide.

Softwood and semi-ripe cuttings

Softwood cuttings are green at the tip and base, and are taken from early spring to midsummer. Many hardy perennials and some small shrubs are propagated in this way. Basal cuttings are shoots formed at the base of the plant and pulled away for use as softwood cuttings in spring. **Semi-ripe cuttings** are green at the top and partly woody at the base — they are usually heel cuttings (see below). Midsummer to early autumn is the usual time and most shrubs, climbers and conifers are propagated by this method.

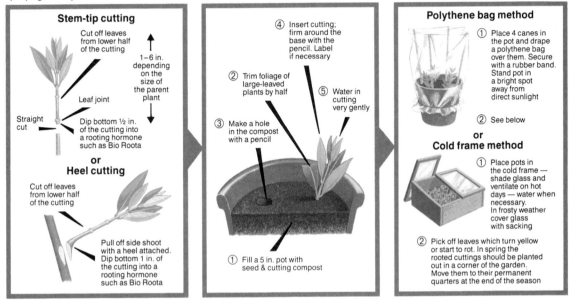

Stem-tip cutting

Cut off leaves from lower half of the cutting

1–6 in. depending on the size of the parent plant

Leaf joint

Straight cut

Dip bottom ½ in. of the cutting into a rooting hormone such as Bio Roota

or
Heel cutting

Cut off leaves from lower half of the cutting

Pull off side shoot with a heel attached. Dip bottom 1 in. of the cutting into a rooting hormone such as Bio Roota

④ Insert cutting; firm around the base with the pencil. Label if necessary

② Trim foliage of large-leaved plants by half

⑤ Water in cutting very gently

③ Make a hole in the compost with a pencil

① Fill a 5 in. pot with seed & cutting compost

Polythene bag method

① Place 4 canes in the pot and drape a polythene bag over them. Secure with a rubber band. Stand pot in a bright spot away from direct sunlight

② See below

or
Cold frame method

① Place pots in the cold frame — shade glass and ventilate on hot days — water when necessary. In frosty weather cover glass with sacking

② Pick off leaves which turn yellow or start to rot. In spring the rooted cuttings should be planted out in a corner of the garden. Move them to their permanent quarters at the end of the season

Hardwood Cuttings

A large variety of trees, shrubs, Roses and bush fruit can be propagated in this way. The usual time is late autumn. Choose a well-ripened shoot of this year's growth.

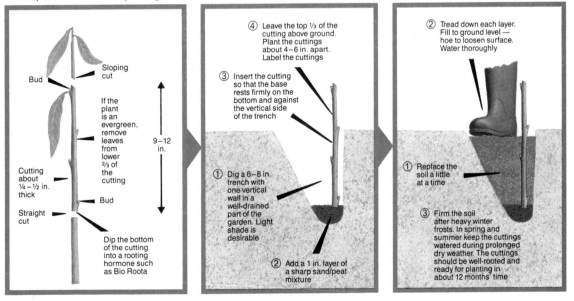

Bud

Sloping cut

If the plant is an evergreen, remove leaves from lower ⅔ of the cutting

9–12 in.

Cutting about ¼ – ½ in. thick

Bud

Straight cut

Dip the bottom of the cutting into a rooting hormone such as Bio Roota

④ Leave the top ⅓ of the cutting above ground. Plant the cuttings about 4–6 in. apart. Label the cuttings

③ Insert the cutting so that the base rests firmly on the bottom and against the vertical side of the trench

① Dig a 6–8 in. trench with one vertical wall in a well-drained part of the garden. Light shade is desirable

② Add a 1 in. layer of a sharp sand/peat mixture

② Tread down each layer. Fill to ground level — hoe to loosen surface. Water thoroughly

① Replace the soil a little at a time

③ Firm the soil after heavy winter frosts. In spring and summer keep the cuttings watered during prolonged dry weather. The cuttings should be well-rooted and ready for planting in about 12 months' time

Plant Material & Planting Methods | Roots with Soil

You will never finish stocking your garden as long as you remain a gardener. There will always be more spaces to fill, old plants to renew and new varieties to try. The easiest way to achieve success at planting time is to use pot-grown specimens or container-grown plants so as to avoid root disturbance. There are times, however, when we must rely on lifted plants, such as hardy perennials dug up at the nursery, bedding plants taken out of plastic trays or rooted cuttings separated from others in a propagator. In these cases some root damage is inevitable, and the rules for planting are designed to reduce this shock to a minimum. The leaves will continue to lose water after planting and so it is essential that new roots are produced as quickly as possible to replace the damaged ones. This calls for thorough soil preparation, careful lifting and then planting at the right time and in the right way.

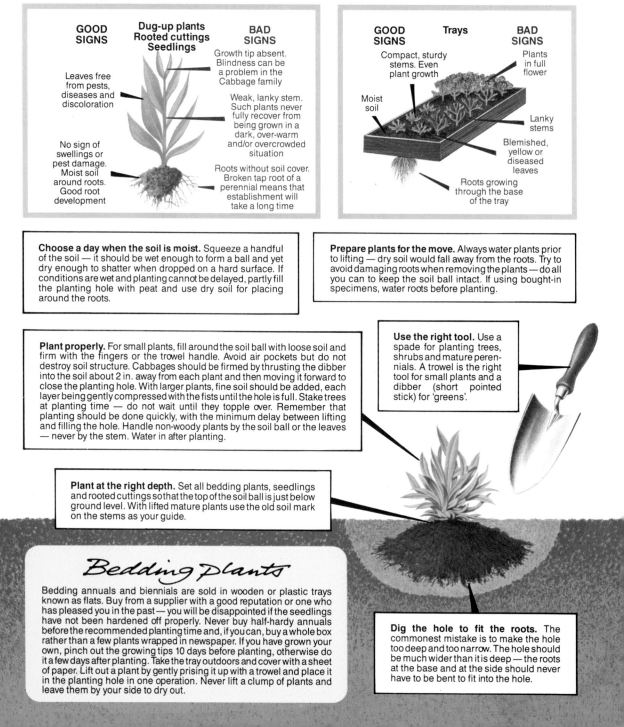

GOOD SIGNS — Dug-up plants, Rooted cuttings, Seedlings — **BAD SIGNS**

Leaves free from pests, diseases and discoloration

No sign of swellings or pest damage. Moist soil around roots. Good root development

Growth tip absent. Blindness can be a problem in the Cabbage family

Weak, lanky stem. Such plants never fully recover from being grown in a dark, over-warm and/or overcrowded situation

Roots without soil cover. Broken tap root of a perennial means that establishment will take a long time

GOOD SIGNS — Trays — **BAD SIGNS**

Compact, sturdy stems. Even plant growth

Moist soil

Plants in full flower

Lanky stems

Blemished, yellow or diseased leaves

Roots growing through the base of the tray

Choose a day when the soil is moist. Squeeze a handful of the soil — it should be wet enough to form a ball and yet dry enough to shatter when dropped on a hard surface. If conditions are wet and planting cannot be delayed, partly fill the planting hole with peat and use dry soil for placing around the roots.

Prepare plants for the move. Always water plants prior to lifting — dry soil would fall away from the roots. Try to avoid damaging roots when removing the plants — do all you can to keep the soil ball intact. If using bought-in specimens, water roots before planting.

Plant properly. For small plants, fill around the soil ball with loose soil and firm with the fingers or the trowel handle. Avoid air pockets but do not destroy soil structure. Cabbages should be firmed by thrusting the dibber into the soil about 2 in. away from each plant and then moving it forward to close the planting hole. With larger plants, fine soil should be added, each layer being gently compressed with the fists until the hole is full. Stake trees at planting time — do not wait until they topple over. Remember that planting should be done quickly, with the minimum delay between lifting and filling the hole. Handle non-woody plants by the soil ball or the leaves — never by the stem. Water in after planting.

Use the right tool. Use a spade for planting trees, shrubs and mature perennials. A trowel is the right tool for small plants and a dibber (short pointed stick) for 'greens'.

Plant at the right depth. Set all bedding plants, seedlings and rooted cuttings so that the top of the soil ball is just below ground level. With lifted mature plants use the old soil mark on the stems as your guide.

Bedding Plants

Bedding annuals and biennials are sold in wooden or plastic trays known as flats. Buy from a supplier with a good reputation or one who has pleased you in the past — you will be disappointed if the seedlings have not been hardened off properly. Never buy half-hardy annuals before the recommended planting time and, if you can, buy a whole box rather than a few plants wrapped in newspaper. If you have grown your own, pinch out the growing tips 10 days before planting, otherwise do it a few days after planting. Take the tray outdoors and cover with a sheet of paper. Lift out a plant by gently prising it up with a trowel and place it in the planting hole in one operation. Never lift a clump of plants and leave them by your side to dry out.

Dig the hole to fit the roots. The commonest mistake is to make the hole too deep and too narrow. The hole should be much wider than it is deep — the roots at the base and at the side should never have to be bent to fit into the hole.

Plant Material & Planting Methods Bare-rooted Plants

Bare-rooted plants are dug up at the nursery and transported without soil — once all our Roses were bought this way. Damp material, such as peat, is packed around the roots to prevent them from drying out and at no stage should the roots be allowed to become dry. Bare-rooted plants are less expensive than their container-grown counterparts and it is not true that they are always more difficult to establish — some shrubs take root more readily when planted as bare-rooted stock.

Pre-packaged shrubs and hardy perennials are the standard planting material sold by hardware shops, department stores and supermarkets. The pre-packaged plant is a bare-rooted specimen with its roots surrounded by moist peat and the whole plant packed in a polythene bag. Labels are descriptive and colourful, and such plants are cheaper than their container-grown counterparts . . . but there are drawbacks. It is hard to see what you are buying and premature growth may occur in the warm conditions inside the shop.

Planting time is the dormant season between autumn and spring — choose mid October-late November if you can, but delay planting until March if the soil is heavy and cold. Cut off leaves, dead flowers, thin or damaged stems and damaged roots. If the stem is shrivelled plunge the roots in a bucket of water for 2 hours. Place packing material over the roots when you are ready to begin planting. If you can't plant straight away, leave the packing material intact and put the plants in a cool but frost-free place. If the delay is likely to last more than a few days, unpack and heel the plants in by digging a V-shaped trench in which the roots are placed and covered.

Planting mixture

Make up the planting mixture in a wheelbarrow on a day when the soil is reasonably dry and friable — 1 part topsoil, 1 part moist peat and 3 handfuls of Bone Meal per barrowload. Keep this mixture in a shed or garage until you are ready to start planting.

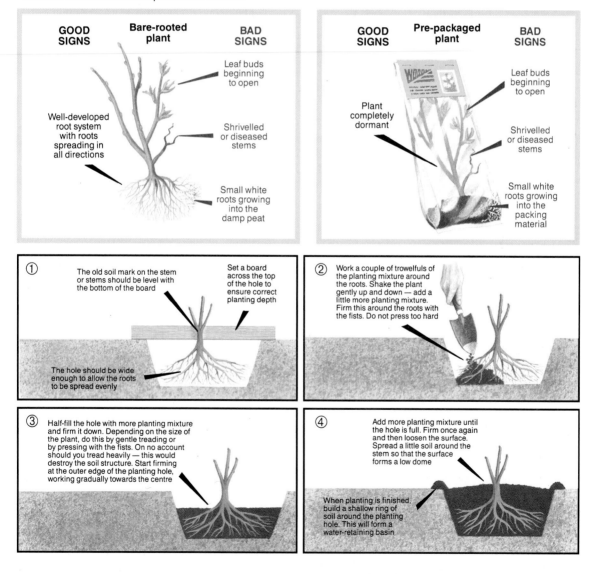

Plant Material & Planting Methods — Containers

A **container-grown plant** will have been raised as a seedling, cutting or grafted rootstock and then been potted on until housed in a whalehide, plastic or metal container. A **pot-grown plant** is a miniature version of a container-grown specimen in a clay, plastic or whalehide pot.

A large container-grown plant should *not* have been lifted from the open ground and its roots and surrounding soil stuffed into the container prior to sale. The test is to gently pull the plant and see if the soil ball comes up easily. If it does, the plant should be rejected.

An evergreen tree or shrub is often sold as a **balled plant**. The tree or shrub is dug up and the soil around the roots is left intact, the soil ball being tightly wrapped with hessian sacking, nylon netting or polythene sheeting. Always carry a balled plant by holding it under the sacking — do not use the stem as a handle.

Container-grown plants offer a convenient way to add flowers and shrubs to your garden at almost any time of the year. But it is not a fool-proof method — you must make sure that the earth around the soil ball is enriched with peat. Roots hate to move from pure peat into a mineral soil which is practically devoid of organic matter.

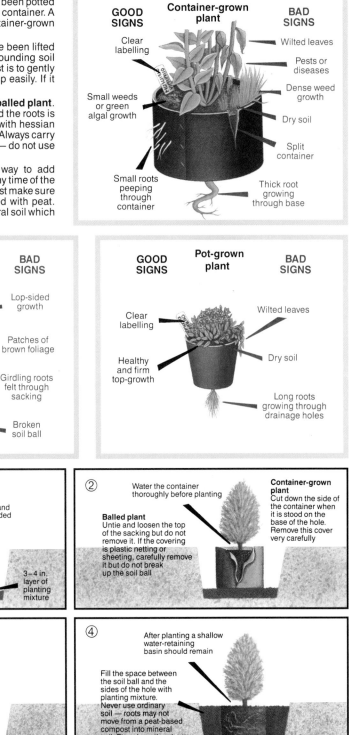

Container-grown plant

GOOD SIGNS
- Clear labelling
- Small weeds or green algal growth
- Small roots peeping through container

BAD SIGNS
- Wilted leaves
- Pests or diseases
- Dense weed growth
- Dry soil
- Split container
- Thick root growing through base

Balled plant

GOOD SIGNS
- Sturdy stems well-clothed with healthy leaves
- Moist soil

BAD SIGNS
- Lop-sided growth
- Patches of brown foliage
- Girdling roots felt through sacking
- Broken soil ball

Pot-grown plant

GOOD SIGNS
- Clear labelling
- Healthy and firm top-growth

BAD SIGNS
- Wilted leaves
- Dry soil
- Long roots growing through drainage holes

① Dig a planting hole which is large enough and deep enough for the soil ball to be surrounded by a 3–4 in. layer of planting mixture

The hole should be deep enough to ensure that the top of the soil ball will be about 1 in. below the soil surface after planting

3–4 in. layer of planting mixture

② Water the container thoroughly before planting

Container-grown plant
Cut down the side of the container when it is stood on the base of the hole. Remove this cover very carefully

Balled plant
Untie and loosen the top of the sacking but do not remove it. If the covering is plastic netting or sheeting, carefully remove it but do not break up the soil ball

③ Examine the exposed surface of the soil ball. Very gently cut away circling or tangled roots but never break up the soil ball

④ After planting a shallow water-retaining basin should remain

Fill the space between the soil ball and the sides of the hole with planting mixture. Never use ordinary soil — roots may not move from a peat-based compost into mineral soil. Firm down the planting mixture with your hands

Sources of Supply

THE GARDEN CENTRE

Three out of every four container plants are bought from a garden centre. You can wander around and look at the perennials, trees and shrubs, knowing that at almost any time of the year you can pick up a container-grown specimen and plant it in your own garden. Selecting a plant is easy but getting it home may be difficult — never bend or twist the stems to get it into the car. Also remember that a plant can get roasted in the boot or windburnt if left next to an open window in a moving car. There are several rules to follow in order to ensure trouble-free shopping. Try to go at the start of the planting season before shortages occur, and try to go in midweek to avoid the weekend crowds. Don't buy on impulse unless you really know your plants — it is much better to take a list and buy the best specimens you can find. If you see an attractive plant which is not on your list, make a note of its name and check its suitability in a textbook when you get home. Buy it on your next visit if it is suitable.

Advantages

● You can see exactly what you are buying. Whenever possible make your selection when a container-grown plant is at its maximum display stage — flowering shrubs in bloom, berrying shrubs in fruit, etc.

● Container-grown stock can be planted straight away. If your first choice is not available, you can immediately pick something else.

● Except for trees it is generally possible to take your plants home with you — no delays, no transport charges.

● Advice is always on hand. However, do check the advice in an Expert book when you get home!

Drawbacks

● The varieties on offer are usually the more popular ones — you cannot expect a garden centre to stock a large number of varieties which might not sell.

● Garden centres are usually some distance from the centre of town, which means that your local one may be inaccessible if you don't have a car.

● Numbers of each variety may be limited, so if you are planning a massed planting or a long hedge you may have to order from a large mail order nursery.

● The main stock-in-trade, the container-grown plant, is generally expensive.

If something goes wrong

If one or more of the plants fail and you are confident that it is not your fault, take it back to the garden centre and explain what has happened. You will need proof of purchase — always keep your receipt when buying plants. If the garden centre is a member of the International Garden Centre Association (you will see the IGC symbol on display) then it guarantees to replace any container-grown plant which has failed within 6 months of purchase, if reasonable care has been taken.

THE MARKET STALL

Bedding plants and bulbs as well as house plants are bought from market stalls throughout the country. Convenient and economical, but do take care. Feel the bulbs to make sure that they are firm and don't buy bedding plants if the bad signs are clearly present (page 62).

Advantages

● Plants are inexpensive — the market stall is often the cheapest source of supply.

● Often conveniently sited, like the High St. shop. The plants are not kept in overheated conditions and the stallholders are sometimes quite knowledgeable.

Drawbacks

● A great deal of inferior stock is offered on market stalls — nursery rejects, half-hardy annuals before the danger of frost has gone and bedding plants in full flower.

● The selection is limited — only fast-moving lines can be stocked and this means the most popular varieties.

If something goes wrong

There is usually very little chance of redress. You cannot expect the stallholder to admit that his bulbs were rotten or that his plants had not been hardened off.

THE HIGH ST. SHOP

In hardware stores, garden shops, department stores, greengrocers and supermarkets you will often see a selection of favourite varieties when the planting season arrives. Seeds are the commonest planting material on offer, but you may also find bulbs, herbaceous border plants, bedding plants and pre-packaged shrubs and Roses.

Advantages
● You can pick up a plant or a packet of seeds without having to make a special trip to the garden centre.

● Unlike ordering by post, you can take your plants or seeds home with you — no delays, no transport charges. Pre-packaged plants are inexpensive, so you can buy many popular ones very cheaply.

Drawbacks
● Warm conditions in the shop can lead to drying out or premature growth — you must always shop carefully when buying store-housed plants. The golden rule is to buy from High St. shops at the start of the planting season.

● The selection is very limited — only fast-moving lines can be stocked and that means the most popular ones.

If something goes wrong
Take the plant back to the shop. The response will depend on the assistant and the policy of the store — there is no guarantee of replacement.

THE MAIL ORDER NURSERY

Despite the attraction of the garden centre, the reputable mail order nursery still remains an important source of supply. Buy from a company you know or one with a good reputation, and order as early as you can.

Advantages
● Many mail order nurseries produce excellent catalogues which enable you to choose plants and seeds in the comfort of your own home. You can check suitability before you commit yourself.

● Unusual and rare varieties can be obtained — the usual source of supply for the latest introductions.

● As near as your postbox — a distinct advantage if you can't get to a garden centre due to lack of a car.

Drawbacks
● You cannot see what you are buying and so you must take quality on trust.

● You cannot take your plants home with you, and they may arrive when the weather is unsuitable.

● One or more of your selections may be out of stock, and you won't know for some time after placing your order.

● Transport involves some stress for the plants and a delivery charge for you.

If something goes wrong
If one or more of the plants fail and you are confident that it is not your fault, write to the company and explain what happened. Many nurseries will return your money if they feel your complaint is a genuine one.

THE BARGAIN OFFER NURSERY

National newspapers and gardening magazines often have advertisements for 'bargain' offers. Good value offers do sometimes occur but you must view such advertisements with caution. Above all, avoid taking some of the more glowing descriptions too literally.

Advantage
● If money is short and you have a large space to fill, a 'bargain' collection is an inexpensive way of filling the border. The plants offered are usually old favourites which are noted for their toughness and vigour.

Drawback
● Bargains do not exist. If the plants on offer are *very* cheap then there is a reason. Shrubs or trees may be small cuttings, which can take some time to produce a worthwhile display, or they may be substandard stock.

If something goes wrong
If the plants fail and you are confident that it is not your fault, write to the company. If the stock is dead or badly diseased on arrival or the plants are not what you ordered, complain bitterly and send a copy to the publication which carried the advertisement. However, if the plants are healthy but are much smaller than expected you have no grounds for complaint ... it was a 'bargain' offer.

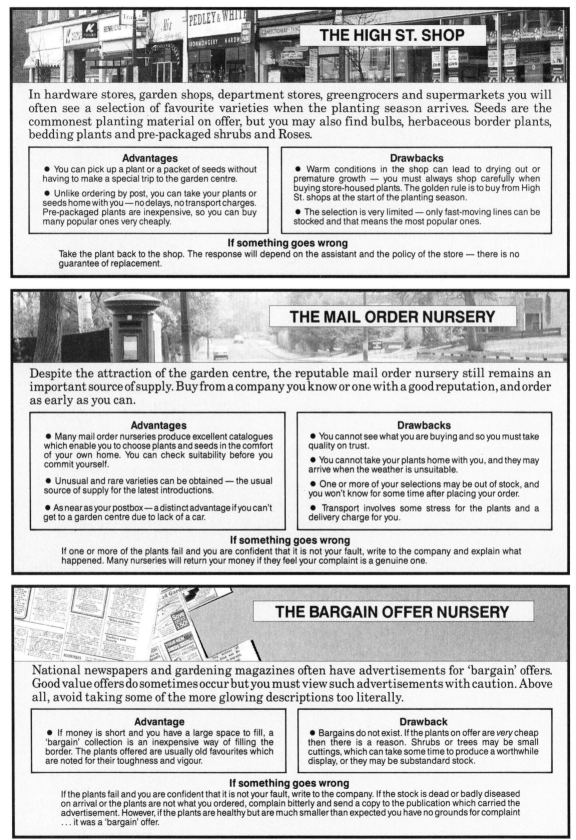

CHAPTER 5
TOOLS & EQUIPMENT

Walk around a large garden centre or DIY superstore in spring and you will be confronted by a large assortment of gardening tools and equipment. You could be excused for thinking that the number of different types of gardening tools must have increased in recent years — but you would be wrong. In a textbook written more than 300 years ago there is a list of well over 100 tools for the keen gardener, and Victorian catalogues offered hundreds of different sorts of hoes, spades, forks, knives etc.

The basic armoury has declined, but the average cost and complexity have greatly increased. There is also a large number of different brands of each item, so you have to choose with care. A well-known name on the handle is a safeguard, but it can mean a higher price. With tools you usually (but not always) get what you pay for, so it is wise to avoid low-priced 'bargains' of unknown origin for tools you plan to use constantly. Stainless steel certainly looks attractive, but ordinary steel is much cheaper and is quite satisfactory if cared for properly.

Your first job is to decide which type of tool or tools you plan to buy. Then look up the appropriate section in this chapter to see what features you have to look for. Having the right equipment for gardening will always make the work easier. For the elderly and the handicapped choosing wisely is even more important — it sometimes means the difference between being able to do a task or not.

Now you know what to look for, you must select a suitable example from your supplier. By all means be guided by the maker's name, the shopkeeper's advice and the manufacturer's advertisement, but for many tools it is essential for you to ensure that the item suits *you*. With spades, forks, hoes, secateurs, shears and so on you must see that both the weight and balance are suitable. A spade which is 'right' for a strong youth would be quite wrong for a small elderly lady.

For the keen gardener with money to spare the most difficult task is to decide just how many tools to buy. On the right is a general basic list for a small garden, but the exact list which would be right for you is something that only you can decide. However, any item on the basic list which you do not buy will undoubtedly increase the chore of gardening.

What people should buy

The BASIC kit for an established small garden	
SPADE	FORK
HOE	RAKE
TROWEL	MOWER
WATERING CAN	

plus
SECATEURS if Roses and/or shrubs are grown
SHEARS if hedges are grown
SPRAYER if Roses, vegetables and/or fruit are grown
HOSE PIPE & SPRINKLER if the lawn is a feature
SPRING-TINE RAKE if the lawn is a feature
LAWN EDGER if the lawn is a feature
GARDEN LINE if vegetables are grown
GLOVES if prickly plants are grown
MOTOR MOWER if the lawn is over 75 sq. yards
WHEELBARROW if plants or manure have to be moved

What people do buy

UNIVERSAL	COMMON
Owned by more than 80% of gardening households	Owned by 40–80% of gardening households
SPADE	HOE
FORK	WATERING CAN
RAKE	SHEARS
TROWEL	HOSE PIPE
MOWER	HAND FORK
SECATEURS	MOTOR MOWER

UNCOMMON	RARE
Owned by 20–40% of gardening households	Owned by less than 20% of gardening households
WHEELBARROW	POWER TOOLS
SPRAYER	ROLLER
GARDENING GLOVES	CLOCHES
LAWN EDGER	LAWN SPREADER
SPRINKLER	LONG-HANDLED PRUNER

Looking after tools

- Clean off all mud, grass etc after use — dry with a rag. Never allow grass mowings to dry on the blades of a mower — removing dried grass and earth with a knife is a laborious task.

- Wipe tools with an oily rag before storing them away — hoes, spades, forks, rakes and trowels can be pushed into a tub of oiled sand if no other method of storage is available.

- Keep hand tools off the floor of the garage or toolshed. Hang them on the wall if possible — keep sharp tools out of harm's way. Turn the lawnmower so that the blades are away from the line of traffic.

- Sharpen tools regularly (see page 80). During winter look for rust on large and expensive equipment. Paint affected areas with Rusty to prevent further corrosion.

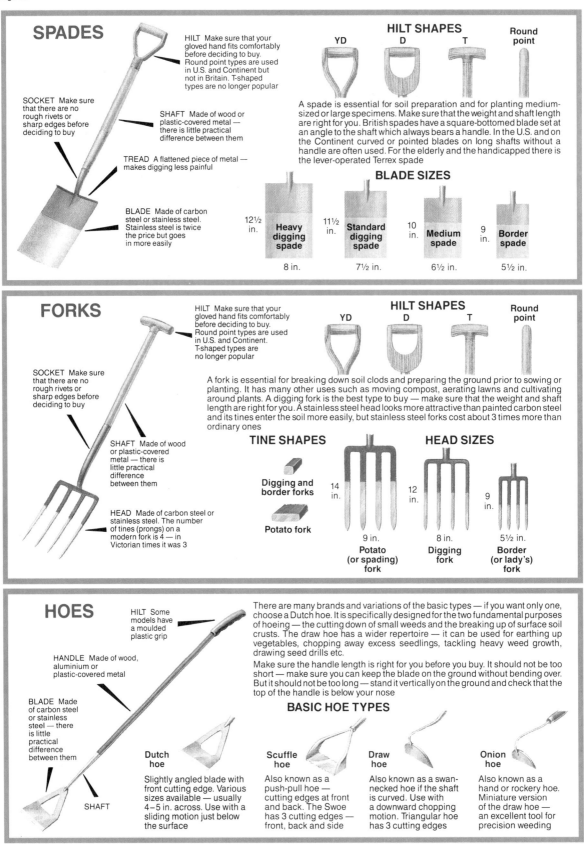

SPADES

HILT Make sure that your gloved hand fits comfortably before deciding to buy. Round point types are used in U.S. and Continent but not in Britain. T-shaped types are no longer popular

SOCKET Make sure that there are no rough rivets or sharp edges before deciding to buy

SHAFT Made of wood or plastic-covered metal — there is little practical difference between them

TREAD A flattened piece of metal — makes digging less painful

BLADE Made of carbon steel or stainless steel. Stainless steel is twice the price but goes in more easily

HILT SHAPES

YD   D   T   Round point

A spade is essential for soil preparation and for planting medium-sized or large specimens. Make sure that the weight and shaft length are right for you. British spades have a square-bottomed blade set at an angle to the shaft which always bears a handle. In the U.S. and on the Continent curved or pointed blades on long shafts without a handle are often used. For the elderly and the handicapped there is the lever-operated Terrex spade

BLADE SIZES

12½ in.	Heavy digging spade	11½ in.	Standard digging spade	10 in.	Medium spade	9 in.	Border spade
8 in.		7½ in.		6½ in.		5½ in.	

FORKS

HILT Make sure that your gloved hand fits comfortably before deciding to buy. Round point types are used in U.S. and Continent. T-shaped types are no longer popular

SOCKET Make sure that there are no rough rivets or sharp edges before deciding to buy

SHAFT Made of wood or plastic-covered metal — there is little practical difference between them

HEAD Made of carbon steel or stainless steel. The number of tines (prongs) on a modern fork is 4 — in Victorian times it was 3

HILT SHAPES

YD   D   T   Round point

A fork is essential for breaking down soil clods and preparing the ground prior to sowing or planting. It has many other uses such as moving compost, aerating lawns and cultivating around plants. A digging fork is the best type to buy — make sure that the weight and shaft length are right for you. A stainless steel head looks more attractive than painted carbon steel and its tines enter the soil more easily, but stainless steel forks cost about 3 times more than ordinary ones

TINE SHAPES

Digging and border forks

Potato fork

HEAD SIZES

14 in.	Potato (or spading) fork	12 in.	Digging fork	9 in.	Border (or lady's) fork
9 in.		8 in.		5½ in.	

HOES

HILT Some models have a moulded plastic grip

HANDLE Made of wood, aluminium or plastic-covered metal

BLADE Made of carbon steel or stainless steel — there is little practical difference between them

SHAFT

There are many brands and variations of the basic types — if you want only one, choose a Dutch hoe. It is specifically designed for the two fundamental purposes of hoeing — the cutting down of small weeds and the breaking up of surface soil crusts. The draw hoe has a wider repertoire — it can be used for earthing up vegetables, chopping away excess seedlings, tackling heavy weed growth, drawing seed drills etc.

Make sure the handle length is right for you before you buy. It should not be too short — make sure you can keep the blade on the ground without bending over. But it should not be too long — stand it vertically on the ground and check that the top of the handle is below your nose

BASIC HOE TYPES

Dutch hoe
Slightly angled blade with front cutting edge. Various sizes available — usually 4–5 in. across. Use with a sliding motion just below the surface

Scuffle hoe
Also known as a push-pull hoe — cutting edges at front and back. The Swoe has 3 cutting edges — front, back and side

Draw hoe
Also known as a swan-necked hoe if the shaft is curved. Use with a downward chopping motion. Triangular hoe has 3 cutting edges

Onion hoe
Also known as a hand or rockery hoe. Miniature version of the draw hoe — an excellent tool for precision weeding

SPRAYERS

Sprayers have many jobs to do in the garden — applying insecticides, fungicides and weedkillers, misting plants in the greenhouse, killing moss on the lawn, spraying foliar feeds on Roses, and so on. Once the popular choice was between a metal syringe and a metal flit gun — now it is between a trigger-operated sprayer and a compression sprayer. Most gardeners need one of each — the simple trigger type for house plants and for small spraying jobs and a hand-pumped compression model for general spraying. It is essential to wash out the sprayer immediately after use. If you plan to use a weedkiller you *must* keep a sprayer solely for that purpose — put a label on the container so you won't forget

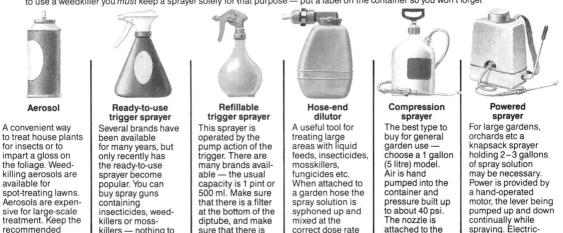

Aerosol

A convenient way to treat house plants for insects or to impart a gloss on the foliage. Weed-killing aerosols are available for spot-treating lawns. Aerosols are expensive for large-scale treatment. Keep the recommended distance away from plant foliage

Ready-to-use trigger sprayer

Several brands have been available for many years, but only recently has the ready-to-use sprayer become popular. You can buy spray guns containing insecticides, weed-killers or moss-killers — nothing to mix, but you pay more for the convenience

Refillable trigger sprayer

This sprayer is operated by the pump action of the trigger. There are many brands available — the usual capacity is 1 pint or 500 ml. Make sure that there is a filter at the bottom of the diptube, and make sure that there is an adjustable nozzle

Hose-end dilutor

A useful tool for treating large areas with liquid feeds, insecticides, mosskillers, fungicides etc. When attached to a garden hose the spray solution is syphoned up and mixed at the correct dose rate with the water stream

Compression sprayer

The best type to buy for general garden use — choose a 1 gallon (5 litre) model. Air is hand pumped into the container and pressure built up to about 40 psi. The nozzle is attached to the end of the spray lance

Powered sprayer

For large gardens, orchards etc a knapsack sprayer holding 2–3 gallons of spray solution may be necessary. Power is provided by a hand-operated motor, the lever being pumped up and down continually while spraying. Electric- and petrol-driven versions are available

SECATEURS

Secateurs are hand-held shears which cut stems when squeezed and spring open when released. They vary in size from delicate flower gatherers to large heavy-duty models. You should need only one pair of secateurs — a general-purpose model about 8 in. long. The curved and anvil types dominate the market — both types have their disciples but there is little to choose between them. There is, however, a great deal to choose between a well-made pair and a shoddy piece of engineering. Economise when buying a rake or hand fork if you must, but never on a pair of secateurs. Use them for stems up to ½ in. in diameter — larger branches should be cut with long-handled pruners or a pruning saw (see page 70)

BLADES Keep cleaned and oiled after use

SPRING May be exposed or hidden. The handles should open quickly after cutting

SAFETY CATCH Make sure that you can reach it easily

HANDLES Check weight and comfort before purchase. Make sure that they are not too big — handles should not push hard against your palm when the secateurs are open

Anvil secateurs

One sharpened blade cuts on to a flat platform (anvil). Always cut *down* on to the anvil. Cuts with less effort than the curved type, but the cut may be a little more ragged

Curved secateurs

One sharpened blade cuts against a broad blade — side anvil secateurs is an alternative name. Generally last longer than anvil type. The most popular type. Double-action versions are available to make cutting easier

Parrot-beak secateurs

Two sharpened blades cut against each other. This scissor-like action gives an exceptionally clean cut, but the blades are easily distorted if forced to cut too-large wood. Not popular

Flower gatherer

A miniature version of the anvil or curved type of secateurs — the flower stem is held by a plastic or metal strip after cutting. Not worthwhile unless you are a keen flower arranger

HOSE PIPES

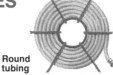

Flat tubing

A recent introduction — lay-flat tubing. It is wound into a cassette-like case for easy storage. A flat hose pipe is worth considering if you are short of space, but there are drawbacks. It is expensive and the whole tube must be unwound before it can be used

Round tubing

The basic type which will last for many years if treated properly. A long length should be stored on a wheeled or wall-attached reel. Half of Britain's hose pipes are not kept on a reel — leaving crushed on the floor can lead to kinks and punctures. Empty and store indoors in winter

Single wall   **Double wall**   **Reinforced**

The usual type of hose pipe is made of PVC and is available in 50 ft and 100 ft lengths. Single wall tubing is inexpensive, but it is not suitable for regions with high water pressure. Double wall tubing is more suitable for general garden use, but reinforced tubing is the best (and most expensive) type you can buy — there is a layer of fibre or braided nylon between the inner and outer tubes. Ribbed tubing is easier to hold than smooth tubing when wet. In recent years Quick Release fittings have largely replaced screw fittings for securing attachments

WATERING CANS & SPRINKLERS
See pages 82–83

LONG-HANDLED PRUNERS & PRUNING SAWS

Ordinary secateurs should not be used on branches which are more than ½ in. across as the tool may be damaged. For cutting larger branches a **long-handled pruner** should be used. This piece of equipment is a pair of heavy-duty secateurs with long (1½–2 ft) handles. This length gives extra leverage, so that 1 in. stems can be pruned. For the keen fruit grower there are **tree loppers** — lever-operated blades on an extended pole up to 14 ft long. These enable high branches to be cut in the orchard. Sounds like fun, but they are difficult to use.

When branches are thicker than a broom handle it is necessary to use a saw rather than an instrument with blades. For the occasional dead branch you can use an ordinary saw, but for the gardener with an orchard there are special **pruning saws**. You can buy straight saws with fine teeth on one side and coarse ones on the other, but the experts prefer the curved **Grecian saw** (illustrated above) which has teeth on one side only. This saw cuts on the pull stroke only. For cutting large branches or main trunks you will need a **bow saw** or a **chain saw**.

GARDEN SHEARS & ELECTRIC HEDGE TRIMMERS

The main use for **garden shears** is the trimming of hedges, although they are also used for cutting long grass, dead-heading annuals, trimming herbaceous perennials etc. Choose a pair with comfortable handles and lightweight blades — holding heavy shears becomes a chore when cutting a long hedge. Serrated edges are more effective than straight ones for cutting woody stems, but they are also more difficult to sharpen. The blades are set at a slight angle to the handles — sloping *towards* you when cutting the face of the hedge and *away* from you when trimming the top. Never cut through finger-thick twigs with the body of the blades — use the pruning notch at their base.

If you have a long hedge to tackle then an **electric hedge trimmer** is a wise investment. A mains model is suitable if the hedge is near a power point — otherwise buy a battery-operated model. Blade lengths vary from 1–2½ ft — a 1½ ft trimmer will suit the average garden. Place the cable over your shoulder so that the main bulk of it is behind you and out of harm's way.

GLOVES & KNIVES

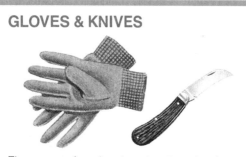

The purpose of wearing **gloves** is not merely to keep your hands clean — a barrier cream applied before going out is the way to avoid soiling your skin. Leather gloves are used to protect the hands from prickles, sharp objects and caustic materials such as lime. But they are heavy, somewhat inflexible and uncomfortable in hot weather. Cotton gloves are much more comfortable, but are no protection against Rose thorns. A good compromise is to buy a pair of fabric gloves with leather palms or a pair of the popular fabric gloves impregnated with green plastic to give a protective suede-like finish.

It is a joy to watch a skilled gardener using a knife, but in the hands of the inexperienced it can be a dangerous weapon. If you have not been trained in its use carry a folding pocket knife for cutting twine etc, but use secateurs for cutting stems. Several types are available — a **pruning knife** has a curved blade and a **grafting knife** has a 3 in. straight one. A **budding knife** is smaller — the 2 in. long blade has a flat tip rather than a pointed one and the flattened handle is used for lifting the bark when budding.

TROWELS & HAND FORKS

The **trowel** is a basic garden tool, essential for planting specimens too small for a spade. It is also used for digging out perennial weeds when minimal soil disturbance is required. The large range available makes choosing difficult, so a few simple rules are necessary. Buy stainless steel if you can afford it, avoid types with channelled blades in which earth can collect, make sure the handle is comfortable and buy two — one of standard size and the other a small narrow type with a blade about 2 in. across. Look for a strong neck and don't buy a long-handled one unless you find bending difficult.

Hand forks are about the same width as trowels, but bear 3–5 short tines instead of a scoop-like blade. They are used for weeding and cultivating soil around plants — buy a long-handled version to reach to the back of the border. The tines are available in various forms — flat, curved and twisted. Choose a fork with flat tines — the other shapes have drawbacks. The hand fork, unlike the trowel, is not essential.

WHEELBARROWS

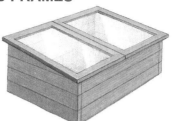

The traditional **wheelbarrow** is illustrated above — a 2–4 cu. ft container carried on a tubular metal frame and bearing a single narrow wheel. Galvanised metal is the usual material — watch for the first signs of rust and treat with an anti-rust paint. Plastic wheelbarrows are available — attractive but liable to break if subject to very heavy treatment. Always test a barrow before buying. Make sure that the main weight is over the wheel and not on your arms when it is pushed, and make sure that the frame does not catch your legs when you walk.

The traditional type is highly manoeuvrable and the best choice for heavy, uneven ground. If your soil is sandy then it would be better to buy one with a wide pneumatic tyre or buy a **ball wheelbarrow** — a standard model with an inflated, ball-like wheel. If your site is fairly flat or if you are elderly or handicapped, it would be worth considering a **two-wheel cart** instead of a wheelbarrow. You will find it easier to push and less liable to tip over, with the added advantage of having a container which can be placed at ground level so that rubbish can be brushed into it.

COLD FRAMES

A **cold frame** is a low unheated structure which bears a sloping roof made up of glazed transparent sections (lights) which can be raised or slid apart. The sides of the frame may be solid or transparent — plastic-sided cold frames are cooler at night than the solid ones. Brick or wooden frames with wooden lights bearing sash bars were once universal, but nowadays metal models are popular.

Cold frames may be movable or fixed and the glazing material may be glass or plastic. They are used for protecting early crops, hardening off half-hardy annuals, striking cuttings and for growing Cucumbers and Melons. Shading may be necessary in the summer — sacking on the glass will cut down heat loss in winter. Adequate ventilation is essential on hot days and when hardening off seedlings. Remember to site the frame in a sunny spot on well-drained soil. The internal warmth is derived from the sun — you can instal electric heating but then it ceases to be a *cold* frame. You can make an old-fashioned **hotbed** by placing the frame on a heap of fresh stable manure topped with a 6 in. layer of topsoil.

COMPOST BINS

Making 'compost' by piling rubbish in the corner of the garden for a few months is worse than useless. The evil-smelling product is of less value than the ingredients in their original state. In recent years a wide variety of **compost bins** have been launched to remove the eyesore and to improve the quality of the end-product.

Before deciding which one to buy you should read the section on compost making on page 23. From this you will see that there are some essential requirements for the container if you are going to make top quality material. First of all, there must be a rainproof cover — rain seeping through compost cools it down and causes evil-smelling decomposition. Get the maximum size for the rubbish available — one large bin will make much better compost than 2 smaller ones. Make sure there is drainage to the soil at the bottom of the bin — retaining effluent will stop the composting process. Look for good insulation — the sides should *not* be well ventilated as the retention of heat is much more important than the entry of air. A brick-sided bin is best of all, followed by straw bales, a stout wooden one and then a firm plastic container. Wire-netting and polythene bags provide little insulation.

MISCELLANEOUS ITEMS

Some of the tools in this chapter such as the spade, fork, rake and trowel are in nearly every gardener's armoury. At the other end of the scale, however, are the small items which are sometimes ignored and are not heavily advertised, but which would make your lot easier. There is the cushioned **kneeling pad** — so vital for the over-fifties when weeding in cold and wet soil. Even better for the elderly is the **kneeling frame** which can be turned over to serve as a stool. A **garden line** is vital — use string if you must, but it is worth investing in a brightly-coloured plastic one mounted on a reel. A long rigid **ruler** is necessary — make one out of a broom handle. A pencil or dowel can be adapted to provide a small **dibber** (see page 73) and 2 flat pieces of **board** are the professional's way of moving rubbish into the wheelbarrow.

A **dribble bar** attached to a watering can is the best way to apply weedkillers to paths — you can buy a **spot weeder** for treating isolated specimens in the lawn, bed or border. The **flame gun** and the **garden roller** have quite rightly declined in popularity, but the need for small items such as **plant labels**, **raffia**, **stout canes**, **lubricating oil** and so on remains as strong as ever.

RAKES & CULTIVATORS

A rake is essential for the final soil preparation before sowing or planting. Its proper use calls for some degree of skill — see page 80. Wide wooden rakes are sometimes used for moving surface rubbish but the popular type has rigid metal teeth (tines) which are about 2 in. long. Spring-tine rakes are for the lawn rather than general garden use. Several types of hand cultivators are available — the usual one bears 3 or 5 curved tines with blade-like cutting ends. Other types have spiked wheels or heavy hoe-like heads. The purpose of the hand cultivator is to cultivate soil to a depth of about 2–3 in. Most gardeners don't need one — forking followed by raking should be quite sufficient

HILT Some models have a modelled plastic grip

HANDLE Made of wood, aluminium or plastic-covered metal. Make sure length is right for you before you buy

SHAFT

HEAD Nearly always made of carbon steel or stainless steel

Rake

A number of short teeth set in a horizontal plate attached to a handle. Choose a 12 in. wide head with 10–14 teeth

Tined cultivator

Also known as a claw hoe — models can be bought with removable centre tines for cultivating along rows. Wheeled models are available

Star-wheeled cultivator

The soil miller combines several starred wheels with a hoe — it is pushed to and fro to produce a fine tilth on light soils

Mattock

This heavy chopping hoe is used to break up the surface of heavy soils — it was once a basic garden tool. The top may bear a 2-pronged cultivator

MOTOR-DRIVEN CULTIVATORS

A motorised cultivator seems like a good idea — a petrol-driven jack-of-all-trades to take the hard work out of gardening. Unfortunately it will not be of much help in the established ornamental garden. The main value of a motor-driven cultivator to the average gardener is the ability to dig over a large area when creating a new garden. If you are going to create a large vegetable garden as well as other features, then it is worth considering purchasing one of the many models available. If, however, the area is not large and most of the cultivated ground is to be turned into lawn and ornamental areas, it is a much better idea to hire one for the job of turning over the soil in your new garden. This will mean less work than digging, but it will also be less thorough. If you buy one there should be an adequate range of attachments — hoes, picks, ridgers, soil aerators etc.

There are 3 basic types. The most popular is the **mid-mounted rotor cultivator** — here the rotors are immediately below the engine and it is the preferred type for digging. Control is difficult when using it as a rotary cultivator. However, you can buy wheels to replace the rotor blades and fit a toolbar with attachments at the rear. Control is much easier when used in this way. The narrowest and generally lightest models are the **front-mounted rotor cultivators**. Here the rotor blades are at the end of a boom at the front of the machine. These machines are easily handled, but they are for cultivating previously-dug ground rather than breaking up compacted soil. The final type is the **back-mounted rotor cultivator**. A fine machine to use, with power-driven wheels as well as a powerful rotor behind the engine. Unfortunately these are heavy machines with a price range (minimum £500) which puts them out of reach for the average gardener.

LAWN TOOLS & EQUIPMENT

If the lawn is a prominent feature in your garden then there are a number of tools which you simply must possess. A **mower** of course, and you have 250 models from which to make your choice. There is no 'right' machine for every situation — a cylinder mower will give the closest cut, a hover mower is generally the quickest and most adaptable to bumps and slopes, and a back roller is essential for a striped look. A lawn up to 75 sq. yards can be tackled with a hand-propelled mower — beyond that an electric- or petrol-driven mower is a good idea.

Overgrown edges are an eyesore and must be trimmed. Hand shears are suitable if you have a pocket-handkerchief lawn — anything larger needs an **edger**. Electrically-driven trimmers are available, but many gardeners find mechanical edgers no quicker or easier to use than long-handled shears. Watering is essential in a dry summer, so a **hose and sprinkler** (see pages 69 and 83) are needed. Remember, of course, that a charge for this is made by the local water authority and a ban will be imposed if a drought is prolonged. A **watering can** is of no use for regular watering, but is an essential piece of equipment for the application of weedkillers, mosskillers and liquid feeds.

Surface debris must be removed, especially in spring and again in autumn — fallen leaves left over winter will ruin a lawn. A **besom** or **spring-tine rake** is the answer, although a **mechanical sweeper** is a good idea if the area is large. Some form of **aerator** is required for cutting through the surface — an ordinary garden fork is the simplest way but there are many tools for this job. The list of additional tools is large — **fertilizer spreader**, **half-moon irons** etc. For a detailed list of tools and equipment see The Lawn Expert.

CHAPTER 6
TECHNIQUES A - Z

BLANCHING

A vegetable-growing technique used for hundreds of years. Light is excluded from some or all of the growing parts of certain types — as a result the natural green colour does not develop. There are several other possible effects — lower fibre content, improved flavour, reduced bitterness and enhanced appearance. The role of blanching is to produce one or more of these responses.

The stems of Celery and Leek are earthed up (see page 74) — the heads of Chicory and Seakale are blanched by covering with a light-proof pot.

COMPOST MAKING
See page 23

CUTTING

Cutting blooms and attractive foliage from flower and shrub borders for arranging indoors is, of course, a basic part of the gardening scene. In this way the fruits of your labours can be enjoyed at any time and in any weather, but there are pitfalls to avoid. Obviously the full beauty of the flower bed or border is diminished, and in the case of newly-planted perennials the loss of stems and green leaves can harm next year's growth. If you have the space and are a keen flower arranger it is a good idea to have a separate bed where plants for cutting can be grown.

In the shrub border this form of spring and summer pruning generally does no harm, but take care during the first year. A newly-planted shrub needs all the stems and green leaves it can muster, so only cut a few flowers and do not remove many leaves. Roses are perhaps the most widely used of all cut flowers — do not remove more than one-third of the flowering stem and always cut just above an outward-facing bud.

DEAD-HEADING

The removal of dead flowers has several advantages — it helps to keep the bed or border tidy, it prolongs the flowering season by preventing seed formation and in a few cases (e.g Lupin and Delphinium) it induces a second flush later in the season.

Use garden shears, secateurs, a sharp knife or finger tips depending on the type of plant. Be careful not to remove too much stem. You must not dead-head flowers grown for their seed pods (Honesty, Chinese Lantern etc).

It is quite impractical to remove the dead blooms from some annuals and perennials and from most trees and shrubs. There are a few large-flowering woody plants, however, which must be dead-headed. The faded trusses of Hybrid Tea and Floribunda Roses should be cut off and the dead flowers of Rhododendrons should be carefully broken off with finger and thumb. Cut off the flower-heads of Lilac once the blooms have faded, but the large heads of Hydrangeas are an exception — remove in March.

DIBBING IN

Dibbing in is a simple and quicker planting technique than using a trowel. The standard dibber is a stout wooden or metal spike, bought from a garden shop or made at home from an old spade handle. These dibbers are for large seedlings. For pot culture and for small seedlings outdoors use a pencil or dowel. The tip of the dibber should be rounded rather than sharply pointed.

Dibbing in (or dibbling) involves inserting the dibber sufficiently deeply into the soil so that the roots will fit comfortably. Place the plant into the hole and then firm the earth by re-inserting the dibber point about 1–2 in. away from the stem. Move the dibber towards the plant in order to press the soil around the roots.

This is a good technique for planting vegetables which have been raised in a seed bed. Brassicas, such as Cabbages, Brussels Sprouts etc, are well-known examples. It is also widely used for planting cuttings, but in all cases you must make sure that the hole is no deeper than necessary. The role of dibbing in is limited — use a trowel and not a dibber for large-size planting material such as bulbs or tubers, and do not use a dibber in heavy, wet soil.

DIGGING
See pages 12–13

DISBUDDING

In general flower buds in the garden are allowed to develop and open naturally to provide the maximum display. For exhibitors, however, and others interested in the size of individual blooms, the flower-stems are disbudded. This calls for pinching out side buds as soon as they can be handled, leaving the central bud to develop into a large specimen to catch the eye of the judge or earn the envy of the neighbours.

Chrysanthemums, Dahlias and Carnations are frequently treated in this way for Show purposes. Many Hybrid Tea Roses produce more than one flower bud at the end of each shoot. With this flower it is nearly always desirable to seek maximum size, so disbudding of side shoots is recommended. Delay removing the side buds if you want to hold back flowering for the day of the Show. If the Rose variety produces very full blooms which spoil badly in wet weather, reverse the process and pinch out the terminal bud so that the side buds develop.

EARTHING UP

There are several reasons for earthing up — the drawing of soil towards and around the stems. Potatoes are earthed up to avoid the tubers being exposed to light. When the haulm is about 9 in. high a draw hoe is used to pile loose soil against the stems to form a flat-topped ridge. The greens (Broccoli, Kale, Brussels Sprouts etc) are earthed up for a different reason — soil is drawn up around the stems of well-developed plants to improve anchorage against high winds.

The stems of Celery and Leek are blanched (see page 73) by earthing up. This begins with Celery when it is about 1 ft high — with Leeks this is done in stages, the height being increased a little at a time by drawing dry soil around the stems.

Earthing up is important on the vegetable plot but it has a place in the herbaceous border. Shoots may appear prematurely during a mild spell in early spring — it is advisable to draw loose soil over them with a hoe so as to prevent damage by severe frosts which may come later.

FERTILIZING

See pages 16–21

FALLOWING

In the old days farmers used to fallow fields occasionally — leaving them bare for a whole season to allow bacteria to build up fertility and to allow the weather to improve the soil structure. This practice has greatly declined in agriculture and has practically no place in gardening, although the vegetable plot is mainly bare in winter and so it can be considered a short-term fallow.

Despite the absence of true fallowing, a special form of fallow is widely used in the vegetable garden. Some forms of soil-borne troubles such as eelworm, club root and white rot can live in the ground for several years. Following an attack, the land must be part-fallowed — that is, no susceptible plant must be grown on it for the period specified in the textbooks.

FORCING

Forcing is the process of inducing growth, flowering or fruiting earlier than normal. To do this there must be a change in the environment, and gentle heat is the most usual stimulant. There are no general rules — the factors which will force one plant may fail miserably with another.

Spring bulbs are forced by keeping the planted bowls cool (40° F) and in darkness for about 8 weeks before moving to warmer conditions — 50° F and then 60°–70° F. Daffodil bulbs for extra-early flowering are prepared by keeping in cold storage for several weeks in late summer.

Rhubarb, Seakale and Chicory are forced by being kept in the dark and at a temperature rising from an initial 50° F to 60° F as growth progresses. Many other plants in pots can be forced at a similar temperature, but require light conditions in a greenhouse or cold frame. Examples include Potatoes, Strawberries, French Beans, Roses, Spiraeas and Azaleas.

FORKING

A garden fork is not really a digging tool, athough it can sometimes be easier to dig a heavy soil with a fork rather than a spade. Forking is really a method of cultivation — lumps are broken down by hitting them with the tines and the surface roughly levelled by dragging the tines across the surface. Forking is also used around growing plants to break up  the surface crust, but you must be careful not to damage surface roots.

The garden fork has several purposes, including moving compost, lifting Potatoes and aerating lawns.

FUMIGATING

Fumigation is a method of destroying pests and/or disease organisms by means of a gas, vapour or smoke. It is practically always restricted to greenhouses and the usual applicator these days is a firework-like cone. Doors and ventilators must be closed after lighting or much of the benefit will be lost.

GRAFTING & BUDDING

A graft is a union between two plants, the roots and lower stem (the stock or rootstock) of one plant uniting with the shoot of another plant (the scion), so that they grow together as one. The main role of grafting in horticulture is the propagation of trees and shrubs where one or more of the following difficulties prevent easier means of producing planting material:

- Varieties which root slowly or not at all from cuttings or by layering.
- Varieties which do not set seed.
- Varieties which do not breed true from seed.
- Varieties which are unsatisfactory when grown on their own roots.

A mystique has grown up about grafting, but the principle is very simple. The stock and the scion must be related — as a general rule the chance of a successful union increases in direct proportion to the closeness of the relationship. Next, there must be physical close contact — it is the thin living layer below the bark which has to knit together. Timing is important — the plants should be just starting to grow after their winter rest, and the union must be protected. This calls for binding with raffia, plastic tape or an elastic tie and then covering the whole area with grafting wax. This will prevent both drying out and infection from air-borne spores.

Although the principle is simple, a large number of systems have evolved over the centuries — saddle grafting, rind grafting, approach grafting, splice grafting and so on. The most popular method is whip and tongue grafting — see below. The stock and scion should be approximately the same thickness — remove the binding material once the graft has taken and new growth has appeared.

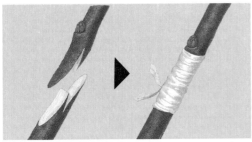

Cacti are the easiest group of plants to graft. All you have to do is to cut the base of the scion in the form of a V. Cut a corresponding V at the top of the stock and push the two grafts together. Push a few pins or thorns through the union and leave the rest to nature.

Commercial Roses are generally propagated by budding — a form of grafting which is carried out in midsummer rather than early spring. A bud or 'eye' of the selected variety is inserted into a T-shaped cut made in the stem of the rootstock — close to the ground for a bush or some distance up the stem for a standard.

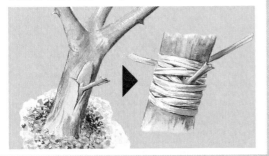

HARDENING OFF

Plants raised indoors or in a greenhouse have tender tissues — suddenly moving them outdoors in spring means a transition to colder conditions and drying winds for which they are not prepared. The result of this shock is either a severe check or death of the specimen, depending on the tenderness of the variety.

To avoid this problem there must be a gradual acclimatisation to the harsher conditions to be faced outdoors — a process known as hardening off. Begin by increasing the ventilation during the day in the greenhouse, after which the plants should be moved to a cold frame. Keep the lights closed at night for several days — then steadily increase the ventilation until the plants are continuously exposed to the outside air for a few days before planting out.

Watch the plants during hardening off. If the leaves turn blue or blotchy and growth stops you will have to slow down the process.

HEELING IN

Occasionally you will find that trees, shrubs, Roses or herbaceous perennials arrive before you are ready to plant them. The ground may be frozen or waterlogged, the site may not be ready or you may be just too busy. If this delay is to be more than 10 days, heel in the plants by digging a shallow V-shaped trench and then spreading them as a single row against one side of the trench. Cover the roots and lower parts of the stems with soil and tread down. Label with some form of permanent tag — paper labels attached by the supplier may rot away. The plants can be left for several weeks — lift and plant in the ordinary way as soon as you are able to do so.

HOEING

The hoe has two important functions. Its main task is to keep weeds under control — hoeing must be carried out at regular intervals to keep annual weeds in check and to starve out the underground parts of perennial weeds. Weeds should be severed just below ground level rather than being dragged to the surface — to ensure success keep the blade sharp at all times. The second important function of hoeing is to break up the surface pan (see page 6) which can be a problem in some soils after rain.

The proper way to use a hoe depends upon the type (see page 68). With a Dutch hoe you push the blade forward as you walk backwards — the blade is held just below the soil surface. The advantages are the avoidance of walking on the hoed area and the superior weed-cutting action. The draw hoe is used with a chopping rather than a slicing motion — the blade is brought down in short chopping strokes as you walk slowly backwards. There are advantages — it is more effective than a Dutch hoe on hard ground and it is safer for use when working near to plants. Draw hoes have other uses, such as earthing up Potatoes and Celery, and the corner of the blade is often used for drawing seed drills.

Hoe with care. Roots of some plants lie close to the surface, and much damage is done by hoeing too deeply. Don't hoe if weeds are absent and the surface is not caked — the 'dust mulch' has now been found to be of no value as a way of cutting down water loss.

LAYERING

Shrubs with flexible stems can be propagated very easily by layering. Some plants, such as Rhododendron and Magnolia, produce new plants naturally in this way. In the Rose garden it is ideal for Ramblers and it can be used for many Shrub Roses.

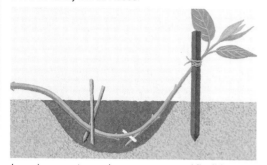

In spring or autumn choose a young and flexible stem. Make a cut about 2–3 in. long on the bottom side of this shoot and then place a matchstick in the cut. Place the cut part of the stem in a hole, fill with a soil/peat mixture and peg down. After about a year sever the stem from the parent plant and transplant the rooted plantlet to the site where it is to grow.

LIFTING

Gardening books dwell at length on digging, planting, pruning and so on ... but not on lifting. However, you must use the right technique when lifting plants or you will damage the roots. If the plants or other items to be moved in the garden are bulky and heavy, you can damage yourself.

Use a fork to lift root vegetables and flower tubers — don't try to harvest fully-grown Carrots, Turnips etc by pulling the foliage. Dig down deeply and prise up gently. Do not store any roots which you accidentally damage. Lifting large shrubs and trees is a skilled job — it is a good idea to cut through the outer roots several months before you plan to lift, and on moving day dig round the root ball and place sacking or wire-netting round it before lifting. Allowing the soil ball to shatter is one of the commonest mistakes at planting time.

Gardening is meant to be a pleasure, but the pain of a slipped disc is all-too-common. Don't try lifting heavy objects at the start of the season when your muscles are out of condition and the weather is cold. Remember to bend your *knees* and not your back. Let your leg muscles do the work — not your shoulder muscles. Know your limitations — use a cart or trolley (or a friend!) when the object is too heavy. Do not overload a wheelbarrow — it can easily tip over when you turn a corner. If it starts to tip over, let go and stand back quickly. It is easier to reload a barrow than nurse a torn ligament.

LIMING
See page 15

MANURING
See pages 22–24

MULCHING

A mulch is a layer of bulky organic matter placed on the soil surface around plants. Mulches are not applied around annuals, but around shrubs, trees and herbaceous perennials they provide several distinct benefits:

- The soil below is kept moist during the dry days of summer
- The soil surface is kept cool during the hot days of summer. This moist and cool root zone promotes more active growth than in unmulched areas
- Annual weeds are kept in check — the ones that do appear can be easily pulled out
- Some mulches provide plant foods
- Soil structure is improved by the addition of humus

Many materials are suitable for mulching — you can use moist peat, pulverised bark, leaf mould, well-rotted manure, mushroom compost, Bio Humus and garden compost. Grass clippings are sometimes recommended and are often used, but a word of caution is necessary. Add a thin layer and stir occasionally — do not use them if they are weedy or if the lawn has been treated with a weedkiller.

The standard time for mulching is May. Success depends on preparing the soil surface properly before adding the organic blanket. Remove debris, dead leaves and weeds, and then water the surface if it is dry. Apply a spring feed if this has not been done, hoe in lightly and you are now ready to apply the mulch. Spread a 2–3 in. layer over the area which is under the branches and leaves — do not take the mulch right up to the stems — a build-up of moist organic matter around the crown may lead to rotting. In October lightly fork this dressing into the top inch of soil — replace in spring. Autumn mulching is sometimes recommended as a way of preventing frost getting down to the roots, but it will increase the risk of dangerous air frosts around the plants in spring.

The benefits of using an organic mulch in the spring are remarkable, but it is still not generally practised. The use of black polythene sheeting as an inorganic mulch in the vegetable garden is even less popular, but its value can be outstanding. Strips of black plastic are laid across the prepared soil and the edges buried under the surface. Slits are cut in the surface to act as planting holes, and growth is stimulated by the moist conditions created. Potatoes do not need earthing up and Strawberries, Marrows, etc are kept off the ground. The greatest boon, however, is in weed-infested land as the plastic sheeting forms a weed-proof barrier.

PROTECTING

Some hardy plants, ranging from the lowly Alyssum at the front of the flower bed to a stately Yew at the back of the garden, may spend their whole life span on your plot without any need of protection. There are others which will need protecting for part or all of their lives — the amount and type of protection will depend on their hardiness and their vigour.

There are three major groups of problems which call for protection:

- Insect pests and fungal diseases
- Unsuitable weather
- Animals

The first group (insect pests and fungal diseases) are controlled by good cultural practice and chemical treatment when necessary — see Chapter 7 for details. The remaining two problem areas (weather and animals) are dealt with on this page.

Frost protection

Never plant out half-hardy annuals until the danger of frost has gone, but the frosts of an average winter will do no harm to the established hardy trees, shrubs, rockery perennials and herbaceous border plants. Perennials which are not completely hardy present a problem — do not cut down the stems until spring if you are going to trust to luck, but you must be prepared for losses if the winter is severe. It is much better to put a blanket of straw, bracken, leaf mould or peat over the crowns. Anchor this cover down with twigs, and don't forget to remove it in spring when new growth begins to appear.

Newly-planted evergreens are at risk, especially when they are known to be rather tender. If it is a choice specimen build a plastic screen around it — make sure the bottom of the plastic sheeting is pinned down to prevent draughts. Alternatively you can put a large plastic bag over the plant when a heavy frost is forecast.

The best protection, of course, is to keep the plants under glass. Pots can go in the greenhouse or cold frame, but for outdoor plants a row of cloches is the answer. Two golden rules — leave a little ventilation when in use and do not remove suddenly when the weather turns mild — increase ventilation for a few days to harden off the plants.

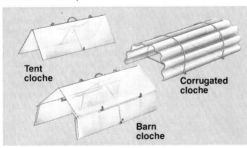

Tent cloche

Corrugated cloche

Barn cloche

For most gardeners the information above will be the counsel of perfection — for them plants must fend for themselves until the gardening season starts at Easter. There is still a hint or two to follow. If a choice plant is white with frost, a spray with *cold* water will cut down the risk of damage. If damage has occurred, don't be in a hurry to use the secateurs. Cutting in late winter may cause tender growth to appear. Wait until new growth appears in the spring — then cut out the dead wood.

Rain protection

It is often the rains of winter leading to waterlogging which cause plants to die, rather than the effect of frost or snow. Obviously there is nothing you can do to protect most plants, apart from proper soil preparation before planting. There is one group where protection is worthwhile — the delicate alpines in the rock garden. Cover these plants with a pane of glass supported by bricks.

Snow protection

It is the weight rather than the coldness of snow which threatens some plants in winter. The load on evergreen branches after a heavy snowfall can cause them to break — if prolonged snow is forecast it may be worth tying the branches of a choice conifer with twine. If you don't and then see the boughs weighed down, brush off or shake the branches. Remember that a blanket of snow can damage a plastic greenhouse and will cut down the light entering through any glass or plastic structure. Brush off this layer or your plants under cloches, in a greenhouse or in a cold frame may suffer.

Wind protection

The direct effect of strong winds is easily seen — plants knocked over and newly-planted specimens dislodged. Always check new trees and shrubs for wind-rock after a storm — re-firm and re-stake if necessary. The indirect effect of a strong prevailing wind is more subtle — growth is lop-sided because of the desiccation of buds on the stems (see page 26). The answer is a windbreak, but never use a solid structure. Hedges are ideal — for more temporary protection use wattle hurdles, sacking stretched between posts etc. Even a wire mesh fence provides some protection. Covering plants with plastic to guard against frost will also provide wind protection.

Animal protection

Cats and dogs can obviously be a problem (page 87), but they are not the only animal pests. Rabbits, hares and deer can be serious pests of young trees. The bark is gnawed and the tree may be killed. Repellents can be tried, but the best answer is fine-mesh wire-netting around the trunk. The top edge of this wire cylinder should be bent down away from the tree.

Rabbits are very fond of young greens, and there is little you can do to protect them. Rose buds are a favourite meal for deer. A 6 ft fence is needed to keep them away — once inside the standard deterrents such as blood meal, moth balls and creosote are only partly successful.

Nylon netting is the best answer to birds in the garden, and a fruit cage is the ideal place for growing soft fruit. Be careful, however, not to leave a point of entry — a bird trapped in a netted area will cause havoc.

Squirrels, mice, voles, moles etc can be pests. It is nice to see this wildlife . . . in somebody else's garden.

PRUNING

Pruning has a very simple meaning — the cutting away of unwanted growth from woody plants. But the purpose of pruning is less easy to understand, as there is nearly always more than one reason for carrying out this work:

- To remove poor quality wood, such as weak twigs, dead or diseased branches and damaged shoots.

- To shape the tree or shrub to your needs. This calls for the removal of healthy but unwanted wood — examples include the pruning of the central leader of a tree to produce an open-centred bush, the removal of a minor branch which is rubbing against a major one and the cutting back of branches which are blocking a pathway.

- To regulate both the quality and quantity of blossom and/or fruit production.

The craft of pruning is perhaps the most difficult lesson the gardener has to learn. Both the timing and the technique depend on the age and type of tree. If you are a novice you must check carefully the rules for the particular plant you wish to tackle. The table on the next page is only a general guide and you should consult the appropriate Expert book for more details.

The Rules of Pruning

- Use good quality tools and make sure they are sharp.

- Cut out all diseased, dead and weak growth. Always prune back to healthy wood, free from the tell-tale staining of infected tissue.

- When pruning any woody plant, realise the difference between light and hard pruning. Light pruning results in **heading back** — the tips of the branches are removed and this stimulates the buds below to burst into growth. The long-term effect is to produce a plant which is smaller but denser than one left unpruned. Hard pruning results in **thinning** — entire branches are removed back to the main stem and energy is diverted to the remaining branches. The long-term effect is to produce a plant which is larger but more open than one left unpruned.

- When pruning a fruit tree, remember that the purpose during the first few years is to establish the mature framework you desire — a process known as training.

- If you are a beginner in the craft of pruning do not attempt any drastic treatment. Too little pruning of healthy wood is safer than too much.

- Collect up all prunings. Compost them if they are soft and healthy — burn them if they are woody or diseased.

- All cuts must be clean. Pare off ragged parts left on sawn surfaces.

- Cut hedges so that the top is narrower than the base. In this way the base will remain clothed with leaves.

Pruning Methods

STANDARD PRUNING The partial removal of the woody structure of the plant, each cut being made individually. In some cases hardly any wood is removed (light pruning) but in others a significant proportion of the stems and branches are cut away (hard pruning).

SHEARING The partial removal of the woody structure of the plant, the cuts being made in wholesale fashion with garden shears or an electric hedge trimmer. This is the method of producing topiary (a decorative-shaped tree) or a formal hedge.

STOOLING The complete removal of the woody structure of the plant. Some shrubs can be pruned back each spring to almost ground level — examples include Eucalyptus, Ornamental Bramble, Coloured-bark Dogwood, Coloured-bark Willow and the Butterfly Bush. This type of pruning is known as coppicing in forestry.

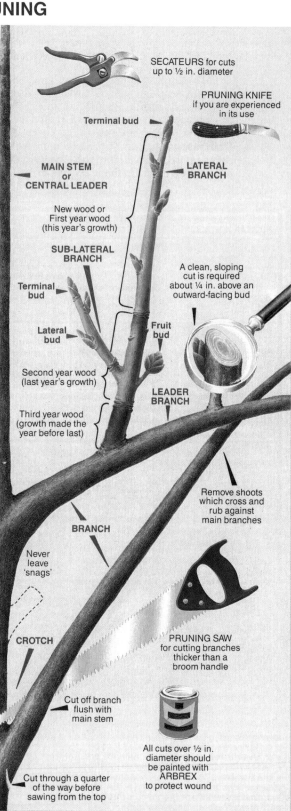

SECATEURS for cuts up to ½ in. diameter

PRUNING KNIFE if you are experienced in its use

Terminal bud

MAIN STEM or CENTRAL LEADER

LATERAL BRANCH

New wood or First year wood (this year's growth)

SUB-LATERAL BRANCH

A clean, sloping cut is required about ¼ in. above an outward-facing bud

Terminal bud

Lateral bud

Fruit bud

Second year wood (last year's growth)

LEADER BRANCH

Third year wood (growth made the year before last)

Remove shoots which cross and rub against main branches

BRANCH

Never leave 'snags'

CROTCH

PRUNING SAW for cutting branches thicker than a broom handle

Cut off branch flush with main stem

All cuts over ½ in. diameter should be painted with ARBREX to protect wound

Cut through a quarter of the way before sawing from the top

PRUNING continued

TREE or SHRUB	HOW TO PRUNE
FRUIT TREES, BUSHES & CANES	
APPLE PEAR	**BUSHES & STANDARDS** If you have bought a maiden (1 year old) tree, cut it back to half its height after planting if it has not been pruned by the grower. In its second year the tree will have produced 3 or 4 branches and an open centre. This is the form in which Apple and Pear trees are usually bought — in winter cut these branches back to half their length. In the third year these cut branches will each have produced 3 or more branchlets. In winter cut these branchlets back to about one half their length. A four year old tree is regarded as an adult or established tree There are several systems for pruning established trees. Time to prune: November – February REGULATION PRUNING is the easiest system to follow. It must be used for the few Apple varieties which are tip-bearing — examples include Discovery, Fortune, Worcester Pearmain, Bramley's Seedling and Lord Lambourne. Remove branches which are crowded, too low, crossing, diseased, damaged or dead. Cut back a few of the upright leaders growing near the top of the tree SPUR PRUNING produces a neater tree but involves more work. Cut back leaders to about half their length and reduce most laterals to about 5 growth buds **CORDONS, ESPALIERS & FANS** Cut back side shoots to about 3 in. from the main stem after planting. Do not prune the main stem. A trained tree with shortened side shoots can be regarded as an established tree Established trees are pruned in August. Cut back each side shoot to about 3 in. Thin out fruiting spurs in winter if they become overcrowded
CHERRY PLUM	Little or no pruning is necessary after the shape of the tree has been established. If branches become congested or damaged, cut out in June – August and paint cuts immediately with ARBREX
RASPBERRY BLACKBERRY LOGANBERRY	See page 45
GOOSEBERRY RED CURRANT WHITE CURRANT	See page 46
BLACKCURRANT	See page 47
OTHER TREES & SHRUBS	
BUSH ROSE STANDARD ROSE	Cut out all weak, dead and awkwardly-placed shoots. Moderate pruning (stems cut back to half their length) is the best method for general garden display. Hard pruning is sometimes used to produce Show blooms on Hybrid Teas. Time to prune: Mid March to early April
RAMBLER ROSE	Ideally all stems which have flowered should be cut out at ground level and new stems tied into the supports. This is not usually practical — the alternative is to cut back lateral branches to about 3 in. from the main stems. Time to prune: As soon as flowering has finished
CLIMBING ROSE	Cut out weak, dead and awkwardly-placed shoots. Shorten some lateral shoots. The correct pruning method depends upon the variety — see The Rose Expert. Time to prune: Mid March to early April
DECIDUOUS TREES & SHRUBS WHICH BLOOM BEFORE THE END OF MAY	Cut out weak, dead and awkwardly-placed shoots. Remove overcrowded branches. Finally, cut back all the branches which have borne blooms. Time to prune: As soon as flowering has finished — do not delay
DECIDUOUS TREES & SHRUBS WHICH BLOOM AFTER THE END OF MAY	Cut out weak, dead and awkwardly-placed shoots. Remove overcrowded branches. Finally, cut back hard all old wood. Time to prune: January – March — do not wait until growth starts
FLOWERING CHERRY CONIFERS	Cut out weak, dead and awkwardly-placed shoots. Remove overcrowded branches. Time to prune: Late summer-early autumn
BROAD-LEAVED EVERGREENS	Cut out weak, dead and awkwardly-placed shoots. Remove overcrowded branches. Time to prune: May
DAMAGED or DISEASED TREES	Carry out tree surgery. Cut back to clean wood. Paint all surfaces immediately with ARBREX to prevent infection. Where there are deep cracks or holes it is advisable to fill them with a mixture of dry sand (3 parts by volume) and ARBREX (1 part)

PINCHING OUT

Pinching out is the removal of the growing point and a small amount of stem by nipping between finger and thumb. The purpose of this technique is to induce bushiness — the removal of the tip of the main stem stimulates the development of side shoots. Many annuals (Antirrhinum, Salvia, Lobelia etc) are pinched out at an early stage to produce well-branched plants. This technique is also used to control the flowering time of Chrysanthemums and Carnations for Show purposes — a technique known as 'stopping'.

PLUNGING

Plunging describes the burying of pot plants up to their rims outdoors. Pots or bowls can be plunged in ordinary soil but it is more usual to construct a special plunge bed filled with peat or sand. Many indoor plants can spend their summers in the fresh air, their roots protected from sudden rises and falls in temperature by the insulating effect of the plunge bed. One of the main uses is for spring-flowering bulbs — the bowls are placed in a plunge bed and covered with several inches of peat, ash or coarse sand in winter. Root formation is stimulated in the cool moist conditions — the ideal preparation for the forcing which takes place later.

PUDDLING

A technique much loved by Victorian gardeners — the roots of herbaceous and woody plants are dipped in a slurry of clay and water before planting. Puddling was supposed to produce a water-holding layer around the roots and to keep pests at bay. Unfortunately there seems to be no scientific evidence for these benefits and it is better to water the planting hole *before* planting if the weather is dry.

RAKING

Raking is often described as one of the skilled techniques of gardening — it takes practice to do it properly. Its role is to create a seed bed after the large lumps have been broken down by forking. Choose a day when the surface is dry but the soil below is moist. Work in long sweeps, drawing stones and rubbish  towards you and breaking down lumps as you push away. After the plot has been raked in this way, repeat the process at right angles. Obviously the lumps must be broken down, air pockets removed and the surface left smooth, but you must know when to stop. Over-raking leads to excessively fine tilth which caps with the first downpour. Spring-tine rakes are excellent for removing leaves and other debris on lawns but cannot take the place of a rigid rake for seed bed preparation. The spring-tine version can only be used as a pull-tool, and so the soil-cultivating effect is lost.

SHARPENING

The neglect of regular sharpening makes gardening so much harder. Hoes, spades and trowels need more than cleaning after use — their cutting edges should be renewed occasionally with a medium file. Shears and secateurs need a fine file and knives are sharpened on an oilstone. Several gadgets are available these days and are worth trying, but there are some jobs you should leave to the expert. Send your cylinder mower off for an annual service once the season is over — don't wait until the start of the season next year. Sharpening saws, like cylinder mowers, calls for special equipment.

SPRAYING

See Chapter 7

THINNING

Thinning is carried out at several stages in the life cycle of some plants — from the time when they are seedlings to the fruiting period of large trees. Despite the often-repeated recommendation to sow thinly you will usually find that the seedlings emerging in the vegetable plot or in seed boxes are too close together. Thinning is  necessary, and this is a job to be tackled as soon as the plants are large enough to handle. Delay means spindly plants which never fully recover. The soil should be moist — water if necessary. Hold down the soil around the unwanted seedling with one hand and pull it up with the other. If the seedlings are too close together to allow this technique, nip off the top growth of the unwanted ones and leave the roots in the soil. After thinning, firm the soil around the remaining seedlings and water gently.

Thinning out of stems may be necessary in the herbaceous border, and it is often required with ornamental and fruit trees when branches become overcrowded. Following the pruning of Roses it is often found that 2 or more shoots develop from a single bud behind the cut. Rub out the weaker shoot.

Several kinds of fruit trees and bushes some-  times set a heavier crop than is required. Crowded fruits do not develop properly, and so thinning is required to allow the remaining ones to develop fully. Recommended distances between fruits are Peaches 9 in., Apples 6 in., Plums 3 in., Gooseberries 1 in. Grapes are thinned by removing some of the fruit with vine scissors from each bunch.

TRAINING & SUPPORTING

Supporting and training are not quite the same thing. Supporting involves the provision of a post, stake or framework to which weak stems can be attached. Training involves the fixing of branches into desired positions so that an unnatural but desirable growth habit is produced.

Some shrubs with lax spreading stems may require some means of support after a few years. Follow the principles described on the left for bushy herbaceous plants — use 3 or 4 stakes with a band joining the top of each stake — never rely on a single pole and twine.

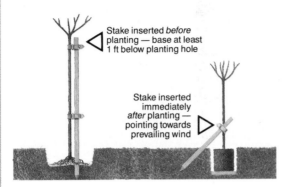

Stake inserted *before* planting — base at least 1 ft below planting hole

Stake inserted immediately *after* planting — pointing towards prevailing wind

Supporting

A tall plant can be rocked by strong winds if its roots are not able to anchor it firmly in the ground. A newly-planted specimen does not have this anchorage, so it can be dislodged or blown over. Staking is the answer — it is a job to do at planting time and not after the damage has been done. Inspect ties regularly — adjust as stem thickens.

Some herbaceous plants, such as Chrysanthemums or Dahlias, are also staked at planting time. Stout bamboo canes or wooden stakes are used. Tie the stems to the support as growth proceeds — use soft twine or raffia. This single-pole method is suitable for plants with spire-like heads, such as Delphiniums. In these cases the stake must be tall enough to support the columnar head.

In most cases, however, tying to a single stake should be avoided. With bushy plants an ugly 'drumstick' effect is produced and is the sign of a poor gardener — the all-too-familiar sight of a tight group of stems attached to a cane and a splayed-out spray of flowers above.

Unfortunately weak-stemmed plants, tall varieties on exposed sites, large-headed flowers and climbers all need support and stakes, wires, canes etc are not things of beauty in themselves. The answer is to choose the type of support with care and try to put it in position when the plant is quite small so that the stems can grow through to hide it.

For many plants all you will need is brushwood or pea sticks pushed into the soil around the young plant when the stems are about 1 ft high. For more robust and bushy herbaceous plants insert 3 or 4 canes around the stems and enclose the shoots with twine tied round the canes at 9 in. intervals. You can buy circular wire frames which are inserted into the soil and produce the same effect. In all cases follow the golden rule — never leave staking until the plant has collapsed.

The only plants which regularly require staking in the vegetable garden are Beans and Peas. Peas can be supported with twigs when young but may require plastic netting when fully grown — Runner Beans are best grown against stout canes, either arranged as a wigwam or as a double row joined at the top by a horizontal holding bar.

When a tree has outgrown its stake it may still need support. This can be provided by fixing a collar to the middle of the trunk and then securing it to the ground by means of 3 strong wires.

Training

Many trees, especially weeping ones, require training from an early stage if a mass of untidy branches is to be avoided. To train a standard, select the branch which will form the trunk and attach it to an upright stake — trim away all low-growing side branches. At the desired height (waist-high for a short standard, shoulder-high for a half standard and head-high for a full standard) let the main stem branch out to produce the head. With some plants (e.g Roses) these branches can be trained downwards over a wire frame to form a weeping standard. Wisteria can be trained as a weeping standard in this way.

Climbers must be trained against a support from the outset to ensure that they remain attached to it and grow in the desired direction. Use trellis work, posts, pillars, pergolas, fences etc. Make sure that all fence posts are well-anchored. For covering walls use plastic-covered straining wire stretched horizontally at 1½ ft intervals — there should be at least 3 in. between the wire and the wall. Many plants can be grown against walls in this way,

including weak-stemmed non-climbers such as Winter Jasmine and Forsythia suspensa. The wire ties used to attach the main stems to the supports should not be tied too tightly. When training climbers up a pole or pillar, wind the stems in an ascending spiral (see illustration) rather than attaching with ties to one side of the support.

The main stems need not all be trained vertically — spreading them horizontally to form an espalier or at an angle to form a fan can dramatically increase the display.

WATERING

Plants cannot live without water — a prolonged dry spell in summer can result in serious losses amongst the plants most at risk — newly-planted shrubs and trees, bedding plants, shallow-rooted vegetables and climbers growing close to the house. Even deep-rooted established plants like Roses can suffer — trials have shown that growth is impaired and the flowering season is curtailed if these plants are not watered during a dry summer.

With all garden plants the battle against water shortage begins well before the dry days of summer. Incorporate adequate organic matter into the soil before planting or sowing, and make sure that the soil is thoroughly moist to a depth of about 9 in. when planting or sowing. Mulch (see page 76) in late spring — you have now done all the preparatory work you can.

The problem

Soil with an average crop of plants loses about 4½ gallons of water per sq. yd per week in summer and 2 gallons per week in spring and autumn. This is equivalent to 1 in. of rain or applied water in summer and ½ in. in spring or autumn. If there is no rain and you have not watered the ground, this water comes from the soil's reserve and drying out occurs.

A point is reached when there is not enough water left in the soil to support healthy plant growth, and foliage starts to look dull. Leaf rolling is soon followed by wilting and leaf fall — the final stage is death.

The high risk areas

- Bedding plants for 4–6 weeks after planting.
- Herbaceous perennials for the first year after planting.
- Shrubs and trees for the first two years after planting.
- Tomatoes, Cucumbers, Marrows, Beans, Peas, Celery and Onions in the vegetable garden.
- Plants growing within 2 ft of the house.
- Plants growing in tubs.
- Plants growing in sandy or low-humus soils.
- Plants with shallow root systems. Not all these plants are small — some (e.g Silver Birch and Rhododendron) are large shrubs or trees.

The answer

The answer is, of course, to water . . . but to do this properly is not as easy as it sounds. Timing, quantity and method all have to be considered. There are, however, a few general principles.

- A plant should never be left to show visible signs of distress during a prolonged period of drought. Wilting means that you have waited too late — the time to water is when the soil below a few inches depth is dry and the foliage appears dull.

- Never apply a small amount of water (less than 1 gallon per sq. yd) and then repeat the watering every few days. This constant soaking of the surface and water-starvation of the lower root zone leads to rapid evaporation, surface rooting which is damaged in hot weather, and germination of weed seeds.

- Choose between **overall watering** and **point watering.** If you have a large area to cover and many plants of various sizes, overall watering must be your choice. This involves watering an area rather than restricting the water to the root zone of each individual plant. Some people use a watering can, but you really do need a hose pipe if watering is not to be a prolonged chore. The usual procedure is to walk slowly along borders and around beds with a hand-held hose and suitable nozzle. A sprinkler makes the job easier and is essential for all but the tiniest lawn. Perhaps the best methods of watering vegetables and shrubs are the sprinkler hoses and seep hoses, but they are expensive. Point watering is used where there is a limited number of large plants to deal with — the methods used are all designed to restrict the water to the immediate zone covered by the roots of each plant.

- Water thoroughly once you decide to water. If you are using a watering can remove the rose. Hold the spout close to the base of the plant and water slowly. If you use a sprinkler water in the evening — never in hot sunshine. With overall watering apply 2–4 gallons per sq. yd, using the higher amount in midsummer, in sandy soils and with high-risk plants. With point watering use 1–4 gallons per plant, depending on the size of shrub or tree.

- Repeat the watering if rain does not fall. There is no easy way to determine the right time for this repeat watering — dig down with a trowel and examine the soil at 3–4 in. below the surface. If it is dry, then water. As a general rule watering will be required about every 7 days during a period of drought.

WATERING continued

Overall Watering methods

WATERING CAN

Impractical for overall watering in anything larger than a tiny garden. Vital, however, for point watering a few plants. Choose the right size and sort of can — 2 gallon with metal rose for garden use, 1 gallon with long spout for the greenhouse and 1 pint size for houseplants.

STANDARD NOZZLE

The most practical method of general watering. For large plants, water around the base of the stems and not over the leaves. Use spray setting for small plants — be careful not to disturb soil and dislodge plants.

STATIC SPRINKLER

The simplest type of sprinkler. Water output is high and pattern is quite even, but area covered is relatively small. Buy stalked model for beds and borders — use a ground-level model for lawns.

ROTARY SPRINKLER

Two or 3 rotating arms produce a circle of fine droplets. Very popular and many brands are available. Some are adjustable for fineness of spray and area covered.

Point Watering methods

SEEP HOSE

Basically a plastic hose pipe bearing a series of pinholes along the sides opposite plants — water seeps through these holes to water ground around roots. Sophisticated types are available with nozzles or small tubes instead of pinholes. Popular with professional Tomato growers but not really for the amateur.

BASIN WATERING

A useful method for large shrubs or Roses growing in well-drained ground which dries out quickly. Build a ridge of soil around each bush and fill this basin using a hose pipe or watering can each time you water.

POT WATERING

A useful method where a limited number of large plants (e.g Tomatoes, Dahlias) are grown. Bury a large pot near the base at planting time — *don't* delay this task until later or roots will be disturbed. Fill the pot slowly with the required amount of water.

PULSE-JET SPRINKLER

Expensive, but a larger area is covered than with other types of sprinkler. A single jet produces a narrow arc of droplets, the jet rotating as a series of pulses. Buy stalked model for beds and borders.

OSCILLATING SPRINKLER

A horizontal tube bearing a series of small holes. A rectangular spray pattern is obtained as the tube slowly oscillates from side to side. All are adjustable for area covered.

SPRINKLER HOSE

Basically a flattened hose pipe bearing a series of fine holes on the upper surface. A long rectangular spray pattern is obtained — excellent for grass paths and rows of vegetables. Check if local authority allows them.

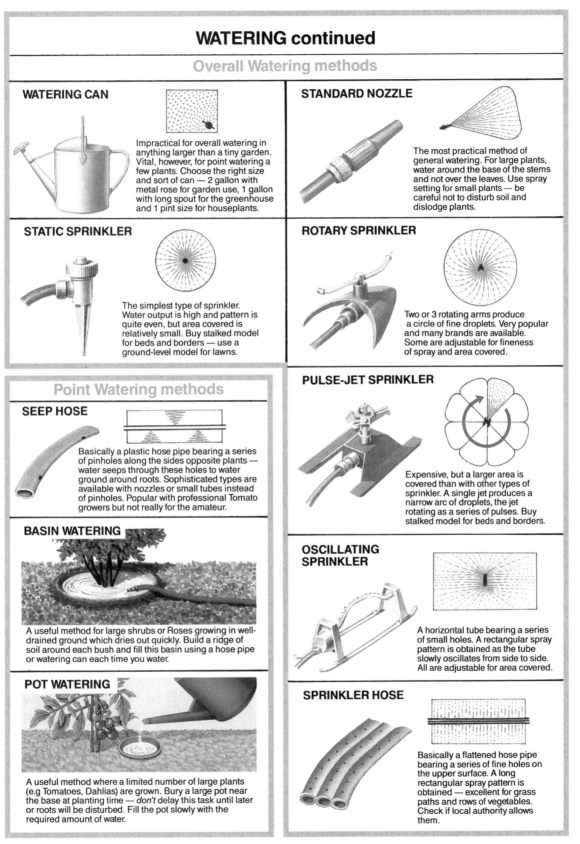

CHAPTER 7

TROUBLES

PESTS are animals, varying in size from tiny eelworms to majestic deer, which attack plants. The general term 'insect' covers small pests — mites, slugs, woodlice and true insects.

DISEASES are plant troubles caused by living organisms which are transmitted from one plant to another. Fungal diseases are the most common. Others are caused by bacteria and viruses.

DISORDERS are plant troubles which have disease-like symptoms but which are not due to a living organism — they are caused, not caught. Common causes are waterlogging and starvation.

WEEDS are plants growing where you don't want them to be. Self-sown annuals in a Rose bed are weeds, dandelions in a wild garden are not.

A variety of troubles are going to occur in your garden. The nature of the plant is important here — some hardy shrubs may remain trouble-free all their lives, an old-fashioned Rose may be host to an assortment of pests and diseases every season. The weather is another basic factor — there will be slugs when it's wet, greenfly when it's dry, frost damage when it's cold and red spider mite when it's hot. So both expert and novice can expect problems. The big difference is that the expert knows what to look for, takes steps to cut down the likelihood of pest and disease attack, and tackles trouble as soon as it appears. Garden troubles are tackled in two basic ways — culturally and chemically. One method cannot replace the other — they both have a job to do in the well-tended garden.

PREVENT TROUBLE BEFORE IT STARTS

CHOOSE WISELY
Reject soft bulbs, lanky bedding plants, old seeds, unhealthy shrubs and disease-ridden perennials

PRUNE PROPERLY
You must learn this essential art. It is obviously necessary for ensuring regular fruit and flower production, but it is also important in the war against pests and diseases. Cut out dead wood. Remove overcrowded branches to ensure adequate ventilation. Paint large cuts with Arbrex

PLAN CAREFULLY
Make sure that the plant is suited to the site. Avoid sun lovers if shade is a problem — avoid tender types if the garden is exposed and prone to frosts. Rotation of crops is essential for many vegetables

SPRAY TO PREVENT DISEASE
Fungicides tend to be protectants rather than cures. This means that you should spray as soon as the first spots are seen. In some cases (e.g rose black spot, peach leaf curl) you must spray *before* the disease is seen

REMOVE DEAD PLANTS, RUBBISH & WEEDS
Rotting plants can be a source of infection — some actually attract pests to the garden. Boxes, old flower pots etc are a breeding ground for slugs and woodlice. Weeds rob plants of food, water, light and space. Hoe or pull — take care if you use a weedkiller

GUARD AGAINST ANIMALS
Use netting to protect seedlings, vegetables and soft fruit from birds. A cylinder of wire-netting around the trunk is the best way to keep squirrels, rabbits, cats and dogs away from the base of trees

FOLLOW THE RULES OF GOOD HYGIENE UNDER GLASS
The humid atmosphere of a greenhouse is a paradise for pests and diseases. Control is often difficult, so prevention is better than cure. Use compost or sterilised soil. Ensure the house is adequately ventilated; dry air encourages pests and poor growth, saturated air encourages diseases. Try to avoid sudden fluctuations in temperature; water regularly. Water in the morning, although you can water in the early evening if the weather is warm. Remove dead leaves and plants immediately

PLANT OR SOW PROPERLY
Follow the rules for sowing and planting (pages 58–64). These rules will ensure that there will be no air pockets around the roots of new plants and will ensure establishment in the minimum possible time. Seed sowing calls for doing the right thing at the right time

FEED THE PLANTS PROPERLY
Shortage of nutrients can lead to many problems — poor growth, undersized blooms, lowered disease resistance and dis-coloured leaves. But take care — overfeeding can cause scorch and unbalanced feeding with too much nitrogen can result in lots of leaves and very few flowers

PREPARE THE GROUND THOROUGHLY
A strong-growing plant is more likely to withstand pest or disease attack than a weak specimen. Waterlogging due to insufficient soil preparation is the basic cause of failure in heavy soils. Add a humus maker when digging. Remove perennial weed roots. Add Chlorophos to the soil if pests have gnawed roots elsewhere in the garden

TACKLE TROUBLE WITHOUT DELAY

BUY THE RIGHT SPRAY

● Chemicals for controlling garden troubles are called pesticides. All of these have been thoroughly tested before sale, and are generally much less toxic than the ones grandfather used. They are safe to use in the way described on the label — but you must follow the instructions and precautions carefully.

● A bewildering assortment is offered by most garden shops. Before choosing look at the label carefully. The front will tell you whether it is an insecticide, fungicide or herbicide. It will also tell you the weight or volume and the active ingredients.

Insecticides

● These products are used to control insects and other small pests. There are 3 basic types.

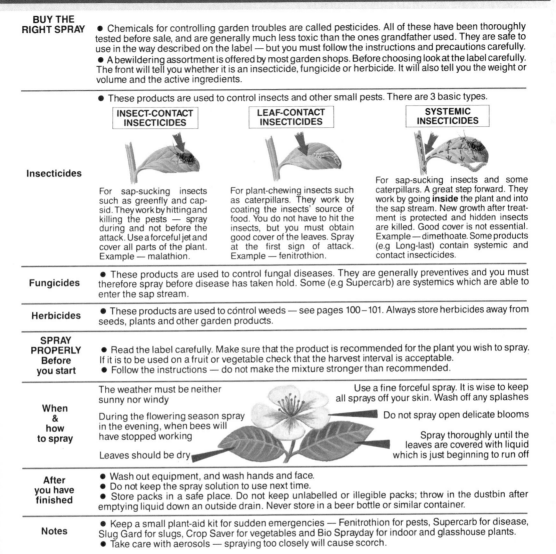

INSECT-CONTACT INSECTICIDES	LEAF-CONTACT INSECTICIDES	SYSTEMIC INSECTICIDES
For sap-sucking insects such as greenfly and capsid. They work by hitting and killing the pests — spray during and not before the attack. Use a forceful jet and cover all parts of the plant. Example — malathion.	For plant-chewing insects such as caterpillars. They work by coating the insects' source of food. You do not have to hit the insects, but you must obtain good cover of the leaves. Spray at the first sign of attack. Example — fenitrothion.	For sap-sucking insects and some caterpillars. A great step forward. They work by going **inside** the plant and into the sap stream. New growth after treatment is protected and hidden insects are killed. Good cover is not essential. Example — dimethoate. Some products (e.g Long-last) contain systemic and contact insecticides.

Fungicides

● These products are used to control fungal diseases. They are generally preventives and you must therefore spray before disease has taken hold. Some (e.g Supercarb) are systemics which are able to enter the sap stream.

Herbicides

● These products are used to control weeds — see pages 100–101. Always store herbicides away from seeds, plants and other garden products.

SPRAY PROPERLY

Before you start

● Read the label carefully. Make sure that the product is recommended for the plant you wish to spray. If it is to be used on a fruit or vegetable check that the harvest interval is acceptable.
● Follow the instructions — do not make the mixture stronger than recommended.

When & how to spray

The weather must be neither sunny nor windy

During the flowering season spray in the evening, when bees will have stopped working

Leaves should be dry

Use a fine forceful spray. It is wise to keep all sprays off your skin. Wash off any splashes

Do not spray open delicate blooms

Spray thoroughly until the leaves are covered with liquid which is just beginning to run off

After you have finished

● Wash out equipment, and wash hands and face.
● Do not keep the spray solution to use next time.
● Store packs in a safe place. Do not keep unlabelled or illegible packs; throw in the dustbin after emptying liquid down an outside drain. Never store in a beer bottle or similar container.

Notes

● Keep a small plant-aid kit for sudden emergencies — Fenitrothion for pests, Supercarb for disease, Slug Gard for slugs, Crop Saver for vegetables and Bio Sprayday for indoor and glasshouse plants.
● Take care with aerosols — spraying too closely will cause scorch.

PICK OFF CATERPILLARS AND DISEASED LEAVES

Minor attacks by caterpillar and leaf miner can often be controlled by hand picking. Mouldy leaves and fruits should be removed at once

EXAMINE DEAD PLANTS

Look closely to find the cause. This chapter and the other Expert books will tell you how to prevent it happening again. Examine the roots and ground for soil pests — take remedial action if found. Make sure that replanting is permissible before replacing

SPEED RECOVERY WITH A FOLIAR FEED

Plants, like humans, can be invalids. The cause may be a pest or disease. Root action may have been impaired by pest, disease or poor soil conditions. The best way to get things moving again is to use a foliar fertilizer, as such food is instantly absorbed. Use Fillip or Instant Bio

CUT OUT DEAD WOOD

During annual pruning all diseased twigs and branches should be cut off and burnt. If canker is discovered at any time of the year it must be cut out immediately and the wound painted with Arbrex

TAKE EARLY ACTION UNDER GLASS

Trouble can develop quickly under glass, so take immediate action. If spraying is recommended never do it in bright sunlight. Place a 2 in. layer of moist peat around stems of Tomatoes and Cucumbers if damaged root action is suspected

EXAMINE PLANTS IN STORE

Get into the habit of occasionally checking bulbs, fruit and vegetables which are being stored. The prompt removal of a rotting specimen may save the rest

RAKE UP AND BURN DISEASED LEAVES & FRUIT

Soil Pests

Many insects live in the soil. Not all of them, however, are harmful to plants. Some are actually beneficial because they feed on garden pests. A rough guide to follow when digging is — **if you can catch it easily, kill it.**

ANTS steal seeds but do no direct injury to growing plants. However, they loosen the soil around the roots so that plants wilt and die. Ants also carry greenfly from one plant to another, and ant-hills disfigure the lawn.

WOODLICE are about ½ in. long, grey, and 'armour-plated'. They hide under decaying refuse, plant pots etc in the garden and come out at night to attack seedlings and young plants.

SLUGS & SNAILS are serious garden pests, specially when the weather is wet and cool. They hide under stones and debris during the day and come out during the night, devouring seedlings and the roots, stems, leaves and even flowers of mature plants. Slime trails are a clue to their presence.

MILLEPEDES are sluggish, dark-coloured grubs which curl up when disturbed. They do a great deal of damage to seedlings and the underground parts of mature plants. This pest should not be confused with the helpful centipede which is brighter coloured and quick-moving.

CHAFER GRUBS are ugly, fat curved grubs over 1 in. long. They feed throughout the year on the roots of trees, shrubs, flowers and vegetables which wilt and sometimes die as a result.

LEATHERJACKETS are legless, dark grey grubs, about 1 in. long and very slow-moving. They are a serious nuisance, devouring the underground parts of a wide range of plants including lawn grasses.

VINE WEEVILS are wrinkled white grubs which attack the roots of many plants. The worst affected are alpines, Strawberries and pot plants.

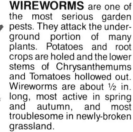

WIREWORMS are one of the most serious garden pests. They attack the underground portion of many plants. Potatoes and root crops are holed and the lower stems of Chrysanthemums and Tomatoes hollowed out. Wireworms are about ½ in. long, most active in spring and autumn, and most troublesome in newly-broken grassland.

CUTWORMS are large grey or brown caterpillars which attack plants at ground level — the leaves wilt and the stems may topple over. Foliage and roots may be eaten. Worst attacks occur in late summer.

Digging, liming and proper rotation on the vegetable plot will help to keep down the number of pests in your soil, but to save your plants from crippling underground attack it is often necessary to use a good insecticide as well.

Soil pest	Treatment
CHAFER GRUBS **CUTWORMS** **LEATHERJACKETS** **MILLEPEDES** **VINE WEEVILS** **WIREWORMS**	CHLOROPHOS will keep your soil free from these pests. Sprinkle the granules evenly over the soil surface at the recommended rate and then rake in lightly. Unlike some soil pest killers, CHLOROPHOS does not taint root crops. For vine weevils in pots or around alpines, water with spray-strength HEXYL
WOODLICE	Remove rubbish where woodlice could hide. Sprinkle SLUG GARD pellets thinly over the soil if woodlice are a nuisance
ANTS	Use an ANTI-ANT dust along the runs and where the insects are seen to congregate. The entrance to the nest should be liberally dusted. To get rid of indoor ants use a liquid ant killer such as NIPPON
SLUGS **SNAILS**	Slug pellets based on metaldehyde are the traditional method of killing slugs and snails. Alternatively a methiocarb/bait pellet (SLUG GARD) can be used — there is the added benefit of leatherjacket, millepede and woodlouse control

Seedling Troubles

SEEDLINGS LYING ON GROUND

Base of stems neither withered nor cut in two	**Cats and dogs** *or* **Seeds sown too close to the surface**
Base of stems withered and blackened	**Damping-off** disease is the most serious seedling complaint, especially under glass. It is encouraged by the use of unsterilised loam, over-watering, and sowing too thickly. The best control measure is to use Cheshunt Compound. Dissolve 1 oz in a little warm water, and then make up to 2 gallons with cold water. Water the seed bed with this solution before sowing, and repeat after the seedlings have come through. Another way of preventing damping-off is to use a seed dressing If damping-off has already appeared, remove and burn all affected seedlings and water the bed or box with Cheshunt Compound solution
Base of stems cut in two	**Cutworms** or **leatherjackets** or **wireworms**. For a guide to recognition and control of these soil pests, see page 86

SEEDLINGS DYING, LEAVES NOT ATTACKED

Wireworms or **leatherjackets** — For a guide to the recognition and control of these soil pests, see page 86

Carrot fly Leaves of affected Carrot seedlings turn reddish

or

Onion fly Leaves of affected Onion seedlings turn yellow and wilt

or

Cabbage root fly Leaves of affected Cabbage seedlings turn bluish-green

Small white maggots can be found at the bottom of the stem and roots. For method of control, see page 91

or

Ants loosen the soil around the roots, see page 86

LEAVES WITH HOLES

Flea beetles attack Cabbage, Turnip, Lettuce, Wallflower and many other plants. Spray vegetables with Multiveg. On other plants use Long-last or Hexyl. Apply as soon as the first signs of damage are noticed

POOR GERMINATION

Soil not disturbed	**Soil not properly prepared** or **seed sown in cold and wet soil** or **seed sown too deeply** or **seed too old**
Soil disturbed	**Birds** are a nuisance, especially in early spring. Use peaguards (arches of fine-mesh wire-netting) over the drills, or criss-cross black cotton 3–4 in. above the bed *or* **Mice** are very fond of Peas and Beans. To avoid loss, dampen seed with paraffin and use Racumin Mouse Bait *or* **Cats and dogs**. A dusting of Pepper Dust will help to keep pets away without doing them any harm *or* **Ants** carry off seeds from seed boxes to their nests. See page 86

SEEDLINGS WEAK & SPINDLY

Seeds sown too thickly

or

Pricking out or thinning out not done at the proper time

or

Seed boxes too far away from light

or

Seed boxes covered with glass or paper too long

SEEDLINGS NOT GROWING

Soil too cold. Treat with sulphate of ammonia or a foliar feed to provide a boost

or

Soil too dry. Lightly water the seed bed

or

Seedlings not hardened off

LEAVES & STEMS EATEN

Slugs and snails or **woodlice** or **millepedes** or **cutworms.** For a guide to recognition and control of these soil pests, see page 86

or

Birds

LEAVES WITH NOTCHES

Pea and bean weevils bite 'U'-shaped notches in young leaves of Peas, Beans and Sweet Peas, so as to give a scalloped edge to the leaves. For the way to deal with this pest, see page 91

Flower Troubles

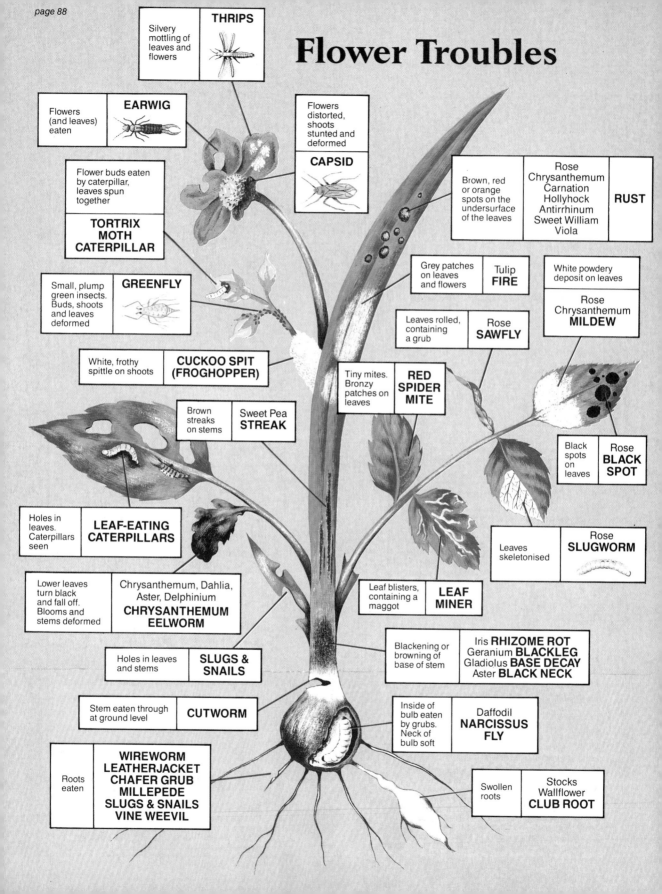

THRIPS
Silvery mottling of leaves and flowers

EARWIG
Flowers (and leaves) eaten

CAPSID
Flowers distorted, shoots stunted and deformed

TORTRIX MOTH CATERPILLAR
Flower buds eaten by caterpillar, leaves spun together

GREENFLY
Small, plump green insects. Buds, shoots and leaves deformed

CUCKOO SPIT (FROGHOPPER)
White, frothy spittle on shoots

RUST
Brown, red or orange spots on the undersurface of the leaves
Rose Chrysanthemum Carnation Hollyhock Antirrhinum Sweet William Viola

Tulip FIRE
Grey patches on leaves and flowers

MILDEW
White powdery deposit on leaves
Rose Chrysanthemum

Rose SAWFLY
Leaves rolled, containing a grub

RED SPIDER MITE
Tiny mites. Bronzy patches on leaves

Sweet Pea STREAK
Brown streaks on stems

Rose BLACK SPOT
Black spots on leaves

LEAF-EATING CATERPILLARS
Holes in leaves. Caterpillars seen

Rose SLUGWORM
Leaves skeletonised

CHRYSANTHEMUM EELWORM
Lower leaves turn black and fall off. Blooms and stems deformed
Chrysanthemum, Dahlia, Aster, Delphinium

LEAF MINER
Leaf blisters, containing a maggot

SLUGS & SNAILS
Holes in leaves and stems

Iris RHIZOME ROT
Geranium BLACKLEG
Gladiolus BASE DECAY
Aster BLACK NECK
Blackening or browning of base of stem

CUTWORM
Stem eaten through at ground level

Daffodil NARCISSUS FLY
Inside of bulb eaten by grubs. Neck of bulb soft

WIREWORM LEATHERJACKET CHAFER GRUB MILLEPEDE SLUGS & SNAILS VINE WEEVIL
Roots eaten

Stocks Wallflower CLUB ROOT
Swollen roots

PULL UP AND BURN IF THE TROUBLE IS INCURABLE

Plants affected by a serious virus disease cannot be cured, but they can serve as a source of infection for surrounding plants. The usual symptoms of virus disease are mottling of leaves, broken colours of flowers and/or stunted growth. Prevention is all-important — buy healthy stock and keep greenfly under control. Once the plant is clearly infected, however, there is nothing you can do — lift and burn. Examples of virus diseases in the flower garden are SWEET PEA STREAK (plant covered with brown streaks) and CHRYSANTHEMUM MOSAIC (centre vein of leaf yellow and thickened. Plant stunted).

GERANIUM BLACKLEG, IRIS RHIZOME ROT, CHRYSANTHEMUM EELWORM, GLADIOLUS BASE DECAY, ASTER WILT and ASTER BLACK NECK cannot be cured. Burn infected plants. Water remainder with Cheshunt Compound solution.

NARCISSUS FLY is destructive — the damaged bulbs are useless and should be destroyed.

TREAT PROMPTLY IF THE TROUBLE CAN BE CURED OR CHECKED

Don't delay. Follow the general rule —

If it is a serious disease — spray when you see the first spots, or put on a protective coat before the disease appears when told to do so by the label.

If it is a serious pest — spray when you see the first signs of attack. Check that the product is suitable for the plant you wish to spray.

Pest	Treatment						Notes
	SPRAYDAY	MULTIROSE	LIQUID DERRIS	MALATHION GREENFLY KILLER	HEXYL	LONG-LAST	FENITROTHION	
ROSE SLUGWORM								Spray serious attacks — otherwise hand pick
RED SPIDER MITE								Keep watch in hot, dry weather
THRIPS								Keep watch in hot, dry weather
GREENFLY								Spray when first colonies appear
BLACKFLY								Spray when first colonies appear
SMALL CATERPILLARS								Spray serious attacks — otherwise hand pick
LEAF MINER								Pick and destroy mined leaves
OTHER CATERPILLARS								Spray serious attacks — otherwise hand pick
CAPSID								Treat plants and surrounding soil
ROSE SAWFLY								Pick and destroy rolled leaves
EARWIG								Treat plants and hiding places
CUCKOO SPIT								Use a forceful jet
CUTWORM, WIREWORM CHAFER GRUB VINE WEEVIL MILLEPEDE LEATHERJACKET	CHLOROPHOS will keep your soil free from these pests. Sprinkle the granules evenly over the soil surface at the recommended rate and then rake in lightly. For vine weevils attacking established plants, water with spray-strength HEXYL							
SLUGS & SNAILS	SLUG PELLETS based on metaldehyde are the traditional method of killing slugs and snails — see page 86							

Disease	Control
RUST	Difficult to control. Where rust is a likely problem, spray with DITHANE every 2 weeks. Pick off affected leaves as soon as they are seen
BLACK SPOT ROSE MILDEW	Spray with MULTIROSE at the first sign of mildew. Repeat as necessary. In bad black spot areas begin spraying as first leaves open in spring
CHRYSANTHEMUM MILDEW MICHAELMAS DAISY MILDEW	Spray with SUPERCARB at the first sign of mildew. Repeat as necessary
TULIP FIRE BULB & CORM ROTS	Dip bulbs and corms immediately before planting in SUPERCARB solution for 15-30 minutes
CLUB ROOT	Dress with hydrated lime (see page 15) before sowing or planting

The flower troubles described on these two pages include most of the serious pests and diseases. There are many other problems which can occur — for a more complete guide consult the appropriate Expert book.

Vegetable Troubles

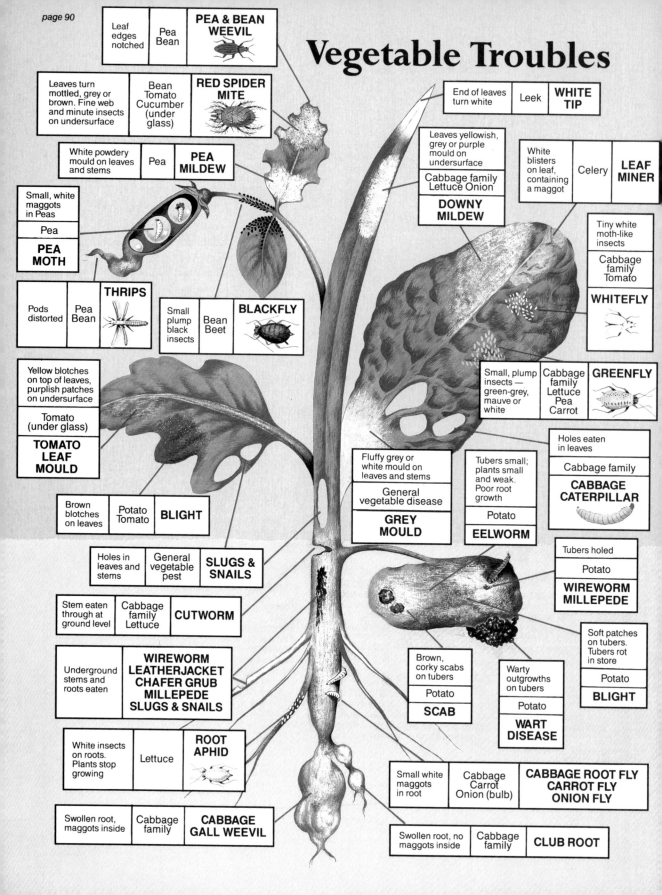

| Leaf edges notched | Pea Bean | **PEA & BEAN WEEVIL** |

| Leaves turn mottled, grey or brown. Fine web and minute insects on undersurface | Bean Tomato Cucumber (under glass) | **RED SPIDER MITE** |

| White powdery mould on leaves and stems | Pea | **PEA MILDEW** |

| Small, white maggots in Peas | Pea | **PEA MOTH** |

| Pods distorted | Pea Bean | **THRIPS** |

| Small plump black insects | Bean Beet | **BLACKFLY** |

| Yellow blotches on top of leaves, purplish patches on undersurface | Tomato (under glass) | **TOMATO LEAF MOULD** |

| Brown blotches on leaves | Potato Tomato | **BLIGHT** |

| Holes in leaves and stems | General vegetable pest | **SLUGS & SNAILS** |

| Stem eaten through at ground level | Cabbage family Lettuce | **CUTWORM** |

| Underground stems and roots eaten | **WIREWORM LEATHERJACKET CHAFER GRUB MILLEPEDE SLUGS & SNAILS** |

| White insects on roots. Plants stop growing | Lettuce | **ROOT APHID** |

| Swollen root, maggots inside | Cabbage family | **CABBAGE GALL WEEVIL** |

| End of leaves turn white | Leek | **WHITE TIP** |

| Leaves yellowish, grey or purple mould on undersurface | Cabbage family Lettuce Onion | **DOWNY MILDEW** |

| White blisters on leaf, containing a maggot | Celery | **LEAF MINER** |

| Tiny white moth-like insects | Cabbage family Tomato | **WHITEFLY** |

| Small, plump insects — green-grey, mauve or white | Cabbage family Lettuce Pea Carrot | **GREENFLY** |

| Holes eaten in leaves | Cabbage family | **CABBAGE CATERPILLAR** |

| Fluffy grey or white mould on leaves and stems | General vegetable disease | **GREY MOULD** |

| Tubers small; plants small and weak. Poor root growth | Potato | **EELWORM** |

| Tubers holed | Potato | **WIREWORM MILLEPEDE** |

| Soft patches on tubers. Tubers rot in store | Potato | **BLIGHT** |

| Brown, corky scabs on tubers | Potato | **SCAB** |

| Warty outgrowths on tubers | Potato | **WART DISEASE** |

| Small white maggots in root | Cabbage Carrot Onion (bulb) | **CABBAGE ROOT FLY CARROT FLY ONION FLY** |

| Swollen root, no maggots inside | Cabbage family | **CLUB ROOT** |

TAKE THE RECOMMENDED ACTION IF THE TROUBLE IS INCURABLE

POTATO EELWORM remains in the soil for a long time. Destroy plants and do not grow Potatoes or Tomatoes on the land for at least 6 years.

POTATO WART DISEASE must be notified to the Ministry of Agriculture. Destroy plants — in future grow a resistant variety.

SPLITTING of Carrots, Potatoes etc is caused by irregular water supply. Do not store affected roots — in future keep soil properly watered during dry spells.

SOFT ROT of Potatoes, Turnips etc results in slimy, evil-smelling roots. Burn affected produce — in future take care not to injure roots at lifting time.

VIRUS diseases can be serious on the vegetable plot — Potatoes, Tomatoes and Cucumbers are some of the crops at risk. There is no cure — lift and burn.

TREAT PROMPTLY IF THE TROUBLE CAN BE CURED OR CHECKED

Pest	Treatment (MULTIVEG / CROP SAVER / LIQUID DERRIS / MALATHION GREENFLY KILLER / HEXYL / LONG-LAST / SPRAYDAY / FENITROTHION)	Notes
WHITEFLY		Repeat spraying is essential
RED SPIDER MITE		Maintain damp atmosphere under glass
PEA THRIPS		Keep watch in hot, dry weather
GREENFLY		Spray when first colonies appear
BLACKFLY		Spray when first colonies appear
SMALL CATERPILLARS		Spray serious attacks — otherwise hand pick
LEAF MINER		Pick and destroy mined leaves
OTHER CATERPILLARS		Spray serious attacks — otherwise hand pick
PEA & BEAN WEEVIL		Hoe around plants in April–May
PEA MOTH		Spray 7–10 days after flowers open
CABBAGE ROOT FLY **CARROT FLY, ONION FLY** **CUTWORM, WIREWORM** **MILLEPEDE** **LEATHERJACKET** **CHAFER GRUB**	CHLOROPHOS will guard your plants against these pests but correct timing is very important — follow the directions on the drum. Sprinkle the granules evenly over the soil surface at the recommended rate and then rake in lightly. Unlike some soil pest killers, CHLOROPHOS does not taint root crops	
ROOT APHID	Apply CHLOROPHOS (see above) or water with spray-strength MALATHION	
SLUGS & SNAILS	SLUG PELLETS based on metaldehyde are the traditional method of killing slugs and snails — see page 86	
CABBAGE GALL WEEVIL	CHLOROPHOS (see above) reduces risk — treatment not worthwhile	

Disease	Control
POTATO & TOMATO BLIGHT **DOWNY MILDEW** **LEEK WHITE TIP**	Spray with DITHANE or MULTIVEG as soon as the first symptoms are seen — repeat every fortnight as necessary. To prevent blight in a wet summer apply the first spray in early July
BEAN CHOCOLATE SPOT (dark brown spots on leaves) **CELERY LEAF SPOT** (brown spots on leaves) **PEA MILDEW, GREY MOULD** **TOMATO LEAF MOULD**	Spray with SUPERCARB or MULTIVEG as soon as the first symptoms are seen — read the leaflet for precise instructions. Repeat as necessary
CLUB ROOT	Make sure the soil is adequately limed and well drained. Before planting dip roots in SUPERCARB solution or CALOMEL DUST paste
POTATO SCAB	No treatment. In future dig in compost but do not lime before planting

The vegetable troubles described on these two pages include most of the serious pests and diseases. There are many other problems which can occur, and some of these are nutritional or cultural disorders rather than the result of insect or fungal attack. Examples include bull-necked Onions, forked Carrots, bolted Lettuces and blown Brussels Sprouts. For a more complete guide to vegetable troubles, consult The Vegetable Expert.

Top Fruit Troubles

FROST

The effect of frost on the foliage becomes apparent as the leaves expand. The lower surface becomes puckered and blistered, and the skin over the blisters cracks. The leaves around the flower trusses are the worst affected, but frost-damaged foliage does not fall. Frost at blossom time is the real menace — flowers turn brown and drop off. In a year of abundant blossom the thinning effect of a slight frost is beneficial — but a late severe frost can be devastating. Planting in a frost pocket should be avoided — see page 26.

BLOSSOM DROP

It is extremely annoying to discover that a healthy tree which was full of blossom has lost its flowers without setting fruit. To find the cause you must know whether this trouble takes place year after year or is an unusual occurrence. If it is an annual event then the most likely cause is the absence of a pollinating partner. Most trees will not set fruit unless another variety of the same fruit with compatible pollen is growing nearby. Your local nurseryman or garden centre can advise you on a suitable variety to plant. If blossom drop does not usually occur then poor weather at flowering time is the most probable reason. Frosting of the blooms is a common problem on cold, exposed plots. Very dry air can result in poor pollination and a wet, cold spring reduces the activity of pollinating insects.

FRUIT DROP

Fruitlets will fall following insect damage — look for grubs in fallen Apples, Pears and Plums. But healthy fruitlets also fall; this may actually be beneficial as a heavy set must be thinned. The first drop of Apples takes place when the fruitlets are pea-sized — the usual reason is incomplete pollination due to a cold wet spring. The major shedding is the 'June drop'. There are several reasons why the fall at this time may be unusually heavy with only a sparse crop remaining. It is normal for newly-planted trees to shed most of their fruit in this way, and some varieties, such as Cox's Orange Pippin, have a notoriously heavy June drop. Irregular water supplies at the root, starvation, frost damage and overcrowding are other causes.

SCAB

A serious disease of Apples and Pears, which can attack all parts of the tree. Leaves bear dark green or brown spots; twigs are blistered and fruits are badly disfigured. The best way to achieve control is to follow a regular spraying programme designed for all the major troubles (page 39). Alternatively spray with Dithane at bud burst, green cluster, pink bud, petal fall and 14 days after petal fall. Rake up and burn fallen leaves in autumn; prune scabby shoots in winter.

SUCKER

The developing buds of Apples and Pears are attacked by young suckers. The blossom trusses turn brown as if attacked by frost, but careful examination reveals yellowish-white insects which look like flattened aphids. Another tell-tale sign is the presence of sticky honey-dew. Spray with Long-last or Fenitrothion at green cluster.

SILVER LEAF

The most serious disease of Plums, which can also attack Apples, Cherries and Peaches. The first sign is silvering of the leaves. Die-back of shoots occurs; wood is stained. Cut out dead branches 6 in. below level of infection. Paint cuts with Arbrex. Dig out tree if toadstools have appeared on the trunk.

BIRDS

Birds can be extremely destructive to flower buds, the main culprits being bullfinches and sparrows. All tree fruit can be damaged, with Cherries, Plums and Pears the worst affected. The outer bud scales are pushed aside and the central portion of each bud pecked out during late winter and spring. Birds can be a problem after the fruit has set, ranging from the total destruction of a Cherry crop to the production of occasional holes in ripening Apples. Unfortunately spray repellents may not keep birds at bay — the best answer is plastic netting wherever it is practical.

MILDEW

Young leaves, shoots and flower trusses of Apples and Pears may appear grey in spring due to infection of this white powdery mould. It is a serious disease — growth is stunted, diseased flowers do not set and leaves may fall. Cox's Orange Pippin is very susceptible. Prune and burn all infected twigs. Use a spraying programme containing carbendazim. See page 39 for a suitable programme.

FALSE SILVER LEAF

A common disorder which looks like silver leaf at first glance. Leaves are silvery, but the effect appears all over the tree rather than progressively along a branch. A cut branch reveals that the staining of silver leaf disease is absent. The cause of false silver leaf is starvation or irregular watering. Put down an organic mulch in spring.

For Apple and Pear growth stages see page 39

LEAF BLISTER MITE

This microscopic mite can be a serious pest of Pears grown against walls. Leaves are spotted with yellow or red blisters which later turn black. Affected leaves fall early, and fruit may be blistered. Pick off and burn diseased leaves as soon as they are noticed.

RED SPIDER MITE

Fruit tree red spider mite

Bryobia mite

The first sign of red spider mite attack is a faint mottling of the upper leaf surface. In warm weather a severe infestation may occur — the leaves turn a bronze colour, become brittle and die. Examine the underside of the foliage with a magnifying glass for the tiny mites. The fruit tree red spider mite is the common species; on Pears you may find the bryobia mite. Spray with Long-last, Malathion or Derris. If necessary repeat 3 weeks later.

PEACH LEAF CURL

Large reddish blisters develop on the leaves. Apart from making the tree unsightly this serious disease of outdoor Peaches leads to early leaf fall and weakening of the tree. The fungus overwinters in the bark and between bud scales, not on fallen leaves. Spray with Dithane in mid February, 14 days later and again just before leaf fall.

SHOT HOLE DISEASE

A fungal disease which attacks Plums, Peaches and Cherries. Brown spots appear on the leaves which turn into small holes. No other symptoms appear and the trees are not seriously affected. Only weak trees are attacked so build up vigour by spraying with Fillip.

CAPSID BUG

¼ in. active bugs

The first signs of damage are reddish-brown spots on the leaves. The spots tear to form brown-edged holes. Young Apple and Pear fruits bear spots which develop into corky patches. Spray with Long-last at green cluster to protect leaves and again at petal fall to avoid fruit damage.

APHID

Greenfly

Cherry blackfly

Several types of greenfly attack Apples, Pears, Peaches and Plums. Some greenfly cause yellowing and curling — others produce reddening and distortion. Spray with Long-last or Fenitrothion at bud burst and again at green cluster. Only one aphid, the cherry blackfly, attacks Cherries, but the effect can be devastating. Spray when they are seen with Malathion or Fenitrothion.

BACTERIAL CANKER

Pale-edged spots are the first sign of this serious disease of Plums, Cherries and other stone fruit. At a later stage gum oozes from the bark and affected branches die back. Tackle the problem quickly to save the tree. Cut out diseased branches and paint cuts with Arbrex.

PEAR & CHERRY SLUGWORM

½ in. black grubs

Both Pear and Cherry leaves are attacked by these slug-like insects between June and October. They feed on the upper surface. Spray with Hexyl if seriously affected.

CATERPILLAR

MOTTLED UMBER MOTH

Smooth 'looper' caterpillar, which attacks trees in spring.

WINTER MOTH

Green 'looper' caterpillar which devours young leaves and may spin them together.

'Looper' caterpillars eat the new leaves in spring and often feed on the petals and flower-stalks later in the season. Protect trees by encircling each trunk with a Boltac greaseband from September to March. If caterpillars are seen, spray with Fenitrothion or Long-last.

VAPOURER MOTH

Colourful caterpillar, about 1 in. long, which feeds on the leaves from May to August. Spray with Fenitrothion or Long-last.

For Apple and Pear growth stages see page 39

CORAL SPOT

Raised pink spots appear on the surface of affected branches. Dead wood is the breeding ground for the fungus, and the spores infect living trees through cuts and wounds. Cut out all dead and diseased branches and paint with Arbrex.

SPLIT BARK

The cause can be a severe frost — another cause is one or more poor growing conditions. Cut away any dead wood; paint with Arbrex to keep out disease. Feed and mulch the tree to restore good health.

DIE-BACK

Begins at the shoot tips and progresses slowly downwards. More common in stone fruit than Apples or Pears. There are a number of reasons, including diseases such as canker. If no disease is present, waterlogging is a likely cause. Cut out dead wood.

WOOLLY APHID

Colonies of aphids live on branches, secreting white waxy 'wool' which protects them. The corky galls they cause are a common entry point for canker spores. Brush off 'wool' with an old toothbrush and methylated spirits. Alternatively, spray with Long-last.

BACTERIAL CANKER

Cankers are flat and may not be easily noticed, but the effect on stone fruit is serious. Attacked branches produce few leaves and soon die. Gum oozes from the cankers. For leaf symptoms see page 93. Cut out diseased branches; paint cuts with Arbrex.

FIREBLIGHT

A devastating disease of Pears which can occur on Apples. Affected shoots wilt and die. Tell-tale sign is the presence of brown leaves which do not fall. Cut out all diseased branches to 2 ft below affected area, but tree is killed once disease spreads to the trunk.

CANKER

The bark shrinks and cracks in concentric rings. Tell-tale sign is the presence of red growths in winter. A serious disease of Apples and Pears, especially on badly-drained soil. Cut off damaged twigs; cut out canker from stems and branches. Paint with Arbrex.

HONEY FUNGUS

Honey fungus (armillaria disease) is a common cause of the death of Apple trees. A white fan of fungal growth occurs below the bark near ground level. On roots, black 'bootlaces' are found. Toadstools appear in autumn. Burn stems and roots; treat soil with Armillatox.

PLUM SAWFLY

The tell-tale sign of this pest of Plums is a hole surrounded by sticky black "frass". Inside will be found the ½ in. grub. Damaged Plums fall before maturity. Cultivate around the trees and spray with Fenitrothion 7-10 days after petal fall.

PEAR MIDGE

Attacked Pear fruitlets become deformed and blackened, usually falling from the tree. Cut fruit reveals a central cavity and tiny grubs. Burn blackened fruit, and keep the soil cultivated. If it was a problem last year, spray with Hexyl at white bud.

STORAGE ROT

Most Apple rotting in store is due to bitter rot (Gloeosporium). If a large quantity of fruit is to be stored, take preventive measures. Spray trees with Supercarb in August and repeat 1-2 weeks before harvest. Remove and destroy diseased fruit immediately.

PEAR STONY PIT

This is a serious virus disease of Pears — affected trees have to be dug out and destroyed. Diseased fruit is small and misshapen with the surface covered with dimples and lumps. The flesh is woody and inedible. The disease is usually restricted to old trees.

For Apple and Pear growth stages see page 39

CHERRY FRUIT MOTH

These green caterpillars can be a nuisance in southern counties, feeding inside the flower buds where they eat both petals and stamens. They continue to feed on the open flowers and then inside the young fruitlets before dropping to the ground in late May. It is not usually necessary to spray against this pest.

APPLE BLOSSOM WEEVIL

A common pest of Apples, which occasionally affects Pears. In spring the grubs feed inside developing flower buds. The stalks remain green but the petals turn brown. If one of these 'capped' blossoms is cut in two, a white grub or brown beetle will be found inside. Spray with Fenitrothion at bud burst.

BLOSSOM WILT

In a mild, wet spring this disease can be serious on Plums, when the tree appears to have been scorched. Apples and Pears can also be badly affected. Blossom trusses wilt and turn brown — shoots are killed in a bad attack. Remove infected blossoms and dead twigs. In summer remove all fruit affected by brown rot (see below).

CODLING MOTH

The grub bores into developing fruit and feeds on the central core. Pears and Plums may be attacked as well as Apples. Grubs can be found inside the fruit in July and August; the telltale sign is sawdust-like "frass" within the Apple. Spray with Fenitrothion in mid June; repeat 3 weeks later.

APPLE SAWFLY

A ribbon-like scar is produced on the surface. Later the creamy-white grub burrows down to feed on the central core which generally causes the fruit to drop in June or July. The grubs go into the ground in July. Sticky "frass" can be seen around the hole. Spray with Fenitrothion at petal fall. Pick up and burn the fallen Apples.

RUSSETTING

The rough scurf which sometimes forms over the surface of Apples and Pears is known as russetting. On some Apple varieties it is natural; on the smooth-skinned varieties it makes the fruit unsightly. The eating quality is not affected. Poor growing weather is the most likely cause, especially if it occurs at petal fall.

BROWN ROT

Most tree fruit can be affected, but the disease is worst on Apples. The infected fruit turns brown and concentric rings of yellowish mould appear. The shrunken mummified fruit may remain on the tree throughout the winter or it may fall. This fungal disease cannot be controlled by spraying and it is necessary to destroy affected fruit as soon as they are seen.

BITTER PIT

Small brown areas appear in the surface tissue, each one marked by a small depression in the skin. The brown areas are occasionally scattered throughout the fruit, rendering it bitter and uneatable. Bitter pit usually develops during storage. The cause is complex, but it is linked to calcium deficiency and a period of water shortage.

NUTRIENT DEFICIENCY

An abnormal change in leaf colour often indicates a shortage of an essential element. Spray the trees with a foliar feed such as Fillip. If the symptoms of iron or magnesium deficiency are severe, water MultiTonic on the soil around the trunks. In spring apply Tree & Shrub Fertilizer.

NITROGEN SHORTAGE
Red & yellow tints

POTASH SHORTAGE
Leaf edge scorch

MAGNESIUM SHORTAGE
Brown between veins

IRON SHORTAGE
Yellow between veins

For Apple and Pear growth stages see page 39

Soft Fruit Troubles

VIRUS

Virus diseases are a major problem of Raspberries and Strawberries. Aphids and other insects are the carriers, and once the plants are infected there is nothing you can do to save them. **Mosaic** is a serious disorder of Raspberries. Strawberries are affected by several viruses — **crinkle** occurs in late spring, **yellow edge** in autumn and **arabis mosaic** in either spring or autumn. Remove and burn diseased plants.

Mosaic

Yellow edge

Crinkle

LEAF SPOT

Leaf spot is the most serious disease of Blackcurrants. Gooseberries may also be attacked. Brown spots appear on the leaves and early defoliation takes place. Leaf spot is worst in a wet season; spraying is a worthwhile precaution. Apply Dithane or Supercarb at the first sign of leaf spotting and repeat at 14 day intervals if weather remains damp. Pick off diseased leaves; rake up and burn all fallen leaves.

CANE SPOT

Raspberries and Loganberries can be affected. Small purple spots appear on the canes, enlarging to form white pits with a purple border. Cut out badly diseased canes in autumn. Next spring spray with Supercarb at 14 day intervals from bud burst until blossom time.

RASPBERRY MOTH

Dead or dying shoots of Raspberries may indicate the presence of the ⅓ in. red caterpillars. They hide in the soil or stakes during winter and move to the shoots in April, where they feed inside the pith. Apply a Tar Oil spray in winter. Cut out and burn withered shoots.

SPUR BLIGHT

Purplish patches appear around the buds on Raspberry and Loganberry canes in early autumn. These patches turn silvery and the buds are killed. Cut out and burn diseased canes as soon as the purple patches start to appear. To prevent attacks spray with Supercarb at 14 day intervals from bud burst until blossom time.

FROST: CANE FRUIT

Some buds on fruit canes may fail to open in spring. If the area around the withered bud is discoloured, the cause is raspberry spur blight. If the surrounding bark appears normal then the most likely reason is frost. This damage is most likely when there has been an early mild spell followed by a frost at bud burst.

STRAWBERRY TORTRIX MOTH

A serious pest of Strawberries in some areas of Britain. Several leaves are joined together by silken threads. Inside this protective cover the ¼ in. green caterpillars feed. These spun leaves should be picked off and destroyed. If spraying is necessary apply Fenitrothion before flowering and repeat after picking.

LEAF SCORCH

Leaves develop brown edges which are sometimes torn and curled. Growth is stunted and the fruit is small. The cause is potash deficiency — water with Instant Bio immediately.

BLACKCURRANT RUST

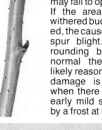

Yellow patches appear on the underside of Blackcurrant leaves in early summer. At the end of summer the leaves turn brown and fall. Spray with Dithane immediately after harvest.

RED-LEGGED WEEVIL

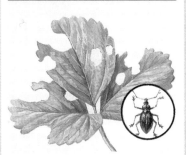

In parts of Britain this distinctive wingless weevil can be a serious pest of Raspberries and Strawberries. The weevils are rarely seen; they feed at night and drop to the ground when disturbed. Control is difficult.

APHID

Many aphids attack soft fruit and their effect can be serious. In some cases there is severe leaf distortion, but the main danger is due to the viruses they carry. Currants are affected by the **currant blister aphid,** producing coloured blisters. Both **lettuce aphid** and **gooseberry aphid** cause severe leaf-curling on Gooseberries. Two aphids attack Raspberries — the **rubus aphid** and the stem-coating **raspberry aphid.** Strawberries can be attacked by many species — the **shallot aphid** which can cripple the plant, and the **strawberry aphid.** In all cases spray with Long-last or Fenitrothion.

Blister aphid   Leaf-curling aphid   Stem-coating aphid

RED SPIDER MITE

Several mites attack soft fruit. The general symptoms are pale or bronze-coloured leaves and the presence of minute 'spiders' on the undersurface. The **red spider mite** infests Blackcurrants and Strawberries in hot summers. On Gooseberries the **bryobia mite** is a common pest, and defoliation is likely to occur in a severe attack. For both these mites spray with Long-last just after flowering if the weather is warm and settled. The **strawberry mite** is much more serious and much more difficult to control. Young leaves turn brown — older leaves are crinkled. Plants are stunted and the crown may die. Lift and burn infested plants.

Bryobia mite   Red spider mite   Strawberry mite

BLACKCURRANT EELWORM

The microscopic pests live on the young leaves and flowers within the bud. The infested buds fail to open, so the branches remain bare. There is no satisfactory method of control, but luckily it is uncommon. Attacks are worst after a wet autumn. Cut off and burn bare branches.

STRAWBERRY EELWORM

Several types of eelworm attack Strawberries and identification is difficult. Leaf stalks may be abnormally long and turn red ('red plant disease') or leaf and flower stalks may be short and thickened. There is no cure — dig up and burn infested plants. Do not replant for at least 5 years.

BIG BUD MITE

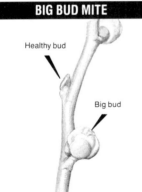

Healthy bud

Big bud

This gall mite is by far the most serious pest of Blackcurrants. Red Currants and Gooseberries are occasionally attacked. In late spring or early summer these microscopic mites are carried by wind or insects to the bushes. By July they have entered the buds, which swell and become less pointed. These 'big buds' eventually wither. Inspect the bushes carefully in winter. Pick off enlarged buds — dig out and burn badly infested plants.

BLOSSOM DROP

It is sometimes found that bushes which have blossomed well set little or no fruit. If the plants are healthy and not suffering from drought then there are two possible causes. Either frost occurred when the bushes were in flower, or pollination was defective due to either wet and cold weather or very dry air at blossom time.

FROST: STRAWBERRIES

Open Strawberry blooms are extremely sensitive to frost. The petals remain apparently unharmed but the central core turns black. Nothing can be done — the flowers wither and fall. The time to take action is before the frost occurs — cover the plants with newspaper if frost is forecast at blossom time.

AMERICAN MILDEW

American mildew is a crippling disease of Gooseberries. White powdery patches appear on the young leaves and shoots — later the fruit is affected. The mould changes from white to brown. This disease is encouraged by overcrowding — grow Gooseberries on an open site and prune regularly. Cut off diseased branches in September. Apply Supercarb next year when the first flowers open and repeat the spray twice at 14 day intervals. Blackcurrants are occasionally affected.

STRAWBERRY RHYNCHITES

Both Strawberries and Raspberries can be attacked. In May and June the stalks of blossom trusses are punctured, the unopened buds wither and occasionally fall. Strawberry rhynchites is easily recognised by its greenish metallic body. The damage is rarely serious.

REVERSION

Healthy   Reverted

cleft   no cleft

This virus disease causes a change in leaf shape. The basal cleft disappears, the main lobe has less than 5 main veins and 10 serrations. The flower buds are red rather than grey. The virus is spread by the big bud mite (page 97) and reverted plants steadily degenerate. Destroy badly diseased plants.

STRAWBERRY MILDEW

This is the commonest disease of Strawberries. Dark patches appear on the upper surface of the leaves, the infected foliage curling upwards to expose greyish mould below. Fruit may also be affected. Spray with Supercarb at 14 day intervals from the beginning of flowering until the fruit starts to colour.

BIRDS

Birds are a menace with all types of soft fruit when the berries or currants are ripening. At the bud stage Gooseberries are most at risk; in many gardens some or all of the dormant buds are stripped off by bullfinches during the winter months. The only really satisfactory answer is netting. Make sure the base of the net is well secured. If netting is not practical, wind cotton thread through the branches and delay pruning until the buds are breaking in the spring.

YELLOWTAIL MOTH

Hairy, colourful caterpillar which can cause a rash if handled. It is sometimes found on Raspberry canes, where it can cause partial skeletonisation if present in sufficient numbers. The yellowtail moth, however, is a solitary feeder and so spraying is rarely necessary. Just pick off and destroy.

GOOSEBERRY SAWFLY

1 in. spotted caterpillar

A serious pest of Gooseberry and Currant bushes which can cause complete defoliation in a severe attack. Identification is easy as the caterpillars generally feed round the edge of the leaf. Keep a careful watch for gooseberry sawfly from May onwards and spray with Fenitrothion or Malathion at the first sign of damage. There can be up to 4 broods a year, so a second spray may be necessary.

STRAWBERRY BLOSSOM WEEVIL

Both Strawberries and Raspberries can be attacked. The flower stalk is partially severed after eggs have been laid inside the flower bud, the unopened flower then withers and may fall. Blossom weevil is easily recognised by its greyish-black body. The damage is rarely serious.

CAPSID BUG

Both apple capsid and the common green capsid can cause severe damage. The small green bugs puncture the leaf surface, producing reddish-brown spots. As the leaves expand ragged brown-edged holes are formed. This pest can be a nuisance on all soft fruit, especially Currants and Gooseberries. Capsid bug is not an easy pest to control — spray with Long-last or Fenitrothion when the first flowers are about to open and repeat after the fruit has set.

MAGPIE MOTH

1¼ in. 'looper' caterpillar

This distinctively coloured caterpillar feeds on Gooseberry and Currant bushes in spring and early summer and can cause defoliation. Fortunately it is no longer common and is only likely to be troublesome in small sheltered gardens. If only a few caterpillars appear hand picking will give satisfactory control. Alternatively spray with Fenitrothion when the flowers are about to open.

LEAF MIDGE

A serious pest of Black-currants, the small maggots feeding on the young leaves at the shoot tips. The foliage becomes twisted, puckered and discoloured. Growth may be checked. This is a difficult pest to control; apply Long-last as soon as damage is first noticed.

CANE MIDGE

The tiny pink maggots feed under the outer layer of young Raspberry canes. Direct injury is slight, but the damaged tissue is suscep-tible to attack by serious diseases. Spray with Fenitro-thion if splits appear — repeat 2 weeks later.

DIE-BACK

The dying back of odd branches of Gooseberries is a frequent complaint — the cause is the grey mould fungus (see below). A branch suddenly dies — the foliage turns yellow and then it withers and falls. Grey mould may be seen. Remove affect-ed branches — paint with Arbrex.

VINE POWDERY MILDEW

White powdery patches appear on the leaves. This covering is often sparse so that browning of the leaf may be more noticeable than the white mould. Fruit is covered with a white powdery mould. Burn diseased leaves and wood. Apply Supercarb when disease is first seen, repeat at 14 day intervals.

SLUGS, SNAILS & BEETLES

Holes eaten in Strawberries may be due to slugs, snails or strawberry ground beetles. Attacks are worst in enclosed gardens. Fortunately these pests are controlled by methiocarb, the active ingredient of Slug Gard. Scatter pellets around plants.

CLUSTER CUP RUST

Minute yellow-edged pits ('cluster cups') appear on the large orange patches cover-ing infected fruit. This dis-ease occurs only where sedges are growing nearby. If it has been a problem in the past, spray with Dithane shortly before flowering.

BIRDS & SQUIRRELS

Animals are usually the cause when fruit is entirely devoured. Birds, such as blackbirds, will eat Straw-berries and squirrels are rapidly becoming the major pest of this crop in many areas. Deterrents are of limited use and the only answer is netting.

STRAWBERRY SEED BEETLE

These beetles are about ½ in. long, greyish, and very active. They bite at the seeds and the attached flesh so that the fruit is disfigured. Keep down weeds, clear away dead leaves and remove garden rubbish. Sprinkle Slug Gard around the plants.

RASPBERRY BEETLE

Raspberry beetle is the most serious pest of Raspberries, Loganberries and Black-berries as the ¼ in. grubs can soon ruin the crop. Spray Raspberries when the first fruits start to turn pink. Use Liquid Derris or Malathion — or Fenitrothion if you can wait 7 days before picking.

GREY MOULD (Botrytis)

This fluffy mould is destruc-tive to Raspberries, Straw-berries, Grapes and Currants in a wet summer. Remove mouldy plant material immediately, but the only answer in a humid season is to spray before it appears. Apply Supercarb when the first flowers open. Repeat twice at 14 day intervals.

Weed Control

Weeds are plants growing in the wrong place — last year's forgotten Tulip bulb growing up through this year's Wallflowers is a weed. Textbooks stress all the different ways in which weeds can harm the growth of garden plants — they steal water, plant foods, light and space plus harbouring pests and diseases. A greater problem than all of these well-publicised effects is the unsightly nature of weeds. Like an unpainted house, they give a neglected appearance ... and no gardener wants that.

So the menace of weeds must be tackled, and it must be tackled *quickly* before the weeds have taken hold. A wide variety of weedkillers have appeared to help in the battle, but they are not the only means of control.

ANNUAL WEEDS complete at least one life cycle during the season. They spread by seeding, and all fertile soils contain a large reservoir of annual weed seeds. The golden rule is that emerged annuals must be killed *before* seeding by hand pulling, hoeing or burning off with a contact weedkiller.

PERENNIAL WEEDS survive by means of underground stems or roots which act as storage organs over winter. The stems usually spread by creeping under the ground. The golden rule is that their leaves must be regularly removed to starve out the underground storage organs or else a translocated weedkiller must be used.

METHODS OF CONTROL

HAND PULLING

The oldest method of control and still a useful technique in certain situations. These include the removal of well-grown but easily uprooted annual weeds in beds and borders, the digging out of isolated deep-rooted weeds in the lawn and the eradication of weeds growing amongst the alpines in the rockery. A technique to consider where there are a few large weeds, but not when the problem is widespread and serious.

HOEING

The hoe is the traditional enemy of the weed, and despite all the advances of science it still remains the most important weedkilling technique around growing plants. It is much quicker than hand pulling, and will destroy large numbers of annual weeds if the soil surface is dry, the hoe blade is sharp and the depth of cut kept shallow. Not really effective against perennials — hoe at regular intervals to starve out roots.

MULCHING

Read the mulching section on page 76. Organic mulches will help to suppress annual weeds, but the use of a black polythene mulch for weed control is even more spectacular. A weed-infested patch can be covered, the surface hidden with bark chippings, gravel or peat, and no weeds will peep through for years.

FLAME GUNNING

An oversized blow torch for burning off the top growth of weeds and destroying surface seeds — once fairly popular but now largely replaced by quick-acting weedkillers. Like a flame gun, these weedkillers will scorch off top growth, but without the smell, smoke and inherent risks. A flame gun is still a good idea if a large weedy area in full flower has to be cleared.

DIGGING

Weed control begins at the digging stage. The roots of perennial weeds should be removed and burnt. The surface layer of annual weeds should be buried by inverting the spadeful of soil. This is not the end of the problem — weed seeds buried many years previously can be brought to the surface by the digging operation.

USING HERBICIDES

During the past 30 years chemical weedkillers (herbicides) have revolutionised farming and commercial horticulture. They have also improved the lot of the amateur gardener, but not to the same extent. Unlike the farmer, the home-owner usually has a collection of different plants in the weed-infested area and few weedkillers are safe as an overall spray on a wide range of plants. Another important worry is that not all weeds are killed and they may take a long time to die — no great worry to the farmer but a point of concern to the gardener who is more concerned with appearances than crop yields.

Weedkillers have become extremely popular in those areas of the garden where no other satisfactory method of control is available (e.g paths) and where specific plants are grown (e.g fruit trees and Rose beds).

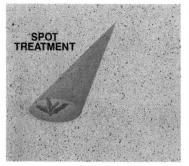

SPOT TREATMENT

Application to a single weed or a group of weeds. Examples are painting the leaves of a perennial weed growing next to a Rose with a translocated weedkiller, and the covering of a deep-rooted lawn weed with a spoonful of Lawn Sand. It is useful for isolated weeds not killed by a previous treatment.

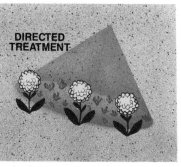

DIRECTED TREATMENT

Application to a group of weeds, great care being taken to avoid contact with nearby garden plants which would be susceptible to the weedkiller. Use a watering can with a dribble bar on a still day. An example is the use of paraquat/diquat in the vegetable garden.

OVERALL TREATMENT

Application to the whole area affected by weeds. The weedkiller may be a non-selective one where the area is either a path or land not bearing plants, or it may be a selective one (for example a lawn weedkiller) where the land bears plants which are resistant to the chemical.

HERBICIDE TYPES

A **selective weedkiller** damages only a limited range of plants — used when the garden plants in question are resistant and some or all of the important weeds are susceptible. Example — lawn weedkillers

A **non-selective weedkiller** damages garden plants as well as weeds — used on uncultivated land. Some can be applied by directed treatment to beds and borders. Example — paraquat/diquat

FOLIAGE-APPLIED WEEDKILLER
A chemical which enters the plant through the leaves. Obviously, weed foliage must be present

SOIL-APPLIED WEEDKILLER
A chemical which enters the plant through the roots. These herbicides have a **residual action**, remaining active in the soil for weeks or even years, depending on the chemical, concentration, soil type etc. They tend to be unspectacular in action, killing the weeds as they germinate below ground

CONTACT ACTION
Chemical only kills those parts which are touched, so complete leaf cover is required. Excellent for annual weeds, acting as a chemical hoe. Translocated action is very limited or absent, so there is no long-lasting effect on perennial weeds

TRANSLOCATED ACTION
Chemical moves in the sap stream, so roots as well as leaves are affected. Complete leaf cover is not required. Effective against many perennial weeds, but action is often slow and results are governed by timing, weather etc

AVOIDING PROBLEMS
● Make sure that the product you buy is recommended for the specific purpose you have in mind
● Keep a watering can specifically for herbicides
● Apply herbicides on a still day
● Read page 85

Herbicide	Foliage applied		Soil applied	Uses	Notes
	Contact	Translocated			
ALLOXYDIM-SODIUM		★		A,B	Grass killer used when grassy weeds are actively growing amongst flowers, shrubs & Roses. No persistence in soil
AMINOTRIAZOLE		★		C,D	Wide-range herbicide effective against grassy as well as non-grassy weeds. Mixed with soil-acting herbicides to make path weedkillers
ATRAZINE			★	C,D	Very similar in composition and activity to simazine — used as a substitute in path weedkiller mixtures. Emerged weeds are not killed
2, 4–D		★		C,D	Hormone-type weedkiller — effective against many annual and perennial weeds but not grasses. Mixed with dicamba etc to produce Brushwood Killer. Avoid drift
DALAPON		★		A,C,D	Grass killer used in spring or autumn around fruit (take care) or on paths and wasteland. Lasts about 2 months
DICAMBA		★		C,D	Hormone-type weedkiller — effective against many annual and perennial weeds but not grasses. Sold as a mixture with 2,4–D etc to produce Brushwood Killer. Avoid drift
DICHLOBENIL			★	A,D	Formulated as a granule — use in early spring around fruit & shrubs (take care) or on paths. Lasts up to a year
GLYPHOSATE		★		A,B,C	Very popular — effective against annual and perennial weeds but acts slowly. Use as a directed spray around growing plants. No persistence in soil
MCPA		★		C,D	Hormone-type weedkiller — effective against many annual and perennial weeds but not grasses. Sold in mixtures with simazine and aminotriazole
PARAQUAT/DIQUAT	★			A,B,C,D	Very popular — effective against annual weeds, which are killed in a few days. Use as a directed spray around growing plants. No persistence in soil
PROPACHLOR			★	A	Formulated as a granule — used on moist soil around resistant plants. Emerged weeds are not killed. Lasts about 2 months
SIMAZINE			★	A,C,D	Mixed with aminotriazole as path weedkiller — use at low strength as a long-lasting annual weedkiller around Roses and some shrubs
SODIUM CHLORATE		★	★	C,D	Old-fashioned method of killing a very wide range of weeds on wasteland and paths. Effective and long-lasting, but there is a risk to nearby plants

KEY
★ Main or only mode of action
A Use around growing plants
B Use shortly before planting or sowing
C Use on neglected areas
D Use on paths and drives

See **THE LAWN EXPERT** *for full details on weed control in turf*

A Gallery of Garden Weeds

AEGOPODIUM PODAGRARIA
(ground-elder) Ⓟ

AGROPYRON REPENS
(common couch) Ⓟ

ANAGALLIS ARVENSIS
(scarlet pimpernel) Ⓐ

CALYSTEGIA SEPIUM
(hedge bindweed) Ⓟ

CAPSELLA BURSA-PASTORIS
(shepherd's purse) Ⓐ

CARDAMINE HIRSUTA
(hairy bittercress) Ⓐ

CERASTIUM HOLOSTEOIDES
(common mouse-ear) Ⓟ

CHAMAENERION ANGUSTIFOLIUM
(rosebay willowherb) Ⓟ

CHENOPODIUM ALBUM
(fat-hen) Ⓐ

CIRSIUM ARVENSE
(creeping thistle) Ⓟ

CIRSIUM VULGARE
(spear thistle) Ⓑ

CONVOLVULUS ARVENSIS
(field bindweed) Ⓟ

EQUISETUM ARVENSE
(field horsetail) Ⓟ

EUPHORBIA HELIOSCOPIA
(sun spurge) Ⓐ

FUMARIA OFFICINALIS
(common fumitory) Ⓐ

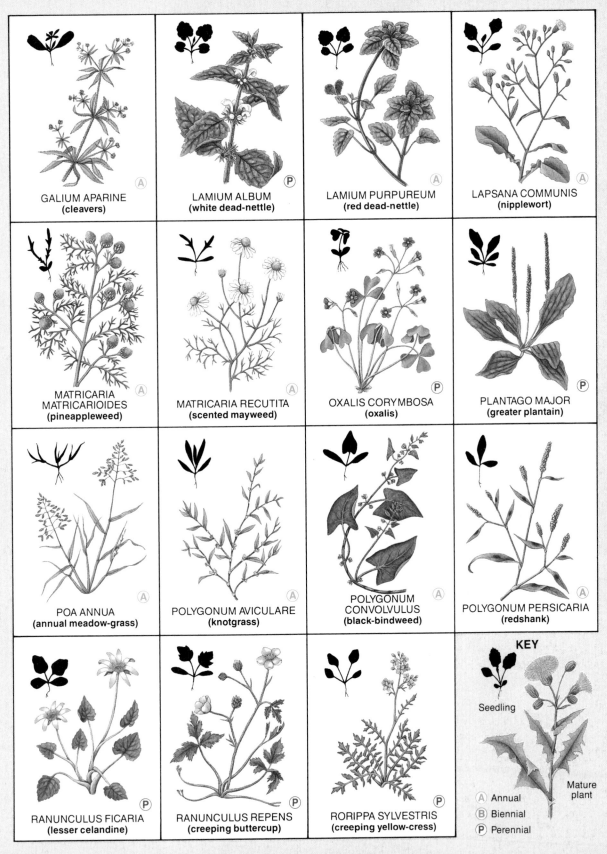

GALIUM APARINE
(cleavers) Ⓐ

LAMIUM ALBUM
(white dead-nettle) Ⓟ

LAMIUM PURPUREUM
(red dead-nettle) Ⓐ

LAPSANA COMMUNIS
(nipplewort) Ⓐ

MATRICARIA
MATRICARIOIDES
(pineappleweed) Ⓐ

MATRICARIA RECUTITA
(scented mayweed) Ⓐ

OXALIS CORYMBOSA
(oxalis) Ⓟ

PLANTAGO MAJOR
(greater plantain) Ⓟ

POA ANNUA
(annual meadow-grass) Ⓐ

POLYGONUM AVICULARE
(knotgrass) Ⓐ

POLYGONUM
CONVOLVULUS
(black-bindweed) Ⓐ

POLYGONUM PERSICARIA
(redshank) Ⓐ

RANUNCULUS FICARIA
(lesser celandine) Ⓟ

RANUNCULUS REPENS
(creeping buttercup) Ⓟ

RORIPPA SYLVESTRIS
(creeping yellow-cress) Ⓟ

KEY

Seedling

Mature
plant

Ⓐ Annual
Ⓑ Biennial
Ⓟ Perennial

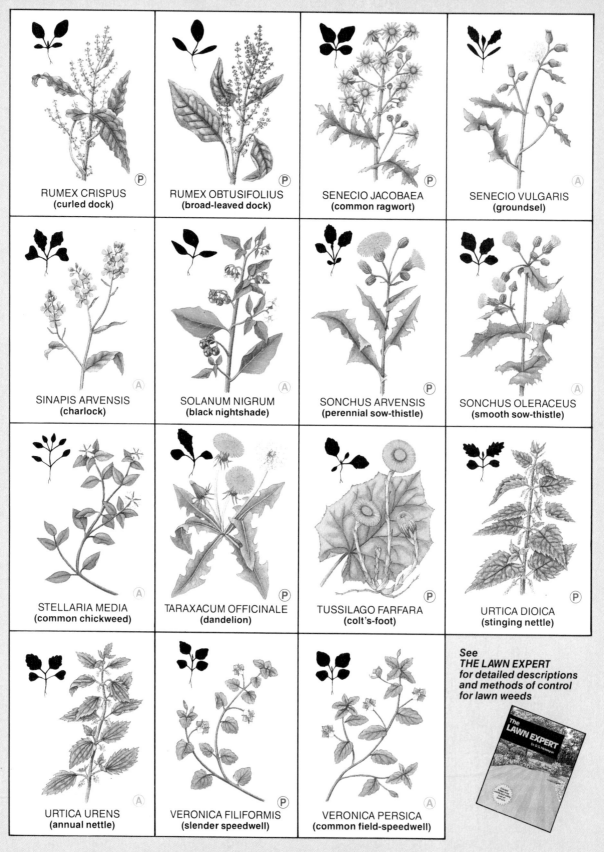

RUMEX CRISPUS
(curled dock) (P)

RUMEX OBTUSIFOLIUS
(broad-leaved dock) (P)

SENECIO JACOBAEA
(common ragwort) (P)

SENECIO VULGARIS
(groundsel) (A)

SINAPIS ARVENSIS
(charlock) (A)

SOLANUM NIGRUM
(black nightshade) (A)

SONCHUS ARVENSIS
(perennial sow-thistle) (P)

SONCHUS OLERACEUS
(smooth sow-thistle) (A)

STELLARIA MEDIA
(common chickweed) (A)

TARAXACUM OFFICINALE
(dandelion) (P)

TUSSILAGO FARFARA
(colt's-foot) (P)

URTICA DIOICA
(stinging nettle) (P)

URTICA URENS
(annual nettle) (A)

VERONICA FILIFORMIS
(slender speedwell) (P)

VERONICA PERSICA
(common field-speedwell) (A)

See
THE LAWN EXPERT
for detailed descriptions
and methods of control
for lawn weeds

The
LAWN EXPERT
Dr D.G. Hessayon

CHAPTER 8
GREENHOUSE GARDENING

It is usual for books on growing under glass and for the catalogues of greenhouse manufacturers to begin with a great hymn of praise. Any garden, however small, can house a glass structure of some type and any greenhouse, however small, will add a new dimension to your gardening.

All sorts of shapes and a wide range of sizes are available, but the fundamental difference between one type and another is the minimum temperature at which it is kept. The cold house is the simplest — no artificial means of heat are provided and so in the depths of winter the temperature can fall below freezing point (32°F). Despite this vulnerability to frost, the cold house extends the growing season by trapping the sun's heat during the day. Here you can work protected from the elements with plants which are sheltered from wind and rain and can enjoy day temperatures which are appreciably higher than the warmth outdoors. Tomatoes are the favourite crop — during the rest of the year there are cuttings to take, seeds to raise and vegetables (Lettuce, French Beans etc) to force. Melons, Grapes, Aubergines, Okra and Peppers can be grown at home — back to the great hymn of praise of the greenhouse textbook!

In fact, the range of the cold house is limited. You cannot grow frost-sensitive plants between late autumn and mid spring unless you provide heat. The usual practice is to turn it into a cool house (minimum temperature 45°F) and so open a whole new world. Now 'greenhouse plants' can be grown — Palms, Orchids, Geraniums, Fuchsias and so on. Half-hardy bedding plants can be raised for the garden and a year-round display of blooms can be created for either greenhouse or living room. The installation of a heater transforms growing under glass into a year-round hobby.

An average-sized house (8 ft long x 6 ft wide) will cost you £150–200 when staging etc has been fitted. Before making this investment, carefully consider the points not made in the textbooks. Constant attention is needed — and this means every day in summer. There is watering, feeding, ventilating, misting and so on. There is also the fuel — keeping an 8 x 6 house at a minimum of 45°F will cost £60–90 during an average winter.

The purpose of the previous paragraph is not to discourage you — it is to avoid adding to the number of greenhouses owned by people with limited time to spare who after a year or two allow the structure to become a home for pots, boxes and various pieces of household equipment.

On a much more encouraging note, most people who buy a greenhouse run out of space for all the exciting things they want to grow. For them there is a different warning. If you have the time, money and are keen on growing things — buy the next size larger than you have planned! Keep it as a cool house — the attraction of having a warm house (minimum temperature 55°–60°F) for exotics is obvious, but your fuel bill will be about £300 per year. Stove houses (minimum temperature 65°F) have almost disappeared.

SITE & ERECTION

- Check with the authorities to see if permission is required.

- Choose a sunny site — never place a greenhouse under a tree. Try to place it close to the house — electric wiring is costly and carrying other forms of fuel to the far end of the garden is a chore in winter.

- Do not site the greenhouse close to the road or a play area — replacing broken panes is always annoying.

- Choose a well-drained site if you plan to grow in border soil. This does not apply, of course, if you propose to use only pots and growing bags.

- The central pathway should run East–West.

- Level and firm the soil a few weeks before erection. Your new greenhouse will arrive with full instructions — follow them exactly.

- Foundations should not be required if the house is 8 x 6 or less. If a concrete base is recommended, follow the instruction leaflet.

- Make sure the frame is perfectly square before glazing. Don't try to use the glass to square up aluminium glazing bars.

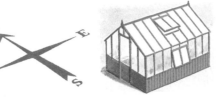

CHOOSING A GREENHOUSE

TRADITIONAL

Vertical sides and an even span roof. Use of space and heat is efficient, and enclosed lower part cuts down winter heat loss. Choose an all-glass model for growing-bag and border crops.

LEAN-TO

Useful for a south- or west-facing wall. Bricks store heat during the day — fuel bill is reduced. Best choice for a conservatory — an interconnecting door makes it part of the house.

THREE-QUARTER SPAN

Lighter and more airy than a lean-to — useful for growing wall plants such as Vines and Figs. Expensive, however, so the choice should be between a traditional house or a lean-to.

DUTCH LIGHT

Sloping sides and an even span roof — angled glass makes it warmer and brighter than a traditional house. Also more stable, but supporting upright plants from floor to roof is more difficult.

POLYGONAL

Many (6–9) sides — attractive when filled with pot plants and sited close to the house. Expensive, however, and not a good buy if you want maximum space for your money.

DOME

Three advantages — attractive appearance when filled with flowers, maximum stability and maximum light absorption. Major drawback is unsuitability for growing tall crops effectively.

SIZE

A wide range of sizes is available. The standard sizes are from 6 to 20 ft long in widths of 6, 8 or 10 ft. The one you choose will depend largely on the money and space available — remember annual running costs as well as the initial outlay. The most popular size is 8 ft long and 6 ft wide — if you plan to have staging on both sides then choose an 8 ft wide model. If you plan to grow Tomatoes, the height to the eaves should be at least 5 ft and the ridge height about 7 ft. Somewhat surprisingly, it is more difficult to control the environment in a small house than in a large one. Increased size reduces the problem of draughts and sudden fluctuations in temperature.

STRUCTURE

Aluminium has taken over from wood as the most popular building material. It is cheaper, easier to maintain and the thin glazing bars mean more light within the house. The drawbacks are quite minor — aluminium houses lose slightly more heat at night than wooden ones and the metal frame is received in bits and so construction is rather more difficult.
Wood is considered by most people to be more attractive. Buy Western Red Cedar, Teak or Oak. Cheap wood must be painted regularly or be treated with a long-lasting preservative.
Galvanised iron houses are no longer popular. Paint with a rust-destroying paint such as Bio Rusty immediately, as the protective coat of zinc becomes scratched after a few years.

GLAZING

Buy **glass**. It is denser, heavier and not as safe as plastic but the advantages far outweigh the drawbacks. More light enters, less heat escapes and it is easier to shade and clean.
Polythene and **PVC** have a limited life — if you do choose a plastic, make sure that it is UV stabilised. Glass has one major problem — it will shatter if hit by a heavy object. If you are near the road or a play zone, consider **polycarbonate** sheet. It has many of the advantages of glass but is light and unbreakable. Unfortunately it scratches easily and is more expensive.

DOORS

Hinged or sliding — both types have their disciples. Sliding doors can be used as an extra ventilator and they don't slam shut. But hinged doors generally fit better and so are less likely to be a source of draughts.

VENTILATORS

The ventilators on the standard model are usually inadequate. You need both a roof and side ventilator — their total area should be 10–20% of the total floor area. Louvred side ventilators are better than the traditional hinged types, but make sure that they close properly.

OPTIONAL EXTRAS

One or two of the so-called optional extras are in fact essential. An example is **staging**. This is required for at least part of the house — constantly stooping to ground level to tend to the pot plants would add backache to greenhouse gardening. Slatted wooden staging about 2½ ft above the ground is the traditional form of bench. A gap should be left between the back of solid staging and the side of the greenhouse to allow free circulation of air. Nowadays you can buy metal staging and shelves as an optional extra. Collapsible types enable you to grow bedding plants at a convenient height in spring and then you can dismantle the staging in summer to grow Tomatoes.

A **power point** is another essential if you are going to take greenhouse growing seriously. Your source of heat for a cool house may not be electricity, but you will need a 3-pin point for a heated propagator (see page 110). Lighting is also a useful optional extra to enable you to work in winter.

Automated equipment is available. The automatic ventilator starts to open when the temperature reaches 70°F, the automatic blinds start to unroll when the light meter records unacceptable brightness and the automatic watering system provides a regular supply of water to the plants. Only you can decide whether the high cost for such wizardry is worthwhile.

HEATING

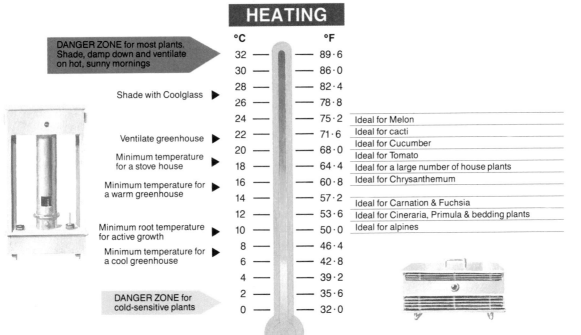

DANGER ZONE for most plants. Shade, damp down and ventilate on hot, sunny mornings

Shade with Coolglass ▶

Ventilate greenhouse ▶

Minimum temperature for a stove house ▶

Minimum temperature for a warm greenhouse ▶

Minimum root temperature for active growth ▶

Minimum temperature for a cool greenhouse ▶

DANGER ZONE for cold-sensitive plants

°C	°F	
32	89·6	
30	86·0	
28	82·4	
26	78·8	
24	75·2	Ideal for Melon
22	71·6	Ideal for cacti
20	68·0	Ideal for Cucumber
18	64·4	Ideal for Tomato
		Ideal for a large number of house plants
16	60·8	Ideal for Chrysanthemum
14	57·2	Ideal for Carnation & Fuchsia
12	53·6	Ideal for Cineraria, Primula & bedding plants
10	50·0	Ideal for alpines
8	46·4	
6	42·8	
4	39·2	
2	35·6	
0	32·0	

The unheated or cold greenhouse is a place for Tomatoes and Cucumbers in summer, Chrysanthemums in autumn and then alpines, bulbs and cacti in winter. Heating is needed to extend its range, and you will require a method of maintaining a minimum temperature of 45°F (cool greenhouse) in the depths of winter. Forget about a warm greenhouse unless you are a greenhouse fanatic — to maintain a minimum of 60°F costs 4 times as much as heating to 45°F.

Make sure that the heater you choose is sufficiently large to heat the greenhouse to 45°F when the temperature is only 20°F outside. There are many formulae to calculate heater size — use the following simple one:

	Size of heater required
Surface area* × 33	British Thermal Units (BTUs) per hour
Surface area* × 10	Watts

*see page 110 for calculation

Examples
8 ft × 6 ft house: 208 sq. ft of glass
requires 6864 BTUs/hr (paraffin, oil or gas heater)
2080 watts (electric heater)
12 ft × 8 ft house: 324 sq. ft of glass
requires 10692 BTUs/hr (paraffin, oil or gas heater)
3240 watts (electric heater)

The danger of winter cold can be minimised by keeping the compost or soil on the dry side — plants in wet soil are prone to damage. Keep the glass clean to ensure maximum entry of the sun's rays — seal cracks to prevent draughts. Lining the inside of the greenhouse with polythene is a simple form of double glazing — fuel bills can be reduced by 15 per cent.

In the late spring and summer the problem is reversed — the temperature has to be reduced to keep the plants cool. Dry heat is more dangerous than moist heat, and several interlinked methods are used to lower temperatures. Damping down (spraying the floors with water on warm summer mornings) and misting the plants lowers the temperature when the house is adequately ventilated. When temperatures continually rise above 80°F it is essential to shade the glass (see page 110).

Fix a maximum/minimum thermometer — it should be set up on the north-facing side at eye level. Remember that plants are harmed by widely fluctuating temperatures and the chance of disease is increased.

Study the range of greenhouse heaters available before making your choice. They come in a wide range of shapes and sizes and the fuel used governs the running costs. Electricity is the most convenient but is also the dearest. Natural gas is the cheapest, and paraffin lies in between these two extremes.

ELECTRIC FAN HEATER The popular choice for a small greenhouse. There are many advantages — no fumes, no transport of fuel and good thermostatic control. These benefits are shared with other electric heaters — fan heaters have the added benefit of circulating the air quickly — warm air in winter and cool air in summer. Place centrally — keep away from delicate foliage.

ELECTRIC TUBULAR HEATER The preferred type for a large house or where high temperatures are required. A bank of 2 or 3 tubes run around the sides of the house, providing a heat which is much more evenly spread than with a fan heater.

CONVECTOR HEATER AND NIGHT-STORAGE HEATER Widely used for home heating, but not really suitable for the greenhouse.

PARAFFIN HEATER Cheap to buy and cheap to run, but the advantages stop there. Carbon dioxide is produced, which can be beneficial, but so is water vapour and this increases the risk of disease in winter. Buy a blue-flame model and trim the wick regularly. The paraffin heater is useful to keep the chill off a small house but is not really a good idea for maintaining a temperature of 45°F. However, it is a useful standby to have on hand in case of a power failure.

NATURAL GAS AND BOTTLED GAS HEATER These flueless heaters have their disciples, but there are drawbacks. As with a paraffin heater, water vapour can be a problem. There are also marked temperature differences in the house. Plants can be damaged by the fumes once the temperature exceeds 40°–45°F, and you must provide the recommended ventilation.

BOILER HEATER The traditional type of greenhouse heater — once the standard and now very much the exception. Water is heated by solid fuel, gas or oil and the hot water circulates along horizontal pipes around the sides of the house. Excellent heat distribution, but costly to instal.

LINKED CENTRAL HEATING Linking the greenhouse to the domestic heating system seems like an excellent idea if the greenhouse is a lean-to or a conservatory. However, most home central heating systems operate during the day and switch off at night — the wrong way round for the greenhouse.

SOIL-HEATING CABLE An electric heating cable on the staging or in the soil is economical — the heat is directed exactly where you want it.

USING A GREENHOUSE

Far too many greenhouses are used to grow a few Tomato plants in summer and a tray or two of seedlings in spring. For the rest of the year there is an array of empty pots, bags of fertilizer, trowels and assorted tools. Make your greenhouse earn its keep every day of the year — below is a calendar to illustrate the many ways you can use an average-sized house.

COLD GREENHOUSE: never heated Minimum temperature below 32°F (0°C)

WINTER

SOW Onion, Lettuce, Radish, Beetroot, Turnip, Carrot
SOW IN A PROPAGATOR Tomato, Begonia, Pelargonium
BRING IN Bowls of spring-flowering bulbs, Strawberry plants
TAKE Chrysanthemum cuttings
POT UP Fuchsia, Pelargonium, Azalea, autumn-sown annuals
GROW Hardy shrubs, alpines in pots
DISPLAY Camellia, Heather
CHECK Dahlia tubers and Chrysanthemum stools — protect from frost

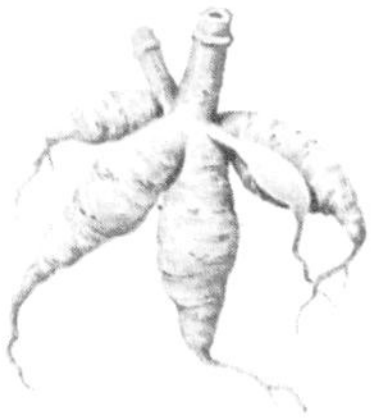

DECEMBER

JANUARY

FEBRUARY

SPRING

SOW Carrot, Lettuce, Radish, Beetroot, Cucumber, French Bean, half-hardy annuals
SOW IN A PROPAGATOR (March) Tomato, Capsicum, Aubergine, French Bean
PLANT (early May) Tomato, Cucumber, Aubergine, Capsicum, Melon
TAKE Dahlia, Fuchsia, Pelargonium cuttings
HARDEN OFF Bedding plants
HARVEST Lettuce, Radish, Beetroot, Carrot, Turnip, Strawberry
DISPLAY Spring-flowering bulbs, hardy shrubs, house plants and flowering pot plants

MARCH

APRIL

MAY

SUMMER

SOW Lettuce, Radish, biennials, French Bean
TAKE Semi-ripe cuttings
HARVEST Tomato, Cucumber, Lettuce, Radish, French Bean, Capsicum, Melon, Aubergine, Carrot
DISPLAY House plants and flowering pot plants, summer greenhouse bulbs

JUNE

JULY

AUGUST

AUTUMN

SOW Lettuce, Radish, annuals, Onion
BRING IN Azalea, Pot Chrysanthemum, Fuchsia, Pelargonium
PLANT Peach, Grape Vine, spring-flowering bulbs in bowls
GROW Spring annuals in pots
STORE Dahlia tubers and Chrysanthemum stools
HARVEST Lettuce, Radish, Tomato, Capsicum, Aubergine, Cucumber, Melon, Peach, Grape
DISPLAY Pot Chrysanthemum, house plants and flowering pot plants

SEPTEMBER

OCTOBER

NOVEMBER

COOL GREENHOUSE: heated during the colder months
Minimum temperature 45°F (7°C)

This is the best general-purpose greenhouse. Instal a maximum/minimum thermometer and try to keep the temperature within the range shown here:

70°F   45°F   80°F   60°F

WINTER   SUMMER

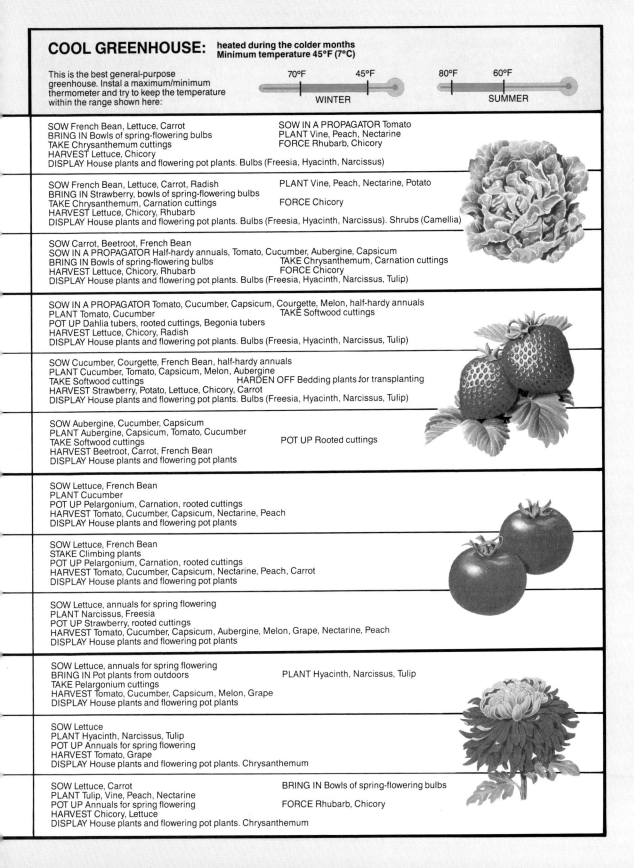

SOW French Bean, Lettuce, Carrot
BRING IN Bowls of spring-flowering bulbs
TAKE Chrysanthemum cuttings
HARVEST Lettuce, Chicory
DISPLAY House plants and flowering pot plants. Bulbs (Freesia, Hyacinth, Narcissus)
SOW IN A PROPAGATOR Tomato
PLANT Vine, Peach, Nectarine
FORCE Rhubarb, Chicory

SOW French Bean, Lettuce, Carrot, Radish
BRING IN Strawberry, bowls of spring-flowering bulbs
TAKE Chrysanthemum, Carnation cuttings
HARVEST Lettuce, Chicory, Rhubarb
DISPLAY House plants and flowering pot plants. Bulbs (Freesia, Hyacinth, Narcissus). Shrubs (Camellia)
PLANT Vine, Peach, Nectarine, Potato
FORCE Chicory

SOW Carrot, Beetroot, French Bean
SOW IN A PROPAGATOR Half-hardy annuals, Tomato, Cucumber, Aubergine, Capsicum
BRING IN Bowls of spring-flowering bulbs
HARVEST Lettuce, Chicory, Rhubarb
DISPLAY House plants and flowering pot plants. Bulbs (Freesia, Hyacinth, Narcissus, Tulip)
TAKE Chrysanthemum, Carnation cuttings
FORCE Chicory

SOW IN A PROPAGATOR Tomato, Cucumber, Capsicum, Courgette, Melon, half-hardy annuals
PLANT Tomato, Cucumber
POT UP Dahlia tubers, rooted cuttings, Begonia tubers
HARVEST Lettuce, Chicory, Radish
DISPLAY House plants and flowering pot plants. Bulbs (Freesia, Hyacinth, Narcissus, Tulip)
TAKE Softwood cuttings

SOW Cucumber, Courgette, French Bean, half-hardy annuals
PLANT Cucumber, Tomato, Capsicum, Melon, Aubergine
TAKE Softwood cuttings
HARVEST Strawberry, Potato, Lettuce, Chicory, Carrot
DISPLAY House plants and flowering pot plants. Bulbs (Freesia, Hyacinth, Narcissus, Tulip)
HARDEN OFF Bedding plants for transplanting

SOW Aubergine, Cucumber, Capsicum
PLANT Aubergine, Capsicum, Tomato, Cucumber
TAKE Softwood cuttings
HARVEST Beetroot, Carrot, French Bean
DISPLAY House plants and flowering pot plants
POT UP Rooted cuttings

SOW Lettuce, French Bean
PLANT Cucumber
POT UP Pelargonium, Carnation, rooted cuttings
HARVEST Tomato, Cucumber, Capsicum, Nectarine, Peach
DISPLAY House plants and flowering pot plants

SOW Lettuce, French Bean
STAKE Climbing plants
POT UP Pelargonium, Carnation, rooted cuttings
HARVEST Tomato, Cucumber, Capsicum, Nectarine, Peach, Carrot
DISPLAY House plants and flowering pot plants

SOW Lettuce, annuals for spring flowering
PLANT Narcissus, Freesia
POT UP Strawberry, rooted cuttings
HARVEST Tomato, Cucumber, Capsicum, Aubergine, Melon, Grape, Nectarine, Peach
DISPLAY House plants and flowering pot plants

SOW Lettuce, annuals for spring flowering
BRING IN Pot plants from outdoors
TAKE Pelargonium cuttings
HARVEST Tomato, Cucumber, Capsicum, Melon, Grape
DISPLAY House plants and flowering pot plants
PLANT Hyacinth, Narcissus, Tulip

SOW Lettuce
PLANT Hyacinth, Narcissus, Tulip
POT UP Annuals for spring flowering
HARVEST Tomato, Grape
DISPLAY House plants and flowering pot plants. Chrysanthemum

SOW Lettuce, Carrot
PLANT Tulip, Vine, Peach, Nectarine
POT UP Annuals for spring flowering
HARVEST Chicory, Lettuce
DISPLAY House plants and flowering pot plants. Chrysanthemum
BRING IN Bowls of spring-flowering bulbs

FORCE Rhubarb, Chicory

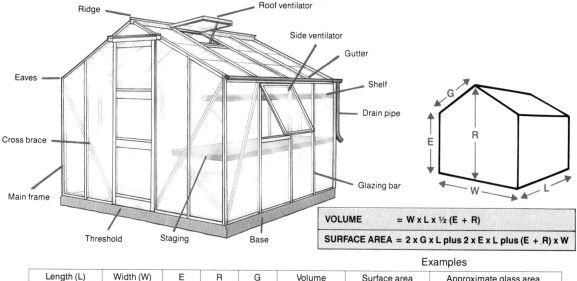

VOLUME	$= W \times L \times \frac{1}{2}(E + R)$
SURFACE AREA	$= 2 \times G \times L$ plus $2 \times E \times L$ plus $(E + R) \times W$

Examples

Length (L)	Width (W)	E	R	G	Volume	Surface area	Approximate glass area
6½ ft	4½ ft	5 ft	7 ft	3 ft	175 cu. ft	158 sq. ft	150 sq. ft
8 ft	6 ft	5 ft	7 ft	3½ ft	288 cu. ft	208 sq. ft	195 sq. ft
8 ft	8 ft	5 ft	7 ft	4½ ft	384 cu. ft	248 sq. ft	235 sq. ft
10 ft	8 ft	5 ft	7 ft	4½ ft	480 cu. ft	286 sq. ft	270 sq. ft
12 ft	8 ft	5 ft	7 ft	4½ ft	576 cu. ft	324 sq. ft	305 sq. ft

PROPAGATING

Cuttings require a moist and reasonably warm atmosphere in order to root satisfactorily. Seeds of some important greenhouse crops, including Cucumber and Tomato, require a temperature of 65°–75°F in order to germinate satisfactorily. Obviously it would be ridiculous to create these conditions throughout the greenhouse — a heated propagator is the answer.

A propagator is a container with a transparent cover. Choose one heated by electricity rather than by paraffin, and make sure that it is large enough for your needs. There are large mini-greenhouses in which you can keep tropical plants under stovehouse conditions, but you will probably require something simpler — a propagator with a thermostatically-controlled base which will hold a couple of seed trays.

VENTILATION

Greenhouse plants are living things which require fresh air. Ventilation supplies fresh air as well as reducing the air temperature. Strong air currents, however, should be avoided — on blustery days ventilate on the side away from the wind.

Ventilation is required almost all year round. In winter opening the roof ventilator an inch or so for a few hours around midday is sufficient, but do not open up the house if the weather is frosty. In spring more ventilation will be required and in summer the ventilators should be open from morning until near sunset. The side ventilators must also be used as about 8 air changes per hour are required.

Nowadays automatic ventilation systems and electric fans linked to ventilators can be used to circulate fresh air. But for most of us, ventilation remains a manual skill to be acquired by practice. Too much can reduce plant growth — too little can allow temperatures to rise dangerously high. As a guide when growing Tomatoes, open the ventilators when the temperature reaches 70°F.

PLANTING

Once there were just 2 ways of growing plants under glass — either in pots or in the border soil. Flowering plants such as Chrysanthemum or Carnation were grown in 3 ft wide beds, and in large greenhouses there were shrubs such as Camellia and Hydrangea in the borders. Vines and Figs, Cucumbers and Tomatoes — all were popular greenhouse border plants.

The problem is that soils can become 'crop sick' when the same type is planted year after year. Yields diminish and disease attacks increase alarmingly. When this happens you have to choose from 3 courses of action. You can change the soil, sterilise it or change over to the modern technique of growing bag cultivation.

Growing bags have revolutionised greenhouse practice. They are consistent and sterile, and capable of giving high yields ... but you must follow the instructions carefully. The rules for watering and feeding are quite different from the way one cares for plants in border soil.

LIGHT & SHADE

Your greenhouse in winter will be short of light. Make sure that the glass is kept clean, and greenhouse hobbyists can instal electric lighting to extend day-length.

Spring is the best time, when your greenhouse becomes a warm sun trap. But in summer it can become a death trap for plants — many plants are harmed when temperatures stay over 90°F. Some form of sun screen is essential, and roller blinds of wooden slats, hessian or plastic are an obvious answer. For the keen grower there are automatic blinds controlled by photo-electric cells.

Another way to protect your plants from sun scorch is to paint or spray the outside of the glass with an electrostatic shading material such as Coolglass. This is not removed by wind or rain but can be easily wiped off with a duster during dull spells or at the end of the summer. When using shading materials you will need to know the approximate surface area of the greenhouse — see above.

FEEDING

As clearly described on pages 16–21, plants require food to keep healthy. With a high-yielding crop, such as Tomatoes or Cucumbers, this need is even more pronounced in order to obtain a good crop of full-size fruit. Commercial peat-based composts contain essential nutrients, but these last for only about 6–8 weeks after planting. After this period regular feeding is essential. The usual technique is to use a soluble fertilizer such as Instant Bio which is diluted and applied through a watering can. Foliar feeding is an interesting technique which can be used when root feeding is ineffective because of disease or injury.

POTS & POTTING

Plastic pots are not just substitutes for clay ones. There are a number of advantages — they are lighter, more durable and easier to clean. They need less water, but there is an increased danger of water-logging. Peat, paper and whalehide pots are available, but they should only be temporary homes for plants until the final potting up or planting out stage.

Learn to recognise when a plant is pot-bound. Growth is slow, even when the plant is fed regularly in spring and summer. Check by spreading the fingers of the left hand over the soil surface. Invert and gently knock the rim of the pot on the staging and then lift off the pot. If there is a matted mass of roots around the soil ball, it is pot-bound and repotting is necessary.

Never use ordinary garden soil for filling pots. Use a peat-based or soil-based compost and never jump from a small pot to a very large one when repotting. If you do the new compost may well become sodden and new root growth will be inhibited. Use a pot which is only one or two sizes larger than the present one.

Put a layer of compost in the bottom of the new pot and place the plant on top of it. Fill around the soil ball with fresh compost, leaving a ½–1½ in. space between the compost level and the rim of the pot. Water carefully and keep in the shade for about a week.

PESTS & DISEASES

The warm and moist conditions in a greenhouse encourage the rapid spread of plant pests and diseases. Troubles often begin under the leaves where they can multiply unnoticed until a serious infestation has built up. Sterile compost plus correct heating, watering and ventilation will help to maintain strong and healthy plants, but action at the first sign of trouble is necessary.

Smokes are available for the control of both pests and diseases. Choose an evening when there is no wind and the foliage is dry. Close all ventilators before igniting the smoke and then shut the door. Ventilate the house next morning. In addition to smokes there are many insecticidal and fungicidal sprays. Read Chapter 7, and make sure that any material you use under glass is recommended for greenhouses.

WATERING

A greenhouse is a rainless place and so the plants must rely on you for water. In summer plants may need watering twice a day — in winter they may require water only once a fortnight.

Water with care. Do not give daily dribbles so that the soil never dries out. The time to water is when the soil or compost is on the dry side, and then water thoroughly. Growing bags have their own special rules — follow the maker's instructions.

Another tip is to water to the weather. Plants need much more water on a sunny day than on a cloudy one. For example, a 3 ft Tomato plant loses only ½ pint on a dull day, but this rises to 2½ pints on a sunny day. Water in the morning — try to avoid watering when the sun is shining brightly.

For watering individual plants, the best buy is a can with a long spout so that you can reach the back of the greenhouse staging. If the house is a large one a watering can is not practical — you will need a hose pipe. Keep the pressure low to avoid washing away compost and exposing roots. Use rainwater whenever possible — never use hard water for Azalea, Orchid, Cyclamen or Hydrangea.

There are several systems available which make watering easier. For pot plants you can use capillary matting — lay polythene sheeting on the bench and unroll a length of capillary matting. Stand the pots on this absorbent material and keep it saturated. A more sophisticated system is trickle irrigation. A narrow plastic hose bears nozzles at intervals — these nozzles drip water into the pots and the flow is controlled by a valve.

On hot days the house should be damped down by spraying the floor and staging with water. The plants should be misted with a fine spray.

GREENHOUSE CROPS

See
THE VEGETABLE EXPERT
for full details on growing
Tomato, Cucumber,
Aubergine, Capsicum,
Carrot and Lettuce
under glass

See
THE HOUSE PLANT EXPERT
for full details on the range
of ornamentals which can
be grown under glass

CHAPTER 9
WATER GARDENING

Water adds another dimension to the garden. Visitors may walk past your flower beds or shrubs, but they will stop by the pool. The sight of water has a fascination which is hard to explain, and the presence of moving water in the form of a cascade or fountain adds sound to the other delights of the garden. Apart from the water there is the attraction of being able to grow a range of new plants (the Aquatics) and to include a group of living creatures (the pond fish).

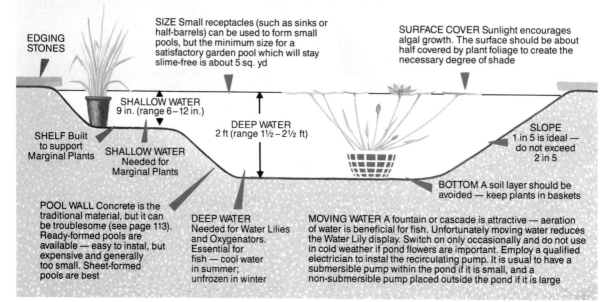

SITE Choose a spot in full sun, sheltered from the east wind if possible. Ponds must be sited away from trees — dead leaves decompose to produce salts and gases which harm fish and encourage algae. Tree roots can break a concrete pool wall

SHAPE Simple shapes with gentle curves are best — avoid fussy shapes and acute corners. Squares and rectangles can be made with concrete but are not easy to produce with sheet plastic

SAFETY FIRST Ponds are attractive to visitors, wildlife . . . and children. Crawling babies and toddlers must be watched or a pond cover used — children can drown in a few inches of water

EDGING STONES

SIZE Small receptacles (such as sinks or half-barrels) can be used to form small pools, but the minimum size for a satisfactory garden pool which will stay slime-free is about 5 sq. yd

SURFACE COVER Sunlight encourages algal growth. The surface should be about half covered by plant foliage to create the necessary degree of shade

SHALLOW WATER 9 in. (range 6–12 in.)

DEEP WATER 2 ft (range 1½–2½ ft)

SLOPE 1 in 5 is ideal — do not exceed 2 in 5

SHELF Built to support Marginal Plants

SHALLOW WATER Needed for Marginal Plants

BOTTOM A soil layer should be avoided — keep plants in baskets

POOL WALL Concrete is the traditional material, but it can be troublesome (see page 113). Ready-formed pools are available — easy to instal, but expensive and generally too small. Sheet-formed pools are best

DEEP WATER Needed for Water Lilies and Oxygenators. Essential for fish — cool water in summer; unfrozen in winter

MOVING WATER A fountain or cascade is attractive — aeration of water is beneficial for fish. Unfortunately moving water reduces the Water Lily display. Switch on only occasionally and do not use in cold weather if pond flowers are important. Employ a qualified electrician to instal the recirculating pump. It is usual to have a submersible pump within the pond if it is small, and a non-submersible pump placed outside the pond if it is large

FORMAL POOL

The outline of the pool is clearly defined and the shape is usually geometrical or gently curved. It is separated from other garden features and is often used as a centrepiece. Floaters and Deep-water Aquatics are essential — Marginal Plants are not really necessary.

INFORMAL POOL

The outline of the pool is not clearly defined — it merges into the adjoining feature or features such as a rockery or bog garden. The outline is irregular — the object is to make the pool look like a natural stretch of water. Marginal Plants are important as they obscure the edge of the pool.

CONSTRUCTION

CONCRETE POOL

The traditional type of pool. It has lost favour in recent years, but still has a few advantages. The concrete pool can be built in any shape or size, and when well-constructed it is certainly the strongest and most permanent. The drawbacks, however, outweigh the benefits. A great deal of hard work is involved and the site must not have been cultivated — settlement will crack the concrete wall. The deep-water section should be square or rectangular. Aim for a wall 6 in. thick — build a wooden frame and instal with a 6 in. gap between wood and soil (see illustration). Fill with concrete, pressing down to fill the corners, and remove wood when set. The shallow-water area can be curved and irregular if desired. When dry, paint the surface with a proprietary sealing compound before filling and stocking — raw concrete is harmful to fish.

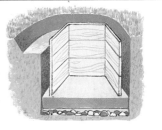

SHEET-FORMED POOL

The pool made from plastic sheeting is by far the most satisfactory. It is easily constructed and can be large enough to accommodate Deep-water Aquatics. One minor drawback is that it is difficult to create the right angles required for square and rectangular ponds — choose a curved shape instead. Do *not* economise when buying the sheeting. Polythene is inexpensive but will only last for a couple of seasons. Nylon-reinforced PVC is much better but best of all is butyl rubber, which should with care last a lifetime.

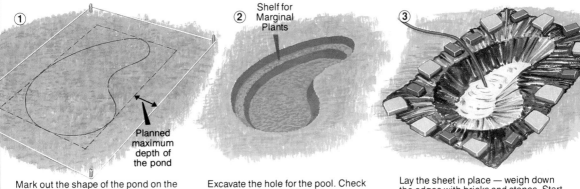

① Mark out the shape of the pond on the ground. Measure the size of sheet required — note the extra requirement for the planned depth of the pond

Planned maximum depth of the pond

② Shelf for Marginal Plants

Excavate the hole for the pool. Check with a board and spirit level to ensure that the top is not sloping. Line the hole with a 1 in. layer of wet sand

③ Lay the sheet in place — weigh down the edges with bricks and stones. Start to fill the pool — the liner will stretch to the contours of the hole. Switch off the water when filled

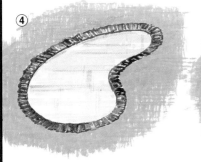

④ Trim the edges with scissors, leaving a 6 in. overlap all round. Pleat the liner as necessary to form a neat edge

⑤ Cover the plastic edge with crazy paving set in concrete or use some other form of paving. Leave a narrow overhang above the pool

⑥ Marginal Plants

Deep-water Aquatics

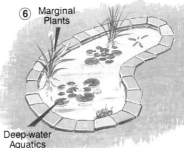

Make sure that all the plastic is covered by the paving. Stock the pool with plants and fish

READY-FORMED POOL

These days you can buy ready-formed pools in all sorts of shapes. Resin-bonded glass fibre is the usual and most satisfactory material, and no other pool type is quicker or easier to instal. Unfortunately, nearly all ready-formed pools are too small to allow more than one Deep-water Aquatic to be grown and the shallow depth makes winter freezing a serious threat to pond life. Despite this limitation of size, they are quite rightly popular for small gardens, incorporation in rockeries, adding interest to patios etc. Small heaters and pool covers can be bought to overcome the icing-up problem. Where space is strictly limited it is possible to build a miniature pool using an old bath, galvanised tank, or half-barrel. Installing a ready-formed pool is simple — just make sure that it is both level and quite rigid in the excavated hole before filling with water.

POND PLANTS

Latin name	Common name	Height	Distance between crown and surface	Flowering period	Notes
DEEP-WATER AQUATICS	Roots submerged — leaves and flowers on or just above the surface. Important for keeping the water clear — the leaves provide shade and this discourages algae				
NYMPHAEA	Water Lily	Surface	4 in.–3 ft, depending on the variety — usual depth 1–2 ft	June–September	Many varieties available. Dwarfs cover 1–2 sq. ft — crown 4–9 in. below surface. Other extreme is the V. Strong Grower group — 60 sq. ft across — crown 3 ft below surface. Many colours available, but not blue. Check the size group before buying
APONOGETON DISTACHYUS	Water Hawthorn	Surface	1–2 ft	April and October	White petals, black anthers. Oval, glossy leaves. Not fully hardy in North
NYMPHOIDES PELTATA	Water Fringe	2–3 in.	1 ft	July–September	Deep yellow flowers. Miniature Water Lily-like leaves 1½ in. across
OXYGENATORS	Leaves, stems and roots submerged — flowers may be above the surface. Important for keeping the water clear. The leaves absorb minerals and carbon dioxide, and this discourages algae				
ELODEA CRISPA	Goldfish Weed	Below surface	Not critical	—	Upright brittle stems — narrow curled leaves. Very effective
TILLAEA RECURVA	Tillaea	Below surface	Not critical	June–August	Dense green mat — used by fish as food. Insignificant white flowers
RANUNCULUS AQUATILIS	Water Buttercup	1 in.	Not critical	June	Surface leaves Clover-like, submerged leaves finely divided. White flowers just above surface
HOTTONIA PALUSTRIS	Water Violet	6 in.	Not critical	June	Ferny leaves — whorls of pale lavender flowers on emerged stems
MYRIOPHYLLUM SPICATUM	Water Milfoil	Below surface	Not critical	—	Bronzy-green feathery leaves on long reddish stems
FONTINALIS ANTIPYRETICA	Willow Moss	Below surface	Not critical	—	Tangled masses of stems covered with dark green, mossy leaves. Grows in shade
FLOATERS	Leaves, stems and flowers on, just below or just above the surface. Important for providing shade if Water Lilies are not present				
AZOLLA CAROLINIANA	Fairy Moss	Surface	Floating	—	Dense green mat of ferny leaves — turns red in autumn
EICHHORNIA CRASSIPES	Water Hyacinth	6 in.	Floating	August–September	Very attractive, but not hardy. Glossy leaves, feathery roots and spikes of lavender flowers
STRATIOTES ALOIDES	Water Soldier	Surface	Floating	July–August	Rosettes of spiny leaves rise to the surface at flowering time
LEMNA TRISULCA	Ivy-leaved Duckweed	Surface	Floating	—	Small translucent leaves — the only Duckweed which will not take over the pond
HYDROCHARIS MORSUS-RANAE	Frog-bit	Surface	Floating	May	Good choice — small Water Lily-like pads and small white flowers
MARGINAL PLANTS	Roots submerged — leaves and flowers clearly above the surface. Purely ornamental. Not required to maintain balance (see page 116)				
ALISMA PLANTAGO	Water Plantain	2 ft	0–6 in.	April–June	Oval leaves — spikes of small pink and white flowers. Remove seed heads
IRIS LAEVIGATA	Blue Water Iris	2 ft	2–4 in.	June–September	Excellent choice — typical Iris flowers in white, blue, purple and pink
MYOSOTIS PALUSTRIS	Water Forget-me-not	9 in.	0–3 in.	May–July	Pale green leaves — bright blue flowers are yellow-eyed
PONTEDERIA CORDATA	Pickerel	1½ ft	3–5 in.	June–October	Spear-shaped leaves — blue flowers borne on spikes
RANUNCULUS LINGUA GRANDIFLORA	Spearwort	2 ft	2–4 in.	June–August	Dark green, narrow leaves — large Buttercup-like flowers
SAGITTARIA JAPONICA PLENA	Arrowhead	1 ft	3–5 in.	July–August	Arrow-shaped leaves — whorls of white Stock-like double flowers
SCIRPUS ZEBRINUS	Bulrush	3 ft	3–5 in.	June–July	An attractive Bulrush with stout stems which are striped green and white
TYPHA MINIMA	Dwarf Reedmace	1½ ft	1–4 in.	May–September	Brown heads on Reed-like stems. Good for small pools
BOG PLANTS	Roots in moist but not waterlogged soil. Can be useful around an informal pool, but only if damp conditions exist. There is no place for bog plants near modern watertight pools				

Examples include **ASTILBE ARENDSII, CALTHA PALUSTRIS, DICENTRA SPECTABILIS, GUNNERA MANICATA, HEMEROCALLIS VARIETIES, HOSTA VARIETIES, IRIS KAEMPFERI, PRIMULA JAPONICA and TROLLIUS VARIETIES** — see The Flower Expert for details

Nymphaea Rose Arey

Nymphaea alba

Pontederia cordata

Ranunculus aquatilis

Eichhornia crassipes

Nymphoides peltata

Myosotis palustris

Scirpus zebrinus

Iris laevigata Variegata

STOCKING & MAINTENANCE

Autumn is the busy time — remove as much debris as possible and cut down all dead foliage. If trees are nearby, fallen leaves must be taken out before they settle to the bottom. If the pool is small and leaves are a serious nuisance, cover the surface with wire-netting until the trees are bare.

Freezing can be a problem in winter — very cold weather in winter can turn all of the water in a very small pool into a block of ice, thereby killing the fish and the plants. To prevent this, cover tiny ponds with boards and sacking if arctic weather is forecast. Surface ice does not affect fish nor plants in large pools or lakes, but the fish may occasionally suffer in the average-sized garden pond. To provide air, stand a pan of hot water on the ice until it melts through. Remove and bale out some of the water through the hole until a ½ in. gap is created between ice and water.

Late spring is the time for planting. Every few years you will have to divide the plants and small Water Lily pools will have to be emptied, the plants divided and then refilled about every 3 years.

At all times watch for carpets of algal threads or water weeds. Remove with a stick and a net — essential equipment for every pond owner.

PLANTING

The modern approach is to plant pond specimens in baskets rather than in soil at the bottom of the pool. In this way growth is controlled and plants can be easily lifted for dividing and re-potting when the soil is exhausted. The usual planting season is from late spring to midsummer.

DEEP-WATER AQUATICS

Plant in Water Lily baskets filled with a mixture of heavy loam and a little Bone Meal. Cover the surface with gravel after planting. Place bricks at the bottom of the pool to support the basket so that the crown of the plant is close to the surface. When new growth starts remove the bricks so that the plant is at the recommended depth.

OXYGENATORS

These should be planted in the sunnier part of the pool — the requirement is one plant per 3 sq. ft of pool surface. Some varieties can be temperamental — plant a mixture. The usual recommendation is to attach a small piece of metal to the base of each clump of stems and then drop the clumps into the pool. It is better to fill a tray with coarse sand or fine gravel and plant the Oxygenators in this medium before placing the tray in the pool.

FLOATERS

Use these plants if the Deep-water Aquatics are too sparse to provide adequate shade. Planting couldn't be simpler — just drop the plants in the water.

MARGINAL PLANTS

These shallow-water plants are not necessary to maintain the balance of the pool but they can be extremely decorative and will soften the transition between the pool edge and paving. Plant into the soil layer on the pond shelf or plant in baskets and stand them on the shelf at the recommended depth.

A question of balance

A pool should require little maintenance provided that it has been constructed at a suitable location and in the proper way. All too often we see murky green and fly-infested water in which few fish can survive instead of the clear water we expect, with healthy fish darting below and attractive plants growing on or above the surface.

Lack of maintenance is not the cause of murky water — the problem is that the pool is not balanced. Each component of the pool — water, plant life, soil, dead organic matter and fish must be so balanced as to keep the water free from the dreaded enemy — algae.

Algae are either tiny microscopic plants or long hair-like strands. They will turn water cloudy and then green if left to develop unimpeded. The secret of successful balance is to create conditions which are suitable for plants and fish but not for algae.

The first need is to keep down the amount of organic matter in the pool. Remove fallen leaves — if they rot they produce minerals and other products which harm fish, discolour the water and encourage the algae. Do not incorporate peat, compost or manure in the soil used for potting pool plants and do not give more fish food than is necessary.

Next, provide some surface shade — algae are sun lovers. This is achieved by growing Water Lilies and other Deep-water Aquatics so that their floating leaves cover about one half of the surface. Introduce Floaters (see page 114) if there is insufficient surface cover.

There is another essential group of plants — the Oxygenators. The submerged leaves do emit oxygen which is utilised by the fish, but that is not their main role. Oxygenators inhibit algae by absorbing both the minerals released by decaying organic matter and the carbon dioxide exhaled by the fish.

Introduce the right inhabitants (plants and fish) at the right time and in the right quantity, as described on this page. Proper balance should then be achieved, but size is important here. It is much easier to balance a large pool than a small one. In spring your pool will be slightly green and cloudy — this happens in even the best-balanced pools, and will soon clear once active growth starts.

FISH

Fish add greatly to the interest and charm of a pool, but they also work for their keep by reducing the mosquito population. The outstanding variety is the **Goldfish** — the metallic gold body is known to everyone but there are more colourful and unusual types — the **Shubunkin**, the **Comet** and the white-and-red **Sarasa Comet.**

The **Golden Orfe** is popular because it swims close to the surface and is very active. The **Koi Carp** is a beautiful (and expensive) fish — it needs a large pool (minimum 7 sq. yd) and it damages the Oxygenators. **Tench** is not a good idea as it is a bottom feeder which stirs up soil.

Do not overstock the pool. The maximum stocking level should be 2 in. of fish per sq. ft of pool surface — achieve this level gradually and not all at once. Despite the advice in some textbooks, water snails should not be added to the pool.

CHAPTER 10
GARDEN DESIGN

The purpose of this chapter is twofold. Firstly it sets out to give you some of the basic principles of good design. Secondly it warns you of the pitfalls — those errors which can create an eyesore, give you a great deal of extra work or cause the plants to fail.

This chapter does not try to give you a detailed description of layouts and planting arrangements which qualify as good designs, nor does it contain plans and photographs of well-designed gardens. The simple reason is that 'good' design does not exist as a matter of fact — it is a matter of opinion.

Recently a group of landscape architects stated that British gardens in general were pretty abysmal. From their professional standpoint they could be right, but in the eyes of the proud owners they are very wrong.

From the standpoint of the householder there are only five elements which make up good design:

- The garden must appeal strongly to you and your family.
- The garden must be labour-saving unless you have lots of time to spare or else lots of money to have someone do the work for you.
- The garden must not cost more to create or maintain than you can afford.
- The garden must provide a suitable home for the plants you have chosen so that they can thrive.
- The garden must not be clearly objectionable to the people who are likely to call. That must include friends and neighbours if not landscape architects.

The essential five elements may be present in your garden. If so, leave things alone and create new interest by introducing different plants rather than by changing the basic design. For many, however, change is necessary because one or more of the vital elements are missing.

You may have moved into a newly-built house with a surround of mud, broken bricks, dead trees and little else — you have the excitement (and hard work) of designing a garden from scratch. Alternatively you may have moved into a house which has an established garden that does not appeal to you.

It may not be a new-house situation — there may be a problem with the garden you have tended for years. If upkeep is taking up too much time, the flower beds are in the wrong place, or if you have decided on a greenhouse, sitting-out area or pond, then a change in design will be necessary.

Whether you are beginning from scratch or just making a few changes, the golden rule is to think carefully and plan thoroughly before you act. Mistakes are costly, so work from Step 1 (this page) to Step 5 (page 122). Then you can put your ideas into action.

STEP 1: PREPARE A PLAN OF THE SITE

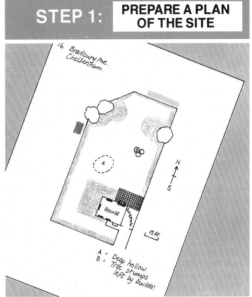

Start with a large piece of paper on a clip board. Make a rough sketch plan of the house and the boundaries of your property. Within this plan mark the main features of the garden and outside the plan draw an arrow indicating north. The features should include more than the obvious things like beds, borders, paths, garden sheds etc. If the site is a new one mark deep hollows left by the builder, dead trees and so on — in an established garden mark poorly-drained areas, frost pockets etc if these are known.

Having marked in the features, look out of the windows of the rooms in which you spend or plan to spend much of your time. See if there are any attractive views beyond your boundary. Mark these on your plan with a yellow crayon — you will not want to block these views when you draw up your design. Now look for eyesores and mark with a red crayon. Almost every garden has an eyesore — the neighbour's dilapidated garden shed or compost heap, a nearby factory chimney etc. In your final design it will be necessary to screen these red areas if possible.

On the rough drawing write down the distances of the corners of the site and each marked feature from both ends of the house. If this is not possible, measure the distances from 2 other fixtures, such as gateposts or trees. There is one more vital task — pick a day when the forecast is for clear skies — ideally this should be in either spring or autumn. In the morning mark the shaded areas in blue on your plan and measure the distances from the object casting the shadows. Repeat this exercise at noon and in the evening — the unshaded area is the 'full sun' area of the garden.

Now you are ready to prepare a scale plan of the garden. Use graph paper and decide on the most suitable scale, such as 1 inch : 10 feet. Draw in the house to scale and then draw in each feature using the measurements noted on your rough sketch plan. To do this accurately, use a compass and a procedure known as triangulation. Set the compass to one of the distances and draw an arc, the point of the compass having been placed on the relevant corner of the house. Repeat the process from the second measuring point with the second distance — draw another arc. The feature is at the point where the 2 arcs cross.

Of course, Step 1 need only be carried out in full for a virgin site or where complete remodelling is planned. However, it is worthwhile even if only a minor change is intended. You will have a reference plan of your garden which can be used for future planning.

STEP 2: DECIDE ON THE TYPE OF GARDEN YOU WANT

This step only applies if you are beginning from scratch after the builders have left or if you have decided to remodel completely your present garden. Few of us have the time, money, skill or courage to change the garden, but it is still interesting to learn that the standard model seen for mile after mile out of any railway carriage window is not the *only* style we can adopt.

SUBURBAN GARDEN

The suburban garden is a particular style which in less than a hundred years has become the standard pattern for home gardens. It is a mixture of formal and informal features — the regimented formal lines of the flower beds are offset by the informal shape and planting arrangement of the rockery and the shrub border.

The style has several basic features. The lawn is of prime importance, and is often placed centrally in the garden. Beds of Roses and annual flowers are as popular as ever, but the herbaceous border is being steadily superseded by the shrub border. As the garden gets larger, the arrangement becomes less formal, the number of trees and ornaments increase but it is the flowers which dominate. This gives the style in its most hackneyed form its charm in summer and its bareness in winter.

COTTAGE GARDEN

The cottage garden has been an essential part of our rural scene for centuries, but it is becoming rarer each year as old houses disappear. Everything about it is old-fashioned ... the plants are generally old-fashioned varieties and little is ever bought.

There is neither clear design nor any formality. Flowers are crowded together and new introductions are planted wherever there is any room. Pots and old sinks, narrow paths and substantial walls make up the framework of the cottage garden. Within this framework scented plants such as Lavender, Shrub Roses, Pinks and Honeysuckle rub shoulders with Beans and Cabbages, and the overall effect is a jumbled mass of colours and shapes beneath old trees and climbing up the walls of the house. At home around a cottage, but distinctly unhappy in a modern suburban street.

ARCHITECTURAL GARDEN

In the architectural garden the designer sets out to produce a non-living skeleton which looks attractive in summer and winter, and into which plants are introduced to add living colour and living shapes. Here paths, walls and containers are chosen for their decorative and not simply their functional role. Trees and shrubs are chosen for their shapes and leaf colours just as much as for their blooms.

This is the way the great French designers such as Le Nôtre regarded their gardens — places for stone, water and architectural living forms with flowers playing a minor role. The best examples of this style can be seen in modern Town Gardens. There are decorative paved areas and a general three-dimensional effect from raised terraces and attractively-planted pots.

MISCELLANEOUS GARDEN

A wide range of layouts, ranging from the beautiful to the bizarre, can be found which do not belong to any of the three basic styles described above. Most important is the grass-and-evergreen gardens beloved by the Scandinavians. Here is an informal and labour-saving arrangement of lawn, conifers, ground cover plants plus bulbs and some flowering shrubs. A common sight in the U.S. and on the Continent, but generally regarded as rather plain for British tastes. The problem is space — grass-and-evergreen gardens and semi-wild gardens rely on splendid stately trees, and a small suburban plot calls for a miniaturised version. Other miscellaneous types include the single-flower types (Roses, Dahlias, Heathers etc) and the Victorian Gardens, with complex beds, Monkey Puzzle trees, Laurel bushes and iron seats. Also included here are 5 per cent of all gardens — the Neglected Plot.

STEP 3: STUDY THE BASIC PRINCIPLES OF GOOD DESIGN

You will be doing nothing 'wrong' if you choose to ignore one or all of the concepts set out on these 2 pages. They represent what *others* regard as good design — they are ways to ensure that the knowledgeable will recognise the presence of accepted good design practice in your garden. But it is *your* garden. The all-important factors are the 5 essential elements (page 117) and the rules for avoiding design mistakes (page 121). This section covers only the design opinions of the experts.

● Aim for something between the over-plain and the over-fussy

For most (but not all) people the austere garden is too dull and tedious for their taste. The conifer gardens of Northern Europe and parts of the U.S. are perhaps more suited to the hills and pines of rural areas than to the brick and concrete of British suburbia. Still, in a sizeable garden in the right setting a splendid effect can be created with grass and woody plants plus only a splash or two of herbaceous plants. Set in the mown turf are several large and irregular-shaped beds or borders of heathers and shrubs. Trees and large shrubs are also grown as isolated specimens — each one carefully chosen for its shape, height and colour.

For nearly everybody something brighter is required. The brilliant red of a Geranium flower has more popular appeal than the subtle, dark red foliage of Acer palmatum Atropurpureum. Aiming for a brightly-coloured effect rather than a blend of greens, creams, white and pastel shades is neither good nor bad, but bright colours should be handled with care. Small beds or borders filled with tiny spots or regimented lines of different colours are frowned upon by the designers. The advice is to plant annuals or biennials in drifts of single varieties, each drift filling a whole bed or blending with others along irregular boundaries. Herbaceous border plants should be set out in groups of 3 or 5 — not as single specimens.

Despite all the good advice, the over-fussy gardens greatly outnumber the restrained ones. The work involved can be enormous. Mowing is a skilful operation, weaving between a complex of flower beds whilst edging and weeding can be never-ending tasks. Dead-heading cannot be neglected and early watering of shallow-rooted annuals is essential in times of drought. It really makes good sense to reduce bedding and increase the use of shrubs and ground cover plants if your garden is taking up too much of your time.

Undoubtedly some designers take this concept too far. The view is sometimes expressed that it is ridiculous to have a pocket-handkerchief lawn and complex bedding in the tiny front gardens of terrace houses — how much better to put them down to paving and tubs filled with flowers. For many people who love gardening but have very little land the over-fussy design gives them the opportunity to potter outdoors for hours. There is nothing wrong with having little beds set in a tiny lawn, but fussiness should certainly decrease as size increases.

● Aim for balance

A garden should be balanced. This does not mean that it should be symmetrical, with the right hand side being a mirror image of the left. In fact, clear-cut symmetry is generally not a good idea and there should be marked differences in design between the two halves. The best way to test for balance is to imagine the left and right sides of the garden on an enormous scale — if one side would quite clearly outweigh the other then the garden is not balanced.

● Avoid a flat-earth policy

The beauty of your garden will be enhanced if you have a mixture of heights. To some extent this can be achieved by having a range of plant forms — tall, fastigiate (column-like) conifers, spreading shrubs, low-growing plants and carpeting ground covers. Proper placing of these various heights and shapes calls for some skill — remember that placing the tallest plants right at the back of your property will make the garden look shorter — a tall feature reasonably close to the house will make the garden look longer. Planting climbers against the house is nearly always a good idea — the garden is extended and the severe lines of the average estate house are softened.

A well-designed garden is a strongly three-dimensional affair. You will need more than a range of plant heights if you are going to avoid the flat-earth policy which seems to affect so many plots. There should be some soil surfaces above the general ground level, and there are several ways of achieving this result. Planted tubs are an age-old method — as valuable as ever for providing colour near the house and for adding interest to plain walls. Rockeries are also popular, but these are usually made to look like a dog's grave rather than a tiered arrangement of planting pockets between horizontal stones.

If you have a sloping site the obvious answer is to create one or more terraces, using brick or stone retaining walls. Spreading rockery perennials can be planted at the front of these terraces to cascade downwards and soften the lines of the wall.

On a level site the answer is to build one or more raised beds. These will help to reduce the monotony of a flat site, but there are other important advantages. Choice plants can be grown on a poorly-drained plot, as the roots are well above the high water table which affect plants growing at ground level. The chore of bending down to weed and plant is reduced — an important consideration as middle age turns to old age. Also the plants are brought closer to the beholder — an advantage if you are growing fragrant or small-flowered varieties. Retaining walls can be built from a wide variety of materials — stone, brick, wood, split logs etc. Using dry stone walling or peat blocks gives the added advantage of allowing plants to be grown in crevices in the retaining wall.

● Create a living skeleton with shrubs and trees

For most people the garden should provide a feeling of maturity, containing a fixed year-round framework rather than looking like an over-sized windowbox. To do this we need permanent objects — ornaments are useful but the answer is to have some shrubs and trees to provide a skeleton. Lack of space is no excuse — there are shrubs and even trees which take up no more soil space than a mature bedding plant.

One of the changes since the War has been the blurring of the lines between the herbaceous border, flower bed and the shrub border. More and more garden designers are singing the praises of the mixed border. Decorative shrubs are planted in the border at wide and irregular intervals — in the large spaces are set groups of plants, selected from such types as Roses, annuals, bulbs, herbaceous border plants and even food crops such as Chives, Parsley and soft fruit bushes. How fashions change — 50 years ago such a mixture would have been regarded as the height of bad taste!

A well-planned mixed border can provide year-round colour and interest. The untimely or natural death of a group of plants simply calls for replacement with a container-grown plant or plants which are in full display. How different when a group of bedding plants die in a flower bed in the middle of summer — the eyesore cannot be removed in the same way.

● Aim for a mixture of evergreen and deciduous woody plants

Gardening magazines and garden design books abound with photographs of the scene in full summer, but the appearance in midwinter is largely ignored. For several months of the year, however, we have to look at the garden when all the flowers and leaves have gone.

Evergreens seem the ideal answer. Living colour is provided when everything seems so dead, and not just in shades of green. Look through the catalogues and books — you will find leaves in steely blue, silvery grey, golden yellow and bronzy purple. There are also variegated types, such as the green-and-white Euonymus radicans Silver Queen and the green-and-yellow Aucuba japonica Crotonifolia.

Of course some evergreens are necessary, but the deciduous shrubs and trees have an equally important if somewhat different role to play. Some of the most beautiful flowering types belong here, and there is the beauty of change. The small and tender leaves of spring mature to summer foliage and finally to the colours of autumn which may be as fiery as any flower.

● Don't try to cram a quart into a pint pot

It is only natural for a keen gardener to try to fill the garden with as many different plants and features as possible. Garden design bureaux look with amazement at some of the lists sent to them — the essentials are there of course — lawn, sitting-out area, washing line, garden shed etc and then all the rest — flower beds, some shrubs please, a Rose bed (of course) and a rockery and a vegetable plot and a place for the children to play and a sundial and a small pond and . . .

If you have an acre of two then it may be no problem, but on a small plot it really is out of the question. Something must go from the list — some areas of open space are vital in every suburban garden if it is not to suffer from horticultural indigestion.

● Create points of interest

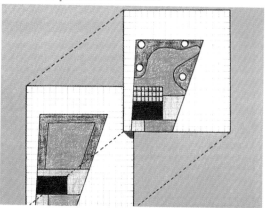

A square green carpet in the centre of the plot with a flower border running around the edge. A style as traditional as fish and chips and a style which may strongly appeal to you, but it is a style which will never win a prize in a design competition.

The problem is that it is so obvious — it can all be taken in with a quick glance and so it lacks interest. The whole secret of good garden design is to create several points of interest in a garden so you have to move your gaze from one to the other. If the garden is of reasonable size there should be several areas of interest so that the stroller comes upon new features when walking around the garden. Ideally one or more of these areas of interest should be out of sight of the house — the 'mystery areas' so beloved by designers.

There is much that can be done on the average-sized plot. Gentle curves soften the line of lawn and border, adding a touch of naturalness. Where possible allow part of the lawn to extend *between* borders so in that part of the garden you walk among the plants. A focal point is a feature which attracts the eye away from the commonplace. It may be a column-shaped conifer, a statue, a Japanese Cherry in full bloom or a stone vase planted with bright flowers. A focal point placed between the window and the furthest point of the garden will make the plot look longer. The reason is simple — the eye is drawn to the focal point and that is where the garden extends to its maximum length. Focal points can have problems — they must attract the eye but not be so dominant as to diminish the effect of or block the view of the rest of the garden. The giant Monkey Puzzle tree in the small Victorian garden is a good example of what not to do.

● Hide eyesores

Some eyesores can of course be removed. Use a neat compost bin instead of heaping up a pile of rubbish, apply a coat of wood preservative and fix a new roof on an aged toolshed and cut down or prune dead or unsightly trees.

For eyesores which cannot be removed you will have to employ some form of screening. The usual answers are a decorative wall, a fence covered with Russian Vine, Ivy or Climbing Roses, or a line of quick-growing conifers such as Leyland Cypress.

These methods of flat screening are not the only ways of hiding eyesores. In fact, flat screening can have its problems — if it is large and eye-catching then it can serve as a focal point. This means that it will actually draw attention to the partly-hidden eyesore! It is sometimes better to have an irregular-shaped and three-dimensional feature such as a bush between the window and the eyesore.

STEP 4: STUDY THE PITFALLS

● DON'T be over-ambitious

Before you draw up your final plan you must face up to your limitations in time, money, ability and health. There is no point in installing a heated greenhouse unless you accept the annual cost of heating and the work involved in regular watering, ventilating, damping down etc.

Changing levels always involves more work than the gardener expects. You can't just cart the excess soil from one spot to raise the height of another area — the topsoil must be first removed, the subsoil graded to the required amount and the topsoil finally replaced. Laying paving slabs, bricklaying, concreting and felling large trees are not jobs to be undertaken lightly if you have never tackled them before. If you can afford it, get a professional. If that is not possible, read about the technique, speak to a knowledgeable friend and try to get him (or her) to help.

● DON'T put plants in the wrong place

When drawing up your plant list, study the scale plan you prepared at Step 1 and look at the characteristics of each candidate plant in a textbook or catalogue. You will want to know the height and spread of the mature specimen and also its soil, light and moisture requirements.

Annuals and rockery perennials will need full sun — some shrubs and border plants will flourish in shade. Some plants will thrive in chalk — others will fail miserably. Make sure that your plant list matches the conditions under which the plants will have to grow.

Make sure that final heights will be in keeping with the garden. This basic piece of advice continues to be given and continues to be ignored. One of the main problems is impulse buying — a Weeping Willow or Deodar Cedar is bought at the garden centre because the small specimen 'looks so nice'. In a few years' time there is the constant need to prune back as the giant tries to get to its natural height.

● DON'T plant too closely

Recommended Planting Distance

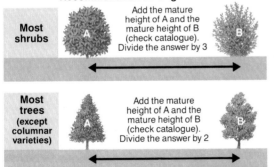

| Most shrubs | Add the mature height of A and the mature height of B (check catalogue). Divide the answer by 3 |

| Most trees (except columnar varieties) | Add the mature height of A and the mature height of B (check catalogue). Divide the answer by 2 |

Always plant at the recommended spacing — the ground may be sparsely covered at first, but the plants will be able to develop to maturity without having to be deformed or constantly hacked back. Shrubs and trees suffer more than other types from too-close planting. The reason is that few textbooks provide planting distances and at first a properly-planted border looks bare and unattractive. Use the distances calculated from the chart above — cover the bare patches with either cheap 'fill-in' shrubs which are later moved or by planting bulbs or annuals.

● DON'T plant trees too close to the house

Foundations are not quite as vulnerable to damage from tree roots as most people think, but you really must be careful when planting trees close to a house on clay soil. The minimum distance from the house should be the height the tree is expected to reach when fully grown. This applies especially to Willow, Poplar and Oak.

You may have moved into a house and found a large tree growing too close to the house. Your re-design programme will obviously include removing the tree, but unfortunately the sudden change in the soil water balance can cause the damage to the house foundations which you are trying to avoid. If the soil is heavy, seek the advice of a tree surgeon.

● DON'T have a large vegetable plot if you have little time to spare

Few aspects of gardening give more pleasure than growing vegetables successfully ... and few take more time. If you have little time to spare for gardening, do not incorporate a large vegetable patch in the design for your new garden. If you have moved into a house which already has a large vegetable garden, grass over part or all of it or turn it into a shrub border unless you plan to employ a gardener.

This does not mean you cannot grow vegetables at all. If the idea of growing some of your own food appeals to you then have a small vegetable patch and grow a few of the types described as 'easy' on page 57. Try herbs and some of the more unusual varieties — no use wasting your limited time on common-or-garden stuff!

● DON'T commit the lawn sins

Just a patch of grass, perhaps, but a lot of thought should go into its design. Its actual shape is up to you, but avoid tight or fussy curves and awkward corners at all costs. You should aim to have a surface free from bumps and hollows, but a gentle even slope across the lawn is acceptable. Grass will grow happily in sun or partial shade, but in deep shade it will never produce a satisfactory, tightly-knit turf.

The first sin is to extend the lawn into a completely sunless area — the second sin is to extend the lawn right up to a wall or path. A clear, grass-free strip should be maintained all round the lawn — this makes edging much easier.

The third sin is having a path which leads directly on to the lawn and stops at the edge. The regular traffic at this point of entry will cause excessive wear and compaction — the first item the visitor sees is a worn patch! Next, avoid narrow strips between beds or between a bed and the edge of the lawn — there should be at least a 30 in. wide gap to facilitate easy mowing.

The upkeep of grassy banks is quite practical these days with the advent of the hover mower. However, you should never extend the lawn over a bank with a slope of more than 30°. Such banks should either be covered with ground cover plants or turned into terraces.

Finally, don't clutter up the lawn with objects which make mowing difficult. Heavy seats and large flower pots are common culprits, but worst of all are large leafy trees which make the sparse, mossy grass below them difficult to mow. If you must have a tree, choose a narrow columnar one or a small-leaved type such as Laburnum or Silver Birch.

STEP 5: DRAW UP YOUR PLAN

You have now reached the final planning stage. A scale plan has been prepared and you have a working knowledge of the main principles of design together with information on the major pitfalls. It is now time to commit your ideas for the design to paper.

Begin by writing down a **Removal List.** This is usually a simple task if only a small amount of remodelling is planned — removing an old garden shed, filling in a fussy flower bed on a lawn, cutting out a dead tree etc. It is even easier when moving into a newly-built house — just get rid of all the builder's rubbish!

The greatest care must be exercised when remodelling an existing garden. The removal of a large feature can so often leave a gaping bare patch which is much more extensive than you imagined. Removing a path seems such a simple idea until you start trying to lift the stones.

Take care even on a virgin site — the remains of an old brick wall can sometimes be turned into an attractive feature. The few remaining trees at the corner of the plot might, when properly pruned, provide a note of maturity which is so often lacking in new gardens.

It is now time to redraw the scale plan prepared in Step 1. Leave out the red, yellow and blue shading and omit all the items on the Removal List — this new plan will eventually be your Design Plan. You are not ready to draw up a final plan at this stage — take several photocopies or tracings so you can record your ideas before making up your mind. You will certainly need several copies as you will undoubtedly have second thoughts!

Look carefully at the plan and see what space you have available. Look at the site — some people find it useful to take a series of photographs at this stage. Now you must make up your mind how you want your new garden to look and what features you propose to include.

You can, of course, copy an example taken from a book of garden plans. There are drawbacks — none of these will fit your site and aspect exactly, and it is difficult for the amateur to visualise the result. It is usually better to visit gardens and look for features and arrangements which appeal to you. Call on friends, walk along streets — there are many examples available for inspection. Take photographs wherever you can — they will be a great help when drawing up your own plan.

Once you have a general idea of what you want in your new garden, you must draw up a **Wants List** — these are the features you plan to introduce. There will be garden features — Rose bed, vegetable plot, mixed border, pond and so on. Add plants which you have seen and would like to include — Pampas Grass, Camellia, Weeping Cherry etc. Don't forget the non-living fixtures — some attractive, like the greenhouse, summer house and patio and others mundane, such as the rotary clothes line and a compost bin.

There are two general rules concerning the Wants List. Don't try to pack too much into your garden. It would be surprising if this list didn't need pruning once the first draft was completed. A garden should not look like a garden centre — there should be large, plain areas to dramatise the busy and colourful spots. The second rule is that you should plan for the future. Include a play area even though the baby is still at the crawling stage. Include a greenhouse even though funds won't allow it for a couple of years. All you have to do is to mark these as 'items to follow' — their presence on the list will remind you to leave a space on the Design Plan.

The **Design Plan** can now be prepared. Draw the features from your Wants List on one of the tracings or photocopies you have prepared. So much is a matter of taste, but remember the aspect pitfalls. Annual beds, greenhouses, ponds and rockeries need sunny sites away from trees. Turf grasses fail in deep shade and patios should be in sunshine for at least part of the day. A path at the back of a large border will make maintenance so much easier, and both play areas and herb gardens are best sited close to the house. Whether you hide away the vegetable plot or leave it prominently exposed as your pride and joy is entirely up to you.

Make sure that you and your family are happy with the completed Design Plan — the first rule of garden planning. If you are new to gardening or if you find design work difficult, you can send off your plan with a note of any misgivings to a Garden Planning Service. Several magazines run such a service and you will find other bureaux listed in directories. Site visits are of course expensive, and if you do not propose to have the plot designed on site then you should go through Steps 1–5 and submit the results to the professional designer. Providing a few vague ideas and not having any idea what you are trying to achieve are the usual causes of disappointment.

It is the last stage, the preparation of the **Planting Plan,** which most worries gardeners. Again you can use a Garden Planning Service, or you can buy a ready-planned collection or copy a plan from a gardening book. Be guided by others if you must but the basic rule remains that you should check the requirements of each plant in a good book and make sure that it will be happy in the conditions to be provided.

Mark the planting spots on your Design Plan and write in the names. The planning phase is over. It is now necessary to reverse the measuring-up process. The distances from the plan must be translated to the garden and the areas marked out accordingly. If you have a change of heart when working on the site, make sure that the plan is altered. Keep the plan for future reference.

CHAPTER 11
NON-LIVING FEATURES

Gardens began as areas of tiles and tinkling water rather than sites for growing plants. To those early Persians the pots of flowers and bushes were incidental to the coolness of the courtyard, and even Le Nôtre, the great French garden designer, was quite happy to use coloured glass beads instead of bedding plants in his complex beds. Now the pendulum has swung the other way — for many people gardens are places for living plants and all non-living objects are an intrusion.

Perhaps the middle course between these two extremes is the ideal one. There are some non-living features we *must* include — walls or fences to mark the boundary where open-plan gardening is not practical, dustbins for rubbish, a shed or garage for the tools, plus a drive and pathways for the car and family. But there are also a host of useful non-essentials — the patio for outdoor living, garden furniture, the pool, barbecue, outdoor lighting, plant containers and so on. Finally, there are the ornaments which have no practical use at all, varying from the life-size marble statue to the tiny gnome.

CONCRETE & MORTAR

CONCRETE is a mixture of cement, sand and small stones (aggregates). Pigments can be added.

MORTAR is a mixture of sand with a binder (cement, lime or a cement/lime mix). Pigments and/or plasticisers can be added.

The strength of concrete after mixing

After 2 hours ▷	Concrete without additives: Workable — no strength at all
After 4 hours ▷	Concrete with setting retardant: Workable — no strength at all
After 3 days ▷	Concrete no longer workable — little strength
After 7 days ▷	Solid concrete — half strength
After 30 days ▷	Solid concrete — full strength

MIXING ON SITE is the traditional method of making concrete and mortar. You can buy the ingredients separately or as bags of ready-packed dry mix. One bag of cement will make about 5–6 cu. ft of concrete. The advantage with mixing on site compared with ready-mix concrete is that you can make up a relatively small batch at a time. This is important if you are a beginner or have limited assistance.

	Proportion by volume				
	CEMENT	SAND	LIME	¼ – ¾ in. AGGREGATE	SAND/AGGREGATE MIX ('Ballast' or 'All-in' Aggregate)
CONCRETE for foundations	1	2½ sharp sand	—	3½	—
			or		
	1	—	—	—	5
CONCRETE for paths & drives	1	1½ sharp sand	—	2½	—
			or		
	1	—	—	—	3½
MORTAR for bedding slabs & laying bricks	1	3 builder's sand	—	—	—
			or		
	1	6 builder's sand	1	—	—

Mix the sand and aggregate into a heap. Flatten, and make a central crater using a spade or shovel. Pour the cement into this crater. Mix and turn the dry materials until the heap is uniform in colour. Flatten the heap once more and make a crater. Add some water to the crater and slowly bring the outer wall into the centre. Mix and turn — add sprinklings of water until the pile is well mixed and thoroughly moist.

THE CONCRETE TEST
Press the top of the pile with the back of the spade and then slide the blade across. The surface should be firm, closely-knit and moist but there should not be a layer of liquid.

READY-MIX CONCRETE is delivered ready to lay. It will save a great deal of time, but remember you will have to use the whole delivery within a couple of hours. Ready-mix makes a longer-lasting path or drive than an on-site mixture. Have everything ready with help standing by when the delivery is made — 1 cu. metre will mean 30–40 barrowloads to be moved.

Paths

A hard walkway is required between A and B when regular traffic occurs between the two points. This is the purely functional aspect of a path, and in out-of-the-way spots or informal surroundings it is quite in order to use purely functional surfaces. Examples are compacted earth, concrete and gravel. Grass paths are not suitable for heavy or regular traffic — they are not hard-wearing and are unpleasant to walk on in wet weather.

In many areas of the garden there is a decorative as well as a functional role for paving. Many attractive materials are available these days — study this page and the catalogues before making your choice. You will have to take several factors into consideration. First of all, the money you wish to spend. Natural stone slabs are often considered the ideal, but they are costly and heavy. Concrete and gravel are much cheaper, but concrete can be somewhat dull and gravel is easily kicked on to the surrounding lawn or flower beds.

Path shape is another factor you must consider — a winding path offers no problems with gravel or crazy paving, a little extra work with blocks and concrete and a stone-cutting nightmare with large slabs.

A few rules. Make the path wide enough — 2 ft is the minimum for a satisfactory path in the average garden, increasing to 3–4 ft in a large garden. The path should slope (minimum 1 in 100) to prevent standing water after rain. If constructed next to the house, the surface must be at least 6 in. below the damp course.

The secret of long-lasting success is to prepare a firm foundation before adding the paving material. Obviously, the depth of this base will depend on the weight of the traffic to be borne, the type of soil (clay, recently-moved soil and loose topsoil will need thorough consolidation) and the type of paving material chosen. A drive is a path which bears 4-wheeled traffic — a 6 in. layer of rubble is required as a base for the surface material.

SLABS — flagstones, crazy paving & pre-cast paving

Natural stone, such as sandstone, provides an air of luxury when used for paving — but there are problems. It is expensive to buy, difficult to handle and extremely hard to cut cleanly. It is much more usual to buy broken pieces and make crazy paving. To avoid fitting problems, lay the larger pieces first in a random pattern at the edge of the path. Then fill the gaps with smaller pieces. The most popular decorative paving material is the pre-cast slab — available in all sorts of shapes, sizes, clever designs and attractive colours. If in doubt, use pre-cast paving.

Take out a trench and ram down the soil. Add a 3 in. layer of hardcore (broken bricks, stones etc) and tamp down firmly. Add a 2 in. layer of sand for large flag-stones, or a 2 in. layer of sand/cement mix if the paving pieces are small. Put a dab of mortar (see page 123) on the underside of the slab at the corners and at the centre. Place in position and press down to the correct level. Brush a dry sand/cement mix into the cracks and the path is finished.

BLOCKS — bricks, stone setts and concrete blocks

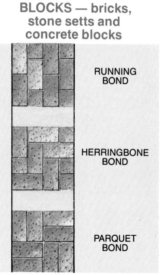

RUNNING BOND

HERRINGBONE BOND

PARQUET BOND

Brick paths add a touch of old-world charm and for the not-so-fit the back-breaking task of lifting, cutting and laying heavy stones is avoided. But a word of caution — outdoor-quality bricks must be used and they must be firmly laid to avoid unevenness. Moss and slime can develop in winter if an algicide spray is not used. Concrete blocks are a modern alternative — you can buy interlocking patterns as well as a wide variety of colours. Another possibility is to use granite setts removed from an old road — new setts are very expensive to buy.

The main attraction of a block path is the scope it provides for making a wide variety of designs — simple bonding, herringbone, parquet, running bonding etc. Lay them in the same way as slabs (see above), but mortar dabs at the bottom of each block are not required. Brush a dry sand/cement mix into the cracks.

CONCRETE

Concrete is criticised by many for its austere look, but it remains a popular paving material for both paths and drives. You can add a colouring agent during the mixing process to improve the appearance, and a non-slip surface can be created by brushing the surface with a stiff broom before the surface has set.

Before you begin it will be necessary to prepare the foundation. Take out a trench and ram down the soil. Add a 3 in. layer of hardcore (6 in. for drives) and tamp down firmly. Place wooden shuttering on either side of the trench — the upper surface of the boards will be the height of the top of the path. Check gradients with a spirit level — one side should be very slightly lower than the other. The foundation should be about 2 in. below the top of the boards for a path (4 in. for a drive).

Place boards at right angles to the path at spacings which are twice the width of the path. These will allow the concrete to expand without cracking.

Work out how much concrete you will require — you simply multiply the height, width and depth of the frame you have constructed. If buying ready-mix concrete, order about 10% more than the calculation. Pour in a small amount of concrete — shovel so that the centre of the load is above the boards. Now you will need the help of an assistant. With each of you holding the edge of a stout board, drag it over the surface with an up and down motion. Repeat the operation with a sawing motion so that the space between the wooden shuttering is completely filled and the surface is smooth. Repeat until the path is completed. Do not lay a concrete path in frosty weather. In hot weather cover the surface with polythene.

GRAVEL

The use of gravel has declined steadily because of the weed problem, but the introduction of fast-acting herbicides may bring this easy-to-use path medium back into favour. It is cheap, easy to lay and adaptable to any shape. Both shingle (small stones smoothed by the action of water) and true gravel (stone chips obtained from a quarry) can be used. A curb on either side is essential and there should be a base of 3 in. of coarse gravel firmly consolidated into the soil. Use a heavy roller or a mechanical tamper hired for the day. Top off this surface with a 1 in. layer of finer gravel or shingle. Roll to form a firm surface.

MACADAM

Macadam is the favourite material for drives — made of stone chippings coated with tar or bitumen and referred to in a number of ways — coated macadam, asphalt, black-top, 'tarmac' etc. Drives are laid using hot macadam and this is a job to be left to the professional. Choose your contractor with care — if you use the man who calls with 'a load left over from the last job' and a bargain price you will have only yourself to blame for the result. For small jobs you can buy cold macadam in bags from your local store. The colours are black, red and green — white chippings can be rolled into the surface to give a 'pepper-and-salt' effect. You will need a heavy roller which should be kept wet during use.

Walls

Walls are built for a variety of purposes. Firstly there is the boundary wall, dividing you from your neighbours or from the street. A wall is chosen rather than a wooden fence for permanence, noise reduction or privacy — you must expect that it will cost more and will be more difficult to erect. A wall makes an excellent boundary, but a tall wall around a small garden can seem oppressive to some people. There are other problems with tall walls. The height may exceed the maximum laid down in the lease or by local or national laws, and piers (brick pillars) or buttresses (sloping supporting walls) will have to be built at intervals if the wall is of brick. A final point about solid walls — they can create a frost pocket or turbulence in windy weather (see page 26).

Internal walls are an important feature in many gardens. There are screening walls to enclose areas or hide unsightly views, and there are retaining walls. A retaining wall may hold back a large area of soil, in which case it should slope slightly backwards and be strongly constructed, or it may merely hold soil within a small raised bed, which requires upright walls and much less robust construction.

The usual walling materials are brick, stone and concrete. The walling materials may be solid or pierced, and the usual practice is to join the blocks together with a cement/sand or a cement/lime/sand mortar. This mortar can be coloured if desired.

A sound foundation is essential — its size and depth will depend on the soil type, building material and height of wall. Finally, you must decide whether to build the wall yourself or have it built by a professional. If it is a high boundary wall and you have never laid bricks before, call someone in. However, there is no reason why low internal walls should not be tackled on a DIY basis.

BRICKS

A low brick wall does not look out of place in any garden, but head-high ones usually belong around large properties. The standard brick is 9 in. x 4½ in. x 3 in. and the mortar thickness is about ⅜ in. This does not mean that all bricks are the same — there is a vast assortment of colours, textures, surfaces and weather-resisting properties. Use either an engineering brick or a facing brick rather than commons.

Do not attempt to build a wall over 4 ft high unless you are an experienced brick-layer. The first step is a solid foundation — dig a trench 15 in. wide and about 9 in. deep. Add a 3 in. layer of rubble and tamp down, after which the trench should be filled with concrete to about 1 in. below ground level. Make sure that the concrete surface is perfectly horizontal.

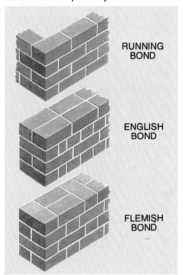

RUNNING BOND

ENGLISH BOND

FLEMISH BOND

Bricks must be bonded so that the vertical mortar joints of one row do not line up with either the row below or the row above. Buy concrete or brick copings to protect the top row of bricks from the weather. Point the mortar before it is dry. With regard to the craft of bricklaying itself, either watch a professional brick-layer at work or ask a skilled friend to show you how. It is not a skill you can acquire by reading a book and unlike most jobs it is not something which you can thoroughly practice before tackling the task.

CONCRETE BLOCKS

The average concrete block is much larger than the average brick, and with the reconstituted stone block has brought wall construction into the DIY range of the ordinary gardener. There are thick cavity blocks which are cheap and both easily and quickly laid to form a head-high wall without piers or buttresses. The solid concrete block is thinner, and is available in many colours and in surface finishes ranging from smooth to rough-stone faced. Although the laying operation is simpler, the same type of foundation is required as for a brick wall (see above) and a protective coping is required to complete the structure.

SCREEN BLOCKS

Square concrete blocks are available which are pierced with a variety of patterns, and are available in numerous colours. They are used to form screen walls, the blocks being stack bonded (each vertical mortar joint lining up with the one above and the one below).

Their use is a matter of personal taste, but some garden designers feel that screen blocks are better used as occasional items in a solid wall rather than on their own to form a lace-like wall.

STONE WALLING

Many types of stone can be used for walling — limestone, granite, sandstone, slate etc. If you have one, you are lucky. If not, then the cost and work involved make it an impractical idea. The usual pattern is a random rubble wall — irregular stones carefully sorted and placed on top of each other to form a tight-fitting wall. Such walls can be constructed without mortar (dry walling), and plants can be grown in the crevices.

RECONSTITUTED STONE WALLING

Reconstituted stone blocks have become the favourite walling material for garden use. Crushed stone is used in place of aggregate in the production of these blocks, and there are many brands. They generally have a textured appearance on the outer face and can be obtained in a variety of shapes and sizes. People who are incapable of making a brick wall quite often have little difficulty with these blocks.

OTHER MATERIALS

Wooden sleepers and peat blocks can be used to prepare dry retaining walls. They have no place in a small formal garden but are extremely effective in a woodland or semi-wild garden. Peat blocks can be used to make a raised bed which is filled with a soil/peat mixture for acid-loving plants. The crevices between the blocks are used for planting Ferns, Heathers etc. Algae and moss develop on the surface of the peat blocks, and no other walling material blends in quite so well with the natural environment.

Fences

Fencing has a number of uses which are shared with walling. It can mark the boundary of the property — important in a country where every man's home is his castle. If privacy is an important factor, a solid fence is erected. Fencing can also be used as an internal feature — hiding unsightly objects, separating sections of the garden etc. It is also employed to provide a windbreak (see page 26) and to act as a support for climbing plants.

The choice of fencing materials is much greater than for walling. The basic materials are wood and concrete for posts; wood and metal (or plastic-coated metal) for the fence itself. You can use these materials in a wide variety of ways — pick a version which is in keeping with the house, position and style of garden. Money is also an important consideration — iron railings may appeal but they are very expensive. Chain link fencing and Chestnut paling are inexpensive, but are not the thing to use on the front boundary of a modern house.

So you must ask many questions. Do I want complete privacy or will a partly open fence do? Must it be child-proof and/or animal-proof? Do I want a low maintenance fence (such as a Cedar Interwoven fence or a plastic-coated one) or am I prepared to paint it every year or so?

Whichever you choose, posts at regular intervals which are set firmly in the ground are essential. They should be 6–10 ft apart and you must remember that tall and closed fences need stronger support than small and open ones. For a tall Closeboard fence you will need posts which are at least 4 in. x 4 in. square.

Wooden fences can be made on site or you can buy ready-made panels. Make sure that the wood has been treated with a preservative and use galvanised nails during erection. Take care of your existing fences — they are expensive to replace. Paint with a long-lasting preservative, such as Woody. Treat corroded metal with Rusty. Secure broken fence-posts immediately or a high wind may bring the whole fence down.

CLOSEBOARD FENCE

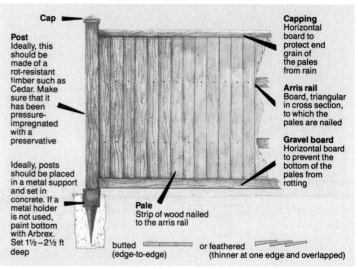

Cap

Post Ideally, this should be made of a rot-resistant timber such as Cedar. Make sure that it has been pressure-impregnated with a preservative

Ideally, posts should be placed in a metal support and set in concrete. If a metal holder is not used, paint bottom with Arbrex. Set 1½–2½ ft deep

Capping Horizontal board to protect end grain of the pales from rain

Arris rail Board, triangular in cross section, to which the pales are nailed

Gravel board Horizontal board to prevent the bottom of the pales from rotting

Pale Strip of wood nailed to the arris rail

butted (edge-to-edge)   or feathered (thinner at one edge and overlapped)

Closeboard fencing is the strongest of all closed wooden fences — made to last for decades but more expensive than either Interwoven or Lapped fencing. It is usually made on site from basic materials or from a kit, although ready-made panels are available.

INTERWOVEN FENCE

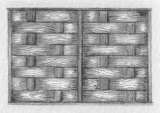

A very popular if unexciting fence, made from thin strips of wood woven between a number of vertical slats. The result is a closed but not completely peep-proof fence which is bought as panels, usually 6 ft wide and heights from 2–6 ft. Interwoven (or Basketweave) fences are usually made of softwood, so treatment with a preservative is essential. The panels are slightly less expensive than Lapped fencing.

LAPPED FENCE

A widely-used alternative to Interwoven fencing, made from straight-edged or wavy- (waney-) edged strips of wood attached to vertical stiffeners. Panels are available in various widths, from 1–8 ft, but the 6 ft panel is by far the most popular. Stout posts are needed (see Closeboard fencing above) and paint with a preservative once the colour has begun to fade. There are various names — Larchlap, Weatherboard and Overlap.

PICKET FENCE

For many the white-painted Picket fence (or Palisade) is a symbol of a cottage in the country, but this type of fencing is not out of place in an urban setting. The stout pales are rarely more than 3–4 ft high and are attached to 2 horizontal rails. The bottom of the pales should be 2–3 in. above the ground to avoid rotting and the tops may be rounded or pointed. The Picket fence is child-proof, but not cat-proof.

RANCH-STYLE FENCE

Strong broad boards are screwed (not nailed) on to evenly-spaced uprights to provide an attractive boundary fence. The cross-pieces are usually softwood (occasionally plastic) and white paint is the favourite finish. The number of horizontal boards (2–9) is a matter of taste and a Ranch-style fence offers little privacy — many children regard it as an ideal climbing-frame! It is popular in the U.S., where it is called Baffle fencing.

TRELLIS

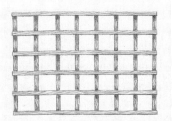

Trellis is made of thin strips of wood (laths) or Larch poles (rustic work) arranged to form a square or diamond pattern. If bought as expanding Trellis, a stout frame is required. It is rarely used as a boundary fence — the main role of Trellis is to support climbing plants. It is employed for internal fencing or at the top of stout boundary fencing such as Interwoven or Lapped panels.

CHESTNUT PALING

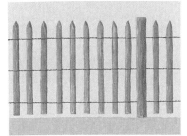

This fencing is bought as a roll — the pointed Chestnut stakes are bound at the top and bottom by horizontal lengths of twisted wire. The fence has little inherent strength, but it provides an effective barrier if firmly attached by wire between stout Larch or Chestnut poles. Chestnut paling is not a thing of beauty, but it is cheap and easy to erect. It is also very simple to camouflage by planting shrubs in front of it.

CHAIN LINK FENCE

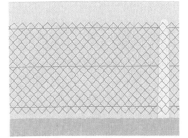

A straightforward utilitarian form of fencing — strong, relatively inexpensive and capable of enclosing the garden at a fraction of the cost of a wooden fence. Squares of galvanised or plastic-coated wire are interlinked to form a net — choose a colour which merges with the surroundings. Firm wooden or concrete posts are needed. Run stressing wires through each chain link square at the top and bottom of the fence.

WATTLE HURDLE

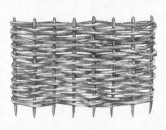

Panels of Wattle hurdle consist of strips of Willow or Hazel woven over upright poles. The panels are usually 6 ft long and are made in various heights. Each panel is nailed to firm supports to produce a fence full of rustic charm. The Wattle hurdle makes an excellent windbreak and keeps animals at bay, but it is not long-lasting and appears out of place in the suburban garden.

WIRE PICKET FENCE

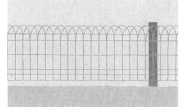

Nearly all of the fences described on these two pages are stout structures, used to mark the boundaries of the property or to set apart clearly sections within the garden. Wire picket fencing is at the other end of the scale — a series of small hoops of plastic-coated wire, each hoop joined to its neighbour to form a low and unobtrusive fence for beds, borders etc. Strong supports are necessary and the Wire picket fence must be drawn taut between them.

POST & CHAIN FENCE

The Post & Chain fence is a purely decorative way of marking a boundary — it provides neither privacy nor protection. Metal posts and chains are the usual form, but plastic versions are available. A less decorative but more practical form is the Post & Wire fence — 2 or 3 strands of wire are drawn between each pair of posts. These straining wires must be kept taut by using straining bolts at the end posts of the fence.

Arches

An archway covered with Honeysuckle, Roses or Clematis can be an excellent garden feature, but there are rules to follow. The material used for its construction should be in keeping with the garden style — an arch made with Pine or Chestnut poles looks attractive in a traditional garden but would look out of place in ultra-modern surroundings. Another point to remember is that it must be large enough for comfort when clothed with plants — the height should be 6½–7 ft and the width 4 ft or more. So you must have room for an arch, and it also must be seen to have a function. It is pointless to place it in the middle of the lawn or at the side of a bed — it should straddle a path and appear to lead somewhere.

Pergolas

A pergola is a series of arches, attached to the side of the house or free-standing in the garden as a focal point. In a large garden the piers can be made of brick or reconstituted stone. In a smaller garden it would be advisable to use wood or metal — pergola kits can be bought from large garden centres. In the traditional pergola the uprights are usually more solid than the roof members, and the uprights are clothed with plants such as Wisterias or Climbing Roses. However, the pergolas which are used to transform patios into outdoor rooms often have narrow supports which bear much stouter beams above. Remember that a pergola with a leafy covering offers a great deal of wind resistance during a gale — the supports must have firm foundations or the structure will be damaged.

Patios

The patio or terrace is becoming increasingly popular in Britain. It is basically a hard-surfaced area which is close to or attached to the house and is designed for sitting out. Purists frown at the use of both words — a patio is strictly an inner courtyard and a terrace is a level area raised above soil level.

Although you will not wish to encroach too far into the garden, it is necessary to make the patio large enough for comfort. It should be a separate area from other features, ideally at a higher level than the surrounding ground and not merely a wide path running the whole width of the property. The shape is usually simple — square, rectangular etc and a wide range of surface materials can be used. Gravel is cheap and simple but rarely satisfactory. Bricks have a rural feel, but paving slabs are undoubtedly the most popular. Buy real stone if you can afford it or pre-cast paving, like nearly everybody else. A patio made of wooden planking is known as a deck — popular in some areas of the U.S. and Continent but not in Britain.

There are some essential needs for every patio. It should receive direct sun for part of the day or it will not be used. It will also need some form of shade for hot, summer days and also some protection from the prevailing wind if the site is exposed. Finally it will require some form of seating, which may be either permanent or temporary.

Consider the optional extras. A screen to provide privacy from the neighbours, a table for dining, a barbecue for cooking . . . for many people the patio has become an extra room in summer.

Lighting

Nothing quite matches the luxury of well-planned garden lighting. Wherever possible it should be installed when the garden is being made, rather than trying to bury cables below existing paving. Really strong illumination calls for mains electricity, and this poses problems. Firstly, the work must be left to a qualified electrician and costly special-purpose cables and fittings will be required. Even more important is the danger of accidentally cutting through the cable when cultivating the ground.

It is therefore usually advisable to buy a 12 V lighting kit. This will contain an indoor transformer to step mains electricity down to a safe voltage. Remember the cardinal rule — the lights should shine on objects and not into the eyes of the observer. Use spot-lighting to illuminate single objects, flood-lighting for large areas, downlighting for pathways and backlighting for dramatic silhouettes.

Containers

Pots, boxes and tubs filled with plants serve many purposes. They can hold trees or shrubs to brighten or soften the lines of the front of the house, or they can hold bulbs to bring outdoor colour close to the window. Containers filled with flowers enliven dull areas, such as stretches of concrete, and of course they are the only means of outdoor gardening for the apartment dweller. Shapes vary — floor-standing pots, vases on pedestals, window boxes, old sinks and so on. Materials are even more variable — glass fibre, stone, reconstituted stone, wood, metal, terracotta etc. Use plastic with care. Choose a simple shape and a neutral colour — avoid plastic containers altogether in an old-fashioned setting. The secret of success with containers is to make sure there is adequate drainage, use a good compost and water regularly in dry weather.

Ornaments

Ornaments are the purely decorative non-living features of the garden. Their purpose is to serve as focal points and are seen at their best in the fine Grand Gardens — large statues in front of clipped evergreens, mock temples standing on small hills, massive stone urns and so on. But ornaments can have a place in the small garden provided you make sure that their size and colour are in keeping with the surroundings. Glass fibre statuary is available, but the favourites are bird baths and sundials. The style of garden is an important consideration. Weathered stone objects can enhance a cottage garden and an abstract sculpture can underline the modernity of an architectural garden. Ornaments are least at home in the small suburban garden, but the painted gnome and concrete donkey will keep their places in many a front garden.

Furniture

Gardens are for living in and not merely places for working, walking and admiring. Some furniture is essential — the size and amount will depend on the extent of the property. Permanent furniture is associated with the large garden. Stone and imitation stone seats need little attention but also offer little comfort — the traditional wooden and cast iron seats require regular treatment or painting to avoid deterioration. Plastic-coated metal is an excellent material although most of the tables and seats sold these days are made of either plastic or glass fibre.

When space is limited the answer is to buy folding chairs and tables to be stored in the shed or garage when not required. The days of the deck chair are gone — now it's the time of aluminium seats with arm rests and removable cushions.